Head Hunter-One Kilo!

by

Dennis Hendrix

TO KATHY,
Thank you for being my friend.
May God bless you for the
rest of your life, you are a
Kind, considerate Woman.
God Bless,
Dennis L. Hendrix
12-17-05

authorHOUSE™

1663 LIBERTY DRIVE, SUITE 200
BLOOMINGTON, INDIANA 47403
(800) 839-8640
WWW.AUTHORHOUSE.COM

First published by AuthorHouse 10/24/05

ISBN: 1-4208-7996-0 (sc)
ISBN: 1-4208-7997-9 (dj)

Library of Congress Control Number: 2005907720

Printed in the United States of America
Bloomington, Indiana

This book is printed on acid-free paper.

I dedicate this book to the "Sky Soldiers" of the 173rd Airborne Brigade, of whom thousands gave their lives when freedom called.

"Airborne all the way, sir!"

Many thanks to the only two people with whom I have shared all these stories for their insistence that I organize them into a book: Charles Josey and William "Bill" Scott Craig. Bill and I spent many hours around campfires in the Georgia deer woods, talking openly and honestly about our Vietnam experiences; Bill in his beloved Marine Corps and me in the Paratroopers. Charles took my stories and helped me commit them to paper, which has been no small task. Thank you both, and God bless you.

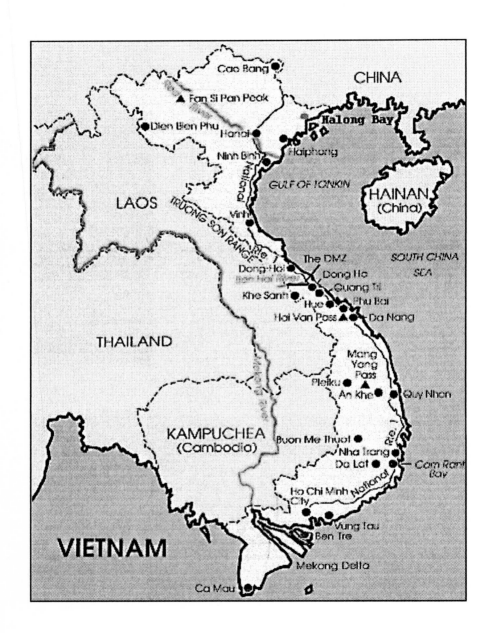

Table of Contents

Introduction

There are numerous thick books that detail the battles we American soldiers fought in Vietnam, books that chronicle military strategy, heroes, and hardships. This book, however, is neither thick nor focused on the successes or failures of U.S. war efforts. It is an account based on memory, rather than on scholarly research; a recollection of what an eighteen-year-old saw, thought, and believed.

Primarily, this is a story about growing up fast and hard, about a terrifying nuclear weapon that has never been used, about atrocities and other horrors of war experienced by a frontline soldier, and the life-altering impact of both the spiritual and the hellish, blood-drenched experiences that came out of time spent in the Republic of Vietnam.

My name is Dennis Lee Hendrix, former paratrooper and former kid searching for some meaning in life.

—•—

Prologue

The sun bore down relentlessly through the single-canopy jungle cover. It wasn't quite 1100 hours and the temperature was already hovering around 100 degrees. The humidity was nearly enough to drown a man. Hendrix lay quietly on the jungle floor, hidden in the rough brush. The camouflage paint was streaking from his beaded forehead in spite of the O.D. green medical bandage he was using as a head cover. The stinging of the sweat in his eyes made him blink constantly, though he dare not move a muscle to wipe it away. *Suck it up*, he thought. A mosquito whined in his right ear, eventually settling down to crawl inside and explore the source of the scent of blood it had found. He could feel something move inside his lightweight jungle fatigues, a lizard, perhaps. *Please don't let it be a scorpion, he thought*. Nothing he could do about it if it was. He would endure the sting quietly if he had to. His squad depended on absolute noise discipline.

Scattered purposefully around Hendrix were nine other men. They were an American fire team in a classic ambush set up on both sides of a jungle trail. Hendrix manned the M-60 machine gun and was covering the bend in the trail. Their mission today, like the day before and the day before that: seek and destroy.

The large foliage moved slightly about thirty meters out; slightly, but just enough for a practiced eye to catch the movement. Hendrix stiffened and blinked once more. Someone was coming. The mosquito began to drill.

Slowly and quietly a figure appeared. It was a small man, maybe even a boy. It didn't matter. The conical hat and black pajamas said farmer. The angry snout of a Russian-authored AK-47, carefully held in his hands, said enemy. He was close enough for Hendrix to see the delicate bone structure of his fingers, too out of place to be holding such a dramatic instrument of death. They should be playing a game of chess or fingering the keyboard of a piano. Life offers all of us strange choices.

The first figure carefully stepped along the path and filled the sight pattern of Hendrix's weapon. A second appeared shortly behind, followed by a third. They were keeping a small spread, no more than a two-meter distance from each other. Inexperienced and too close, in his opinion, but it was to the American advantage.

The face drew nearer. It was a boy, a young boy at that. It was sometimes hard to tell age in these people, but certainly no older than thirteen or fourteen years. His skinny frame seemed too small for the weapon he carried. He was nervous, glancing hurriedly from side to side and raising his nose, beagle-like, to sniff the air for a clue. Hendrix inhaled quietly and let out half a breath, squeezing the trigger as he did. Brief thoughts flashed through his mind of similarly aged young boys laughing and diving off the dock of a lake he knew hundreds of years ago. He squeezed tighter and the weapon erupted.

Chapter 1
The Light

Awake, you who sleep. Arise from the dead, and Christ will give
you light.
Ephesians 5:14

April 20, 1969. My unit, Charlie Company of the First Battalion, 503rd Infantry, 173rd Airborne Brigade, was working in the lowlands of Vietnam. Less than a third of the U.S. troops sent to Vietnam ever saw battle, but by the spring of '69, I had seen more than my share. At the time, I was an eighteen-year-old with seven months of frontline combat under my belt as an Airborne Spec 4 who was beginning to seriously wonder if there was any way to win that war.

The NVA (North Vietnamese Army), although continually short on arms and rations, fought with the fierce tenacity of the obsessed. They knew that wretched jungle better than I knew my favorite hunting spots back home in Georgia. Furthermore, they had furrowed Vietnam's vine-entangled terrain with a maze of tunnels that, in spite of our state-of-the-art reconnaissance, kept us guessing as to where they were and when they would suddenly attack.

That hot April day, we were near Bong Son, which is north of Qui Nhon. Nearby was Highway 1, which follows the coast of the China Sea. At times, we were close enough to the shore to glimpse the water, but that particular spring day was not one of them. My company had broken down into platoons, and we had been searching the abandoned villages near Bong Son. Our government had evacuated those villages because we had so much trouble with the Vietcong (South Vietnamese Communist guerrillas) moving into those little circles of dirt-floor huts that they called "hooches" (also spelled "hootches") and trying to take over the local population.

To the jungle natives, war was ever present, like disease and hard times. For centuries—no matter who claimed victory—the jungle natives' lives seemed no better, no worse. So they just lived from day to day, loyal to no one other than themselves, and ignoring, as best they could, the fighting around them. If we paid or fed them, they were momentarily on our side; if the Vietcong paid or fed them, they were momentarily on their side. They didn't seem to understand or care about the differences between Communism and democracy and just wanted to be left alone.

My unit had been operating in the foothills of the coastal lowlands, looking for the North Vietnamese Army's Eighteenth Regiment, which had been working in and around the central highlands and back to the coastal lands, as well as near Bong Son and Pleiku. To expand our search, we broke down into four platoons. The first platoon and my platoon, the second, had gone into the perimeter of the lowlands, while the third and fourth platoons moved to our west about two klicks (kilometers) away.

We made no contact with the NVA during the three days we were in that area. Our new platoon sergeant, all muscle and very much a man, had been in the military since he was old enough to volunteer, which must have been twenty-five or thirty years earlier. Even he was getting as frustrated as the rest of us.

At about 1500 hours, we pulled into one of the deserted villages. Our plans were to set up a listening post and take a break, while five men were sent up a trail to a point that overlooked the abandoned village in order to scope out the situation. In the process, the detail uncovered a cache of rice the NVA had stashed in a cave. Knowing that where you find one critical supply stored you're likely to find others, our sergeant sent me and some more grunts to join in the search. We found no weapons; however, we did find more rice, several hundred pounds of it, tucked here and there in tunnels and caves. Like mice, it seems, they continually scurried about in the dark, storing what supplies they could find for a time of greater need.

We also discovered a little structure that sent chills up our spines that sweltering day. It was a cage on stilts, a bamboo cage with a four-by-four floor and an interior height of no more than five feet. Although empty when we found it, there was a chain lock on the door, which told us this cramped space had likely served as NVA guest quarters for one or more U.S. soldiers who had fallen into enemy hands.

We scouted until sunset, eventually satisfying ourselves that a large contingency of NVA was using the area. However, precisely where they were at the moment remained unknown to us.

When we ended the search, we headed back down toward the village and its dry rice paddy. Between the paddy and us was a gully, which was about six feet wide, four feet deep, and was also dry at the time. One look told you it was the village latrine, as well as a means of controlling the water that poured down from the mountains during the rainy season. Using the villagers' rickety wooden footbridge, we crossed the gully, selected the highest section of the dry paddy, and dug a ring of foxholes in the soft, rich soil, a circle of burrows each large enough to hold two men. Anti-personnel mines, called claymores, were laid out in front of each foxhole, and a guard was posted. Then we settled into our nightly fighting position to eat some cold rations and get a little sleep.

Claymore mines are surprisingly deadly for their size. Weighing only two pounds, each of these little eight-by-six-inch green killers saturates an area about six or eight feet wide and over an area of sixty degrees across its front with 750 steel ball bearings when detonated. Since they were small, we could conceal claymores fairly well— especially at night—and aim them in the direction from which the enemy was most likely to approach.

In preparation for firing a mine, a blasting cap was inserted into it. In turn, the cap was connected to a length of wire. At the other end of the wire was a handgrip firing device that looked similar to a pair of vise-grip pliers. When you squeezed the handgrip, it created and sent enough electrical charge down the line to detonate the mine and pulverize anything in its path with a volley of steel balls. Simple. Efficient. Deadly.

That April night I learned that more could be done with those mines, as I watched a seasoned guy in the other platoon take the blasting caps out of a half-dozen hand grenades and replace each with a claymore mine blasting cap. To his claymore, he wired a series of hand grenades, much like a string of Christmas tree lights. The grenades were placed every five or six feet in front of his foxhole and tucked into either the sand or grass. The idea behind such a rig was that anyone who got beyond the mine's area of attack would find himself standing in a firestorm of shrapnel from the hidden grenades. All this firepower could be unleashed by a single squeeze of a claymore firing device.

The obvious downside of a claymore was that if the enemy came at you from a direction other than the one anticipated, the mine was useless. And those mines were also dangerous to us when an enemy managed to get to one while a guard dozed; the enemy could turn the mine around so that it fired at the person who set it off.

That night, guard duty was conducted from our foxholes, rather than a forward post. About 2230 hours it became my turn on watch, so I motioned to the guy on duty that he was relieved to get some sleep. Only a few minutes of my hour on duty passed before I spotted something, the silhouettes of three crouched men against the night sky. They were moving ever so slowly and silently through the undergrowth about forty yards from my foxhole. At the sight of them, I reached for my claymore firing device and gave it a firm squeeze.

BLAM!

The mine's blast was followed by silence. All again became still out there. Motionless. No fire was returned, leaving me with a choice of conclusions: I had killed the trio, or I hadn't killed them. They were alone—which wasn't likely—or others were out there, too. No fire returned could also mean they preferred to wait until dawn to attack.

When the blast roused both of our platoons we went to full alert. The new sergeant came to my foxhole wanting to know my sit rep (situation report). I told him what I had seen and that my assumption was the gooks (derogatory slang for both Vietcong and North Vietnamese Army) were probing our perimeter, trying to see what we would do. He said, "Good work," and returned to his position.

Nothing else happened and hours passed. Nonetheless, at daylight, we were particularly wary because that was the Vietcong's favorite time to attack. Dawn gave them just enough light to see at a time when our soldiers were often still asleep or at least groggy after just having awakened. But there was no attack; so, as the sun climbed higher in the sky, we were allowed to heat some water, using our canteen cups and a few Sterno pellets. I took out an LRRP Ration (Long Range Reconnaissance Patrol Ration, the packets of the dehydrated food that we carried), poured the cup of boiling water into the bag, stirred it, and waited for my breakfast to be ready.

There was one LRRP Ration that I really liked: shrimp with rice, and that's what I had for breakfast that day while trying to forget the previous night in that kill-or-be-killed world we had invaded.

Once it seemed safe to find out exactly how much damage my claymore had done, our sergeant went with us to the area where I had spotted the three figures. Freshly trampled grass told us I had definitely spotted activity; however, there were no bodies to be found. Disappointed that I had failed and simultaneously relieved that I hadn't taken three more lives, I kept my emotions to myself as we packed to move out.

When we left and headed up the trail, my squad was in the lead, with me as point (the lead soldier of the patrol). Following me was my slack (the second man in a patrol). Behind my backup followed our squad leader and the rest of platoons one and two. As I headed toward the dry gully ditch to lead the troops across the footbridge and onto the trail, I noticed that the gully below cut through red clay, clay as red as that back home in Georgia. But I didn't think about red clay long. As soon as I reached the far side of the bridge and my slack man was starting to cross, there was a loud explosion.

Afterwards, I was told that, during the night, the Vietcong had taken the string of hand grenades and claymore mines that I had watched being assembled and, somehow unnoticed, dragged all that firepower away from the foxhole of the sleeping soldier who had rigged the intricate series of explosives. The collection of firepower had been repositioned on the trail that led from the village, with its firing device in the hands of our enemy.

Stolen weapons were seldom reported because being involved in that situation got you into big trouble, so the theft wasn't admitted. When that jerry-rigged device was exploded, it was lucky for our platoon that the NVA soldier squeezed the control early, wounding only one man.

Unfortunately for me, I was that man.

The explosion drove a lot of metal into my belly, while other fragments embedded themselves in my right hand and cut my throat. The blast also knocked me to the ground, which is where I should have stayed. Instead, I tried to rise and did make it to my knees. Seeing the Vietcong heading up the trail, I struggled to raise my rifle and tried to shoot. That's when I felt a stinging in my right wrist and looked down to see that a bullet had plowed through it, as well as through the stock of my rifle. The rifle stock was in splinters, and there was a gaping wound at my wrist; I could see the white of the bone.

The rest of the troops were instantly prone, in fighting position, but the gooks were through for the morning.

I collapsed—and probably passed out. The next thing I was aware of was somebody grabbing me by the back of my shirt and pulling me. At first I didn't know who had me, friend or foe. What I could see was blood covering my stomach and legs. To my left I heard a familiar voice hollering; it was a buddy of mine from Philadelphia, Francis Hyman.

"We need a medic! Hendrix has been hit."

A medic rushed over and put a bandage on my bleeding throat, while giving instructions to some soldier who was eager to help. The volunteer grabbed my belt and lifted me up so that the medic could wrap my midsection with a tight bandage to minimize the bleeding.

"I'm gonna give you a pop," the medic told me as he stuck a needle into my arm. Within seconds, morphine was dulling my pain. Next came the lieutenant, assuring me, "You're going to be fine, Hendrix. We have a dust-off coming in."

While I waited for the dust-off (helicopter ambulance), Francis came over, lit a cigarette, and put it in my mouth. I can only wonder why he did that since he knew I didn't smoke; just wanted to do something for me, I guess. When I started coughing he decided the cigarette was a bad idea, threw it away, and reached into my shirt to take out my wallet.

In my morphine haze, I couldn't figure out what he was up to. I only knew I was helpless to do anything about it. He removed my wallet from the cleaned, recycled plastic food pouch I carried it in to keep it dry, stuck a twenty-dollar bill into the wallet, rewrapped it in plastic, and stuck it back into my pocket. "Hendrix," he said, "when you get to where you're going, drink one on me." I did my best to smile, and watched him return to his duty.

What I recall as being only minutes later, I heard the thump-thump-thump of a dust-off headed my way. The large green helicopter marked with a red cross skimmed across the treetops with a clearance of no more than four feet between its skids and the tips of tree branches. That beautiful olive-drab bird made a circle to make sure it wasn't going to get any enemy fire, then landed. Any Vietcong who shot down a helicopter was rewarded with a break for R&R (rest and recreation); so helicopters were prime targets and took precautions.

In preparation for dust-off, I had been placed on a stretcher, which was loaded aboard the helicopter. Morphine or no morphine, when we took off, I could feel the jarring thump-thump-thump of the blade being transferred from the metal floor through my thin stretcher to my aching, bleeding body. It seemed I bounced an inch off the metal galvanized floor of that helicopter with each thump of the blades.

I don't know how far we were from a firebase—probably no more than thirty minutes—but I do remember, before we set down, I saw that our destination was an unfamiliar landing zone, and I tugged on a medic's shirt. "Where are we?"

"At LZ English," he said, "the hospital closest to where you were hit."

From relief, exhaustion, and morphine, I passed out.

I awoke, looking into the face of a young, light-complexioned black man with short hair and smooth skin. When I asked him if the doctor was going to see me, he said, "I am the doctor."

"Sir, am I going to make it?"

"You're going to be all right, but we can't do here what you need done so we're sending you to Qui Nhon." He gave me a reassuring smile and moved on.

There was plenty to keep him busy. To my right were about twenty-five men on stretchers, lined up along the walls of the rectangular building we were in. To me, the place looked like a commercial chicken house, long and narrow, with walls up about three feet, then curtains over screen wire to the roof.

Two male medics picked up my stretcher and put me in line with the other wounded. Some had IVs attached to their arms, some were moaning, and most had blood on their sheets. I thought, *Denny, you've got company; you aren't the only guy to get shot up after breakfast this morning.*

The medics loaded up some of us for transport to Qui Nhon. If I'm not mistaken, they could take up to four per helicopter. Somehow I managed to sleep—at least avoid consciousness—for the majority of the ride.

What I remember next was awaking on a cold, aluminum gurney. I know there was a blanket under me, but I could turn my head and see the metal. More to the point, I could feel it under me, icy and hard. I remember looking to my right and seeing a young man whose left leg was gone. There was blood on the floor, blood everywhere. A Vietnamese man ambled about with a hose, washing streams of red into the drains on the floor. I could see the doctors and nurses and medics scurrying around—not panicky, but definitely with more on their plates than it seemed possible for them to handle.

I became aware of the large warehouse-like building where we were stored. Although surrounded by people I felt very much alone. Nobody seemed to be checking on me or doing anything about me. Then suddenly, without saying a word, two medics dressed in white grabbed my gurney and took me on a fast trip through a doorway into a room off the main area.

As we went through the door of the room I could see a large light fixture hanging from a cantilevered stand. An attractive, fair-haired, young nurse in her twenties directed the medics concerning the position of my gurney so that the light concentrated on my abdomen. Her white mask hung down so I could she how pretty she was.

"Where are you from?" I asked.

Startled at first, neither expecting words to come out of a throat wrapped in bandages nor aware that I was awake, she smiled and said, "Oh, hey. I'm from New Orleans, Louisiana."

"I'm from Atlanta, Georgia," I replied.

"Well, this is going to be simple," she assured me. "You're going to be fine. Two of the best doctors in the business will be operating on you. We're going to take care of you."

Remembering the man with the amputated leg, I wondered if I would still have two hands when this was over.

She continued talking in a warm, reassuring voice. "Don't be afraid. We're going to give you anesthesia. The anesthesiologist is going to put a mask over your face. He'll be sitting directly behind you, and I'm going to be right over here."

Before the mask could be positioned, I managed to say, "Wait a minute. Will you hold my hand?"

She said, "Sure," and wrapped my good hand in hers. The anesthesiologist positioned the mask and said for me to count from 100 backwards to zero. But I was so groggy, I probably couldn't have counted from one to ten forwards.

As my eyes shut, I heard two men talking about my stomach wound. I caught the occasional words "objects in the abdomen … damage … exploratory."

I thought, *Exploratory? Are they just going to look inside?* The last thing I recall while lying under that light was wondering why they didn't mention my throat or my wrist.

The next thing I remember was floating, floating above the two surgeons, the anesthesiologist, the nurse, and my body. I floated face down in a warm cloud of brilliant, white light, whiter than any white I could have ever imagined. Weightless in a womb of tranquility, I watched the activity below.

The surgeon to the left of my body had a scalpel in his hand and made an incision from my breastbone to my navel. The other surgeon held a sponge in one hand and occasionally swabbed my chest. In his other hand, he held an instrument that looked similar to a pair of scissors. With it, he occasionally pinched and moved my skin about. At times, he set the instrument aside but would quickly reach for it again.

I remember noticing that the doctor who was doing the cutting had the hairiest arms I'd ever seen. From the rubber gloves that he wore to the cuffs on the short sleeves of his scrubs, his arms were covered with black hair that was so thick you couldn't see his skin, unless he turned or lifted an arm, revealing its white underside.

I felt no emotional attachment to the activity below, just a keen interest in watching something I had never witnessed before. The surgeon on the right side of my body kept talking about a piece of metal he said the x-ray showed was lodged in the abdomen, and he poked and probed about in my midsection, determined to locate and remove it.

After a time, I lost interest in their activity, but recall noticing every detail about the light fixture that hung over the scene below. There were two hexagon bolts on each side and one in the center, holding the fixture in place. To myself I said, *Somebody ought to clean this light, it's so dusty and dirty.*

The activity below continued as the surgeons moved from my abdomen, to my wrist, and to my throat. But what fascinated me more than the operating-room activity was my glorious feeling of calm, of peace, of serenity, of salvation. The white light that encircled me was intense—but not glaring or unpleasant in any way. Its ethereal cocoon of tranquility was the most wonderful thing I had ever experienced, a sensation you could relish for eternity.

Then I heard a voice. Male. Authoritative. Forceful. It came from behind me, above me, everywhere. Calm and decisive it said, **"It's not time now**."

That was all the voice said, and it seemed that I was instantly back in my patched-up body.

When I next opened my eyes, I was furious, furious that I had been sent back to deal with pain. I was extremely upset, belligerently mad. I felt cheated, cheated out of the contentment I had tasted. But there was no one around to rail at.

On top of all the pain from my wounds, I felt as if my kidneys were about to explode. I looked around the ward and became aware that I was just one of many connected to IVs. The only good thing I could find about my situation was clean sheets.

It was a struggle to sit up. By turning to my left, I eventually managed to touch the tile floor with my left foot. By the time I managed to maneuver my right foot to the floor I was exhausted. My gut ached, my head ached, and everything about me ached. Holding on to the curved footboard of my metal hospital bed, I eventually shifted my weight to my feet. But standing straight was out of the question. I gripped the IV pole to which I was attached and made it my rolling cane.

Realizing that another patient was watching me, I asked him, "Where's the latrine?"

He pointed at a door that seemed miles away, but I headed for it bent double, inching my way there with baby steps. Eventually I made it the thirty or forty feet from my bed to my destination.

Inside there was a row of urinals, my reason for making the trip, but something else drew me to it. Over a line of sinks were mirrors, one per basin. I stared, stared at the stranger I saw in them. Inching my way toward the image, I studied the emaciated, zombie-like man who stared back at me. There was a bloody bandage on his neck, blood on his ears and in his hair. For the first time, I also became aware of the bandages on my wrist and neck and how much beard I had grown. No more than 130 pounds of me was left on my six-foot-one-inch frame.

With shaky hands I reached down and lifted the hospital gown I wore and stared at the reflection of a row of shiny metal staples that marched down my body from my breastbone to my navel. I stared and stared for a long time before resigning myself to the fact that I had become the person I saw in the mirror.

When I began inching my way back to my bed a concerned nurse appeared and helped me settle into bed again. That's when I learned that I had been unconscious for four days following surgery.

During that time, I developed an infection that required my taking shots of streptomycin three times daily. After three weeks of those shots, I had bruises the size of silver dollars on my hips and arms. My fifth week in bed, I became able to sit up and make the trip to and from the latrine on my own, so it was time to move on.

They sent me first to Cam Ranh Bay, then on to a hospital in Japan via a Strategic Air Command C-141, which carried up to 150 walking wounded and stretcher patients. When we landed and my stretcher was being offloaded, I heard a voice holler, "Hendrix!"

I rose up to see tall, lanky Francis Hyman, with his arm in a sling and his chocolate-brown face beaming.

"Man, I got hit three days after you. Look at me. Look at daddy. Got the big hit. I'm outta here, headed home to Philly. I'm finished!"

Unlike Francis, I had more stops to make. My stay in Japan was at just one of a string of hospitals between me and my eventual return to duty at 699 Ponce de Leon Avenue, in Atlanta, the induction center where my military stint began.

And on August 1, 1970, having come full circle, I was honorably discharged.

The days I spent in those hospitals gave me plenty of time to think about my experience in the operating room, yet outside my body and in a far better place. Would I say that during the time I spent cloaked in that glorious white light I was in heaven?

No.

Heaven's waiting room?

Something like that.

Wherever I was, it was as real as the dust on top of the operating room light fixture and the hexagon bolts that held it above the surgeons' heads.

What I took from the experience was a clear understanding that the voice was right; it wasn't time for me to abandon my body. I had a purpose, a reason to be taking up space on this planet, and it was my duty to uncover that purpose and fulfill it.

My multiple hospital stays also gave me time to look back on the first nineteen years of my life, time to dig through a garbage pile of experiences. Like a friend once told me, if you want to know where you're going, you better know where you are and how you got there. So the remainder of this account tells how I became a soldier and what kind I became.

—■—

Chapter 2
The Making of a Soldier

Whoever receives one of these little children in my name, receives me.

Mark 9:37

Under the banner of patriotism and just causes I have taken many lives. Looking back, it now seems I spent my entire childhood preparing for jungle combat, devising ways to move silently and attack swiftly. I spent those years figuring out how to be self-sufficient, never depending on others for my needs. I also learned to filter out pain, my own as well as the pain of others. For me, that's what took the place of ordinary children's games, as I spent my early days subconsciously getting ready to be the best, most independent and effective soldier I could possibly be.

That said, I continue my war story, laying out raw truth. In order to do that, however, some names have to be changed in order to protect the guilty, as well as the innocent.

I was born July 27, 1950, Dennis Lee Hendrix, son of Ira Presley Hendrix, Jr., and Betty Louise Hendrix. She was slender and tall—about five ten—with dark hair, eyes, and complexion, a classic Mediterranean appearance topped by a perpetual smile that seldom faded, no matter how she felt inside. He was a slightly taller, muscular guy, with blue-green eyes and wavy blond hair. One look at his hard hands told you that he didn't shy away from work.

When my parents took me from Atlanta's Crawford Long Hospital to the mill village in nearby Roswell, Georgia, I began my hard-knocks education the moment we passed the town limits sign.

In essence, there were two Roswells. On one hand, it was a place of wealth and privilege, a town widely known for its elegant houses and historic churches. My family lived in the other Roswell, a town of modest-to-substandard housing populated by people who struggled just to get from one day to the next.

While there are no longer any mills or factories in Roswell, and the picturesque town and Atlanta's posh north side are linked by a continuous chain of affluent subdivisions and clusters of upscale retail outlets, there were, in the 1950s, miles of woods and farmland separating the two. In fact, although all the apartments and houses in which I lived were near the center of town, it was never more than a short walk from wherever we lived to the fields and woods that became my early training ground for a soldier's life.

My home was also my training ground for battle. When I was born, Mother was a child of sixteen, and Daddy was only three years older—just kids, really. While she matured, he never did. Initially, Daddy worked at the Roswell Seating Company, sometimes helping make church pews, usually delivering and installing them. Mother, from time to time, worked in a textile mill that was only a couple of blocks from the elegant mansion where Theodore Roosevelt's mother grew up. We spent my earliest years in one half of a wooden duplex across from the textile mill, and my mother's parents, Claude and Louise Stoddard, lived in the other half. For more than forty years, my grandfather worked in the textile mill as a maintenance man, making certain the noisy machinery never ground to a halt. My grandmother also worked in the mill, even though she already had a full-time job keeping house, cooking meals, and washing and mending clothes for her husband and three daughters. My mother was their middle child.

Two years after I was born, my sister Debbie came into the picture. So, by age eighteen, Mother had a baby in her arms and a toddler at her side everywhere she went. She loved us dearly, but the same can't be said for Daddy. He looked on both Debbie and me as little more than inconveniences and unnecessary mouths to feed. Over the years, Debbie managed to work out a more or less congenial relationship with him, something I have never accomplished.

The duplex that temporarily housed us Hendrix's and Stoddard's was just one of the substandard places we lived. Some were less desirable than others. For example, at about age six, I helped Daddy dig a septic field so that we could have an indoor toilet at one of the rental properties.

For a few years, we lived in a small, two-bedroom, brick house that my parents and grandparents jointly bought for $13,600. Night after night they sat around the kitchen table talking about how expensive it was. The house had two bedrooms, a little den, a kitchen, and a small living room that featured a large plate-glass window with a view of the cornfield across the way. The house was small but nice, and the best roof I ever had over my head as a child. Still, it was horribly crowded with two families there. Mother's parents turned the den into their living quarters while I shared a room with my sister Debbie.

We were never anything but poor. It did not help the situation having my daddy squander much of the little he earned on liquor, women, and whatever else caught his roving eye. None of his escapades succeeded in giving him more than momentary relief from his negativism, depression, and anger. Once, when he came home with a car that he certainly couldn't afford, I remember Mother's rage and exasperation. She picked up a ceramic knickknack, chased him out of the house with it, and threw the trinket at the car's windshield as he backed out of the driveway and sped down the street. On impact, the windshield shattered into a web of broken glass.

Time after time, he came back, and I assume the main reason Mother always permitted that was monetary; at least he would go to work. Maybe there was still some physical attraction that drew them to one another because it must be said they were an attractive pair. But any semblance of caring, nurturing love was long past by the time Debbie entered the picture. I could not possibly count the times I heard Mother yell at him after he had squandered the grocery money or hit her, "As soon as these children are big enough, I'm gonna divorce your ass."

But she never did, and violence was daily fare at the Hendrix household. I looked forward to the times when Daddy would go away on trips to deliver and install church pews, even if it did mean Mother worried about what trouble he might get into and what might happen to us without his being there to provide for us. From a child's perspective, however, his inevitable return was always a disappointment.

Despite her perpetual smile, my few memories of Mother being happy involve times when a girl from the neighborhood, who was a friend of hers, came to visit. She and Mother played records on a small phonograph, danced, and laughed. But the moment my father returned, the laughter and dancing stopped. Then bedlam reigned.

There was never a day without a fight. My parents fussed and fought so much I used to pray Daddy wouldn't come home until all of us were in bed and asleep. At other times, I hoped to die and have all I knew of life finished. I just didn't want to see or hear their anger anymore. As the years passed Mother learned to suppress or neutralize her fury and rage; Daddy, however, never did.

Through all of this, Mother found time to instill in us some principles that I continue to try to live by. Over and over, she told us, "Never beg, never steal, never lie, and always keep your integrity."

In 1959, teachers sometimes paid home visits to the parents of their students. Before my grandparents moved out, my fourth-grade teacher, Mrs. Miller, came to visit and brought her little daughter who was a loud-mouthed, question-asking little girl. While Mother and Mrs. Miller talked, I was left with the daughter who kept repeating, "Denny, where is your bedroom? Where is your bedroom? Where is your bedroom?" I was embarrassed to say that I had to share a room and a bed with my sister.

Although I made passing grades, Mrs. Miller held me back and did not promote me to fifth grade. Whether her decision had to do with a lack of maturity on my part, my home situation, or something more that she saw or sensed, I guess I'll never know.

The crowded living conditions in the little brick house at 444 Norcross Street became even worse because my aunts and their families developed a habit of showing up for the weekend. There were pallets everywhere, mouths to be fed, and growing resentment on the part of my parents. The additional squabbling the situation generated prompted my grandparents to move, which left us with an empty den.

After a lot of prodding from me, Mother bought an iron-frame bed and put it in the empty room, finally giving me a space of my own and allowing Debbie a bit of privacy as well.

It seems strange saying it, but those years of having to share the same room, the same bed, and the same continual domestic strife didn't create a bond between Debbie and me; instead, it seemed to push us apart, prompting each of us to live in our separate worlds.

At school, I had friends, but each time the bell rang, signaling that school was over for the day, those friendships were put on hold until the next morning. And, even at school, friendships often revolved around military games. When I was in the third grade we played an ongoing game of army each day at recess. I was in charge of one squad and a kid named David Cole was in charge of the opposing squad.

We did not allow girls to play our little macho game, but we couldn't prevent them from watching or having opinions. The teachers were so accustomed to the racket we made, they really didn't keep a close eye on us. That left, as our foremost observer and commentator, a girl named Sue Cook. Sue had a full head of kinky, dishwater blonde hair, which looked as if it had never met with a brush or comb. If her hair had been red she would have been a dead ringer for Little Orphan Annie … at least in the looks department. But when Sue spoke, it was with a Southern drawl that was so thick and so slow she sounded like a bad Yankee parody of how Southerners talk.

One day as Sue was evaluating our military skills things got out of hand, and we boys started throwing large rocks at each other; rocks we found along the edge of the playground's chain-link fence. One end of the fence was next to a long flight of concrete steps that led down to a lower playing field. At the other end, there was a break in the wire, so our rock gathering took place on both sides of the fence. We were strictly forbidden to go on the far side of the fence because there was only a narrow ledge of dirt behind it before a steep and high embankment began. The embankment consisted of piles of rock under a tangle of kudzu vines. Nevertheless, the narrow strip of ground next to the far side of the fence had a well-worn path that you could travel by sticking your fingers through the fence wire to prevent yourself from tumbling down the embankment.

As our battle continued, several well-thrown rocks rained down on my troops who were out in the open. One or two were even bleeding a bit. Realizing my squad was not the better bunch of rock throwers in this contest, I started yelling at the top of my voice, "RETREAT, RETREAT!"

Figuring that the safest way to join them was to take the fence path, I ducked through the hole in the wire and worked my way along the narrow trail, gripping the chain-link fence with my fingers. Somehow a thrown rock went through the fence wire and found its target: the back of my head. I felt as if a mule had kicked my head. My vision became blurred, my knees would no longer hold up my forty-five-pound body, and my grip on the chain-link fence gave way as I passed out. Like a rag doll, I tumbled head over heels down the steep bank, striking large rocks along the way, as well as tearing my clothes. I finally came to rest on my back, out like a light. When I finally managed to open my eyes, and stare up at the sky, I thought that I must still be alive because I couldn't hurt that much if I was dead.

That's when the face of Sue Cook came into focus. She leaned over, filling my range of vision with a close-up of her face and mop of messy hair. We were practically nose to nose as she drawled, "The next time you say 'retreat,' I guess you'll retreat, won't ya?"

I would have throttled her if my wobbly knees could have held me up. After Sue said her piece, she nonchalantly walked back up the steps, passing hysterical teachers on their way down. As my teacher dusted me off, she chewed me out for falling down the hill—as if I did it on purpose—and declared our little playground "war" ended for good. That neither surprised nor bothered me as much as Sue's on-target military critique.

Sue definitely taught me a lesson, one I've never forgotten. The playground war ended with my first and only retreat in life. I continue believing that it's better to stand and fight than to retreat, fall down a steep, rocky embankment, and have a girl taunt you.

When school wasn't in session, I remained a loner and usually played by myself. Room of my own or no room, I quickly learned the hard way that it was difficult to develop friendships with people you can't bring home. The few times I did ask another kid over, there was either no food to share or my parents launched a violent fight over the most inconsequential of things, screaming and hitting one another, both oblivious to others being present. I quickly decided that I would rather be alone than subject myself to the certainty of being humiliated by the circumstances under which I lived. Being a loner was the most appealing option I had.

When I absolutely had to be inside our house, I drowned out the turmoil around me with television, flipping the dial back and forth in search of war movies and television series such as *Combat*. Those black-and-white images of a life with purpose, honor, and hero status filled my head with colorful visions of a world I hoped to experience.

If I didn't have to be inside, I went as far away as I could and created a preferable world that did not include my family and the chaos they continually generated. I developed a loner's mentality and skills that were beyond those of a normal childhood. When not in school, I left early in the morning, usually around seven, not returning until five or five thirty for supper. After class on school days, I headed straight for the sanctuary of the forest to play army by myself.

I learned the woods and the skills for surviving there. In addition to climbing trees, learning the habits of animals, and being more comfortable in the forest than anywhere else I had ever been, I assigned myself complex military projects. For example, I dug at least a dozen deep, underground bunkers that I roofed with eight-inch tree trunks, which I hacked down with a machete. Tough work for a little kid, but I did it. After cleaning away any branches, I roofed my bunkers with the long, straight pine logs, fitting them close together. A topping of sod, plants, and leaves created hideaways that were virtually impossible to spot, well insulated, and that stayed dry when it rained.

I learned to be as good a shot as you can be with a BB gun, and remember tracking a rabbit, repeatedly shooting it in the neck until I caught it. I then felt sorry for the little creature, cleaned him up, and took him back to the woods where I let him go.

When I was eight years old, my father actually did one thing for me that was special; he went to the Western Auto Store in Roswell and bought me a thirteen-dollar .22 long rifle, the only thing he ever gave me. I have it to this day, having held onto it through good and lean times. It continues to receive the quality care usually reserved for rare, valuable arms.

Although he bought the gun for me, he never took me anywhere to shoot it. I eventually persuaded my mother to allow me to buy a box of .22 shells, the kind we called "snake shot" or "rat shot." They function like a high-powered BB gun. After convincing her it was safe to allow me to fire the .22 unsupervised, I frequently took it to the cornfield to hunt doves. Since rat shot was not for distance firing, I had to sneak up on the doves by being very, very quiet. I got to the point that I could almost catch those birds with my hands. Looking back, my proficiency at eight and nine continues to amaze me. At times, it took me two hours to move just fifty yards, but during those two hours, I never made a sound. My goal was to get that dove, and while I wasn't successful every time, I usually was.

When I was older, I played in a cornfield at night and also went deep into the adjoining woods long after dark. The night never scared me; I wasn't afraid of the dark or the forest or what might or might not have been behind the next tree. I knew my terrain, was a good shot, and became a fairly accomplished woodsman.

What I didn't realize then was I was honing skills that would one day help me survive in the jungles of Vietnam.

When I graduated to a shotgun, a friend of my parents, Johnny Dean, took me quail hunting a few times. I also occasionally hunted with a boy my age, named Jimmy Maltsby; yet, most of my hunting was done alone. Everywhere I went, I walked or rode my bicycle, and there were times I walked all day long. The combination of the two forms of exercise built for me massive, powerful legs and physical stamina that have seen me through ordeals too exhausting for others to survive. During my early hunting days, I also learned to skin and clean animals, which I usually passed on to Jimmy, who had a healthy appetite for wild game such as squirrel, rabbit, doves, and quail.

My main childhood attempts at being with others came out of my love of sports and my ability on the playing field. Baseball was my first love, and I wanted to play Little League baseball, but my parents said they couldn't spare the three-dollar fee necessary for me to sign up. That didn't stop me; when I really wanted to do something, I found a way. I went from house to house, cutting grass to earn that money.

From the age of seven, I was accustomed to earning my own spending money. For example, during plowing season, the farmer who owned the cornfield across from our house paid me a hefty twenty-five cents a day to sit on top of his plow, which was further weighted with sacks of rocks on both sides. Collectively, the rocks and I forced the plow deep in the often cement-hard ground. The mule pulled, the farmer guided, and I provided ballast at the cost of a sore rump.

Only after I had accumulated the small-boy fortune necessary to play Little League did my grandfather take me to the community center in Roswell so that I could sign up. I proved to be pretty good at the sport. Being the hind catcher meant I played all the time. Hitting some home runs and generally batting well, I built the highest batting average in the Roswell league: .657 that year. Our neighbor Ricky McCluskey played on the Roswell team. Ricky was good, too, but he didn't play as well as I did.

Near the close of each season, the coaches got together and picked an all-star team to play other towns around Georgia, and I was chosen to be the all-stars' catcher. Ricky, however, didn't make the cut.

I remember the afternoon I came home with my big news. The family was sitting on the porch, which was how most families survived Roswell summers before air-conditioning came into their lives. When Daddy heard the coach's selections, he never said, "Congratulations, Denny, I'm glad you're on the team," or any words that showed so much as a smidgen of pride in or love for me. Instead, "Ricky McCluskey should have been picked for the team" is what he said. And he repeated it over and over and over.

Throughout the years that I played sports, Daddy occasionally showed up at a game; however, there were no words of praise or fatherly advice. A ride home was as good as it got, and all I grew to expect. While the coaches were quick to praise my accomplishments and spur me on, Daddy's single comment about my performance on the field came during my days as a middle linebacker on Roswell High School's football team. "You ain't nothin' but a little hothead. When things don't go your way, you get down on the ground and kick and carry on."

Yes, I did butt heads and roll on the ground; that's what middle linebackers do because football is a violent game. But even the toughest boys want and need to hear something from their dads that I never heard; those simple, all-important words, "I love you."

Prior to my high school days, I was one of the first Roswell Midget Football players when Coach Fincher, the seventh grade math teacher at Roswell Elementary School, created the Roswell Midget Football League. I played end. Ricky McCluskey, our quarterback, threw me the very first touchdown pass that was scored in the league.

As a teenager I became friends with Louis Wingo, Jr. Louis dearly loved, and I highly respected, his father, Chief Louis Wingo of the Roswell police department. Once, when my sister Debbie was severely cut by broken glass while she and I were playing tag, Chief Wingo took Debbie at breakneck speed to Grady Hospital in Atlanta for treatment. He was greatly admired and respected, so it was a sad day when he was later killed in a traffic accident.

Louis, Jr., became very disturbed by the loss of his father and never got over it. He felt suddenly screwed by life, as I had from the beginning. I guess having that in common was one of the reasons Louis wanted to be my friend.

Shortly after Chief Wingo's fatal accident, Louis, Jr., and I started to run with the wrong crowd, the beer-drinkers and hell-raisers, which included some of my cousins. At age fifteen, I could walk into a package store in Roswell, buy a six-pack of beer, and walk out. Louis, on the other hand, couldn't; he looked too young and was too well known. At the time, a six-pack cost $1.35 so Louis and I would pool what change we could scrounge up, and I'd head for the package store. That was about as bad as it got initially—at least for Louis and me. My cousins and their buddies, however, went on to set new Roswell records for delinquency.

Even though I had started drinking, I was able to maintain my physical agility, stamina, and phenomenal endurance of pain. I continually pushed my body to see how far I could take it. I've been asked if there was a death wish under that. Maybe. I know I had one earlier in my life. Also, coming from a dysfunctional family where consideration of others was not an issue, it didn't bother me if I hurt another player. Coaches noticed my physical ability and determination. In eighth grade I was playing varsity football.

I was also making good grades, A's and B's. I had developed an aptitude for studying, concentrating, and learning. High school also brought me the accolades that go to high achievers in sports. Still, I was itching to be done with school and done with my dysfunctional, violent home. I think that hearing "As soon as these children are old enough, I'm leaving your ass" every day of my life built in my mind an obligation to help Mother escape, and at the same time bring about my own escape. I was just waiting for the right moment.

By the mid-1960s Roswell was growing rapidly, and housing near the center of town was becoming very desirable and out of our budget, so we were then living nearly four miles from the school. After football practice one evening, as twilight was setting in, I stood waiting for someone in my family to come pick me up. After a thorough workout on the practice field, the distance was more than I wanted to walk, so my parents usually picked me up. I knew if my father came and I had already accepted a ride, he would go into a rage over the waste of his time. On the other hand, if I managed to get home on my own and dared say anything about his not having bothered to come for me, I'd be attacked. During one of our physical altercations he actually tried as hard as he could to kick me in the groin.

Coach Ray Shepard noticed I was the last player left and asked, "Denny, how are you getting home?" When I told him that one of my parents was supposed to come for me, he said, "I'll just wait here a minute with you."

As we sat, watching the streaks of color in the sky fade to black, Coach Shepard started talking about how Roswell was being ruined by all the apartments going up and trailers that were being allowed in the city limits. Then he went on and on about how the people who lived like that were low class, not community oriented, and definitely not the kind of people a community should be attracting.

After he had finished his speech (one I suspect he had delivered to just about anyone who would sit and listen), he looked at the night sky and said, "It's dark, Denny. Let me give you a ride home." Knowing what was likely to happen if I took him up on his offer I reluctantly said, "Okay. I live on Mimosa Boulevard."

We got into his car and headed for what my family then called home. Debbie and I packed many times after our parents sold the little brick house. For a time, they rented a house at 1066 Green Street, which was across from the public school's playing field, but when my father took a job in Texas, we temporarily moved into the government projects with my grandparents. When it seemed Daddy's Texas job might last, we headed for Texas; however, it was virtually a turnaround trip because that job vanished. So it was back to Roswell, where we settled into a two-bedroom apartment, number 1-A, 756 Mimosa Boulevard, one of the most undesirable apartment buildings in town. We had just two bedrooms and not much else. Mother shared her room with Debbie; my father shared his with me. To pay the bills, he landed a job driving a truck for Fulton County's Bellwood Prison on Jefferson Street in Atlanta, which was as good as a man who could neither read nor write was likely to do. It was a job he kept for twenty-five years before retiring.

When I told the coach, "Stop here," the look on his face let me know he wanted to apologize for what he had said earlier about the white trash that inhabited buildings such as the one where we stopped. But he didn't. "See ya tomorrow," was all he said.

That incident wasn't the reason I dropped out of high school three months before turning seventeen. Perhaps it was one of the straws that eventually broke the camel's back, just part of the great accumulation of reasons I had for wanting so desperately to get away to another life.

At first, I didn't get far. I took a temporary job as a bobber in the mill. There I spent my days in the dark, damp basement, which was inhabited by cat-size rats. My solitary job was removing remnants of yarn from wooden bobbins. This entailed wrapping the ends of the yarn around my arms, holding my arms out, and letting the heavy bobbins spin to the floor. Over and over I did that until each bobbin was cleaned and ready for reuse.

When word of my decision to drop out circulated at school, every coach at Roswell High called or came to see me, asking— practically begging—me to reconsider and return to school. They kept emphasizing that I had a good future ahead of me in sports and that colleges would be looking at me. But I just didn't care anymore. I couldn't see that my life was going anywhere. The other young males in my family were by then into drugs, heavy drinking, and—if not already there—were well down the road to prison.

I thought that if I stayed on in the family, I would surely end up like the rest of them, dodging the law, doing whatever it took to survive, and as miserable as the rest.

My primary concern about escaping our life was Mother. She worked hard to keep Debbie and me fed, clothed, and focused on seizing the opportunities that came our way. Any free moment she had was spent reading, and she encouraged us to discover the better and brighter world that was hidden in books.

I knew there was a better world out there, and I was an impatient teenager who couldn't see hanging on in Roswell for a shot at a college education earned on the football field. That possibility was too far off, too remote for me to place faith in it; therefore, the best opportunity at hand seemed to be the military. I was in great shape and a cut above average intelligence. If I didn't help myself, if I didn't leave, neither my sister nor I would have had a chance. If nothing more, I could make it possible for Debbie to have her own room again. At the time, I also thought that my leaving might help Mother escape. Sad to say, that never happened.

But I did escape. On my seventeenth birthday, July 27, 1967, I went to see the recruiter, got all the necessary paperwork, took it home, and confronted my parents. "I want to join the army," I said, "and I want the two of you to sign, giving your permission."

Mother balked a little, but within a couple of days, both parents had signed.

Two days later, on the first of August, I had to be at the downtown recruiter station in Atlanta. I got up early that morning so that my father could drop me off before heading for work at the prison. We pulled up in front of the recruiter's office, I got out of the car, said, "I'll see y'all later," and Daddy drove off.

After reporting to the recruiter, a group of us were taken to 699 Ponce de Leon Avenue. There we were sworn in and loaded on a bus. My next stop was Fort Benning, Georgia.

—■—

Chapter 3
A New Beginning

The years others knew as youth, I spent learning the meaning of death.

An unknown Vietnam soldier

The basic training I took at Fort Benning was not much different from the basic training all new army recruits and draftees took in 1967. However, at seventeen, it was all new to me. Apparently our cadre was selected on the basis of how wide and deep their sadistic streaks ran. When we were ordered to do something, it seemed they took great pleasure in belittling our best efforts. While I was accustomed to the pressure of football coaches and listening carefully to instructions, army basic was, nonetheless, a new level of harassment. But, like football practice, it has its purpose. It made some of us determined to prove we were better than they thought we were. It made those who thought they were too smart to learn anything worthwhile change their minds. And it made those who weren't inclined to follow orders quickly rethink their approach to dealing with others.

We had about half volunteers and half draftees. And, as you might expect, the volunteers didn't talk to the draftees and vice versa. It seemed to me that the draftees tended to gripe a lot more than the volunteers; still, both groups did their share.

Being something of a loner, I made only one friend during basic, a volunteer from West Palm Beach, Florida, whose name was Huber. The two of us made a pact to meet on the steps of the Georgia capitol three days after our discharge from the army; however, the one time I did see him after basic was near Cam Ranh Bay in Vietnam. We were there to board caribous (unarmed transport planes used for ferrying troops) that would fly us north, him to one destination, and me to another. So, until our flights left, we stood and talked in the field house that served as an airport lobby. Although I tried contacting him after returning home, that was the last time I ever saw Huber.

From the time our feet hit the floor at four in the morning until dark, we marched here, we marched there, and we marched everywhere we went, moving like a bunch of ducks at first. We were issued two of this, one of that, and so on, until we had all the clothing and bedding the army felt we needed. Heads were shaved, stacks of papers were signed, shots were given, and weapons were issued: M-14 rifles (the standard-issue 7.62 caliber semiautomatic/automatic rifle that predated the M-16, which was the mainstay of U.S. ground forces in Vietnam). My arms ached when we exercised with that M-14. Those rifles didn't look that heavy when John Wayne was swinging one around on some late-night movie. The calisthenics, thanks to years of football practice, were something I was already accustomed to; still, each night, like all the rest, I was physically drained. It was all too much for a few. Two guys from my platoon were sent to the fat farm, and one was delivered to a military hospital when he broke under the pressure.

We were taught to march in formation, military protocol, as well as the fundamentals of the Geneva Convention, and military tactics. On the rifle range, I shot Expert, qualified with machine gun, and received bayonet training. It was a grueling routine which is exactly what it was meant to be. The United States was at war in Vietnam, so we weren't being trained for desk jobs.

I have one memory of basic that most who went through training at other bases were spared. Fireguard. We pulled fireguard every night because our barracks were so old, having been quickly erected during World War II. That meant taking your turn walking around both the interior and exterior of your firetrap barracks until time for you to be relieved. One night while pulling fireguard, I glanced over toward the next barracks to see if I could spot their guard. Instead, I saw something that made me step back into the shadows and watch; a man was throwing clothes out a first-floor window. When he jumped out and scooped up the clothes, I recognized him as a great big North Georgia guy, a draftee. He ran across the grounds to an intersection and waited no more than a couple of minutes before a car pulled up and stopped just long enough for him to hop in. I thought, *This army life that I've looked forward to for so long sure doesn't live up to my expectations, but where would I go if I left?*

During our third week of training, a lieutenant came to the parade field where we were and said, "Everyone here who doesn't have a high school diploma, raise your hand."

In my platoon, there must have been fifteen or twenty of us who raised our hands. The lieutenant continued, "The state of Georgia has an educational facility on base. If you go over from six o'clock to eighty thirty and pass a test every night for five nights, you will receive a GED, a General Education Degree, which is the equivalent of a high school diploma. For those interested, we'll make it possible for you to attend every day for five days. Who wants to go?"

I was one of those who raised his hand. English was my toughest challenge; however, I made perfect scores in history, math, and science. Out of a possible 500, I scored 485. When I was awarded my GED, I mailed the certificate to Mother and asked her to put it away in case I ever needed it. I didn't realize it at the time, but that piece of paper was an important step toward a non-military future.

And, so it went throughout basic training; you're muddy one day, clean the next, and always treated like a fool. However, by the time you have basic behind you, you've learned a lot about military procedures and a great deal more about yourself. It's a process that fosters self-discipline, quick thinking, confidence, and a clear understanding that the instruction offered might one day save lives—one of which could be your own.

After we completed training and a routine battery of tests, I was selected to go to Fort Dix, New Jersey, to AIT (Advanced Individual Training). The day before we were to ship out, Huber and I went with a couple of other guys to the post bowling alley, where we collectively downed four dozen 3.2 Budweisers. By the time we polished off our last round, it was too late to catch a cab, so we had to hoof it back to the company area. The first sergeant collared us, took us to the orderly room, and made us stay up all night, stripping, mopping, and waxing floors. As we took turns throwing we completed our cleaning detail and eventually loaded onto the buses for Fort Dix with no sleep and horrible hangovers. Despite our intensive training we all had a considerable amount of growing up left to do.

The first leg of my trip north was via a Delta flight to LaGuardia. Not only was that my first flight, it was my second trip out of Georgia. (The previous one was a weeklong visit to Washington, D.C., for school crossing guards.) Following two bus rides, I was inside the gates at Fort Dix, New Jersey, reporting for AIT.

My most vivid memories of Fort Dix are of the sea-blue skies and crisp, clean winter air. Unlike Fort Benning, with its pollution from factories and cars, running at Fort Dix didn't make your lungs hurt. Another difference was the style of the training. Our platoon sergeant, a twenty-year man, was into thorough training—not harassment. Under his guidance, I learned advanced weapons such as M-60 machine guns; hand grenades; and survival in combat including defense against booby traps and chemical warfare. We even learned how to construct bombs. He was the kind of person who made you want to learn. But I'm not saying everything at Fort Dix was military perfection, especially not the recordkeeping.

Anyone who has ever tried to straighten out a paperwork error in military records has run into this brick-wall reply: "The U.S. Army doesn't make mistakes." That's what they usually tell you, but it would be more accurate to say, "The U.S. Army never admits mistakes."

While at Fort Dix, I was assigned an incorrect MOS (Military Occupational Specialty). While my MOS should have been 11-B, which is army infantry, I was listed as 11-C, which stands for 81-mm mortars. I never did manage to get this little error corrected, and it caused me problems on down the road. It's even listed on my discharge papers.

I imagine my AIT experience was not unlike the experiences of other soldiers; however, one particular event put me on a special path. Just before my AIT was complete, we marched to the post library to hear a recruiter pitch going airborne. The big, burly guy started with a very enticing offer: "Any man in this room who elects to go to jump school to be a paratrooper will get a thirty-day leave when he leaves this post."

That got my attention; then he showed a movie that romanticized the airborne, making it sound like the most exciting thing in the world. He even dangled the prospect of an extra $55 a month in addition to the whopping $240 I was already being paid. Then came the clincher: "And if you decide jump school's not for you, just say so, and they'll put you right back into the regular army."

Man, oh man! A no-obligation, thirty-day leave was like holding a sizzling steak under the nose of a starving man. And if I didn't like it, I could quit; that's what I understood the man to say. I may have been young and naive, but I wasn't stupid; so to make certain I had all of the conditions straight, I repeated them to the recruiter: thirty-day leave, then if I didn't like jump school, I could quit.

"Absolutely. You got it. This is volunteer army, *volunteer*. If you don't like it, you get out."

I wasn't the only one who immediately saw the opportunity to grab a thirty-day leave, report to jump school, say, "This just isn't for me," and go back to the regular routine of an enlisted man. My California friend Chico had exactly the same idea, so we put our names on the airborne recruiter's dotted line.

When we finished AIT and graduated, the platoon sergeant walked into our barracks, accompanied by the two corporals in his cadre, who lugged boxes filled with thick manila envelopes, all labeled with a name and duty station. Each time a name was read off an envelope, the guy named would holler "here," and with a shout of "air mail!" the sergeant tossed the envelope in the soldier's general direction.

My name was one of the first called. I grabbed my envelope out of the air and immediately saw that it listed Fort Benning, the location of the airborne school, as my duty station—but it had a report date of the following Monday. As soon as I noticed that report date, I went to the sergeant and said, "There's a problem here; my report date is wrong."

"Army don't make mistakes," was his reply.

I hollered at Chico, "Is your leave on there?"

"No. I have to be at Fort Benning Monday morning. There's a travel voucher in here and a bus ticket."

I asked the platoon sergeant if we could go see the airborne recruiter, and he said, "Yeah. But this is Friday, and they leave early over there on weekend pass."

I never ran faster, but when we got to his office, no one could find him; furthermore, the front orderly said there was no way to contact him until Monday. With a mean grin, he added, "Guys, go pack your bags, roll your bunks up, and be ready to catch that bus."

Like a couple of whipped pups, we plodded back to the barracks to hear others in our squadron jabber about their assignments in

Hawaii and various forts throughout the other states. But for Chico and me, it was straight to jump school.

When we reached Fort Benning early Monday morning and went to the barracks for early arrivals, I was still scheming how to get one of those great assignments in Hawaii that I was convinced originally had my name on it. "Chico, here's what we'll do," I said. "We'll go over to the first sergeant of this training company and tell him that, since we didn't get our thirty-day leave, we're just gonna quit."

Chico liked that, and off we went to the orderly room. It was freezing outside, but the door was wide open; only a screen door filtered out the cold. And our reception was about as chilly as the air inside and out. After a nerve-wracking wait, a sergeant came by, wearing a black hat, and boots you could eat off, and barked, "Hendrix, let me see your orders."

He squinted hard at my orders and hard at Chico's orders, and then thrust them back at us. "Okay, you two are assigned Airborne Training Brigade, Class Number 53."

"Sergeant, there's a mistake," I said.

"What kinda mistake?"

"We didn't get our thirty-day leave."

"So?"

"So, we want to withdraw and be reassigned."

"So?"

"The sergeant at Fort Dix said we could withdraw if we want to."

This time, he didn't say "so." "Shut your damn mouth, you whiny wimp, and get down to the training barracks before I kick your ass! You are in jump school, soldier. The only way you're gonna get out early is if they take you out on a stretcher."

When I turned to Chico for support he was out the door and on his way to the training area. So, we were in airborne, whether we liked it our not.

Airborne training is tough as hell; anyone who has survived—or didn't survive it—can vouch for that. It was twice as tough as basic, each day starting with a member of the cadre beating metal trash can lids together, as a gentle hint to hit the floor in high gear, even though it was hours before daybreak.

You learned fast not to call them "cadre," which is technically what they were; however, they had gone the extra mile and qualified to wear their black baseball-type caps. No one else in the military shared their distinctive headgear or had such dominance over the men under them; therefore, if they wanted to be known as Black Hats, that's what we called them.

Their sergeant, who was among those who always carried a two-by-four the length of his forearm, was something to behold. I don't think ten of us could have taken him down. Like him, his half-black, half-white Black Hats formed a vicious bunch. You couldn't talk to them; all we could do was keep our mouths shut and do exactly as they said, while they poured the torture on. I never before or since went through so many push-ups, sit-ups, monkey bars, and runs in T-shirts in below-freezing weather, chanting sentiments such as:

I want to be an Airborne Ranger,
Live the life of guts and danger.

I want to rape and kill and plunder.
I want to burn a VC village.
Airborne every day.
Airborne all the way, SIR!

And all our training was in high gear. Run, do calisthenics, run some more. Run, do calisthenics, run some more; again, and again, and again. We ran everywhere we went—even to and from the chow line—being cursed and threatened every step of the way.

My first airborne "meal" was literally over before I had time to pick up my fork, so I routinely kept from starving by cramming my food into my sweaty fatigue pockets and sneaking bites till it was gone. Besides, I loved Army food and had no problems with it. I used to think that it was a safe bet that the complainers had no better before they came into service.

The first guy to be released from airborne was hauled off to the hospital in the middle of the night with a raging fever. The incident was never mentioned; the next day, it was as if he had never been there. That was not how I wanted to depart, so I decided, at least for the time being, to take whatever punishment they dished out.

The second week, we trained at the jump towers. Monday through Wednesday, following a modified version of our all-day endurance training, we learned everything there is to know about a parachute, how to sit in a plane, how to stand up, how to hook up to the static line that pulls your primary chute when you jump, how to airborne shuffle to the plane's door, and how to jump out of the mock planes. I don't think anyone's attention wandered for even a second. By this point, we all knew that our lives could depend on grasping every single thing we were taught.

Thursday, we progressed to the 250-foot-high towers. As I stood there, looking up at the faraway top, my lifelong fear of heights was in full play, and I was kicking and cursing myself for ever getting into that predicament.

A long cable lowered from the top of the tower and was hooked to my parachute. The cable hauled me to the top of the tower and then released me to drop the equivalent height of a twenty-five-story building. After a couple of drops, they said we were ready for our series of actual jumps from a plane. I didn't think so.

Even though I had made it beyond the jump tower hurdle, I went back to see the first sergeant at the orderly room and told him I wanted to quit. By then, he had definitely pegged me as a troublemaker and derived considerable pleasure in abusing me verbally and threatening me physically. So, with his "encouragement," I continued the process of becoming airborne.

Every day it became more of a challenge. I wondered, could I do this? Am I man enough? Each time I noticed how much the others wanted to make the grade, the more I wanted to do the same. I knew I could run, I could jump, I could get in top physical shape, and thought, If these other guys can do this, by God I'm gonna prove I can do it, too.

We didn't talk about it; we just did it. There was no bragging about accomplishments or ragging others who were having a tougher time than you were. There wasn't strength or energy to spare for that sort of thing ... or time to be concerned about the problems of others. Every minute was critical; there was no time to worry about what happened yesterday, last night, or a minute earlier. You just did

47

whatever it took to get through the moment and be ready for those first five jumps that allowed you to wear parachute wings.

The goof-off kid in me occasionally surfaced. That second week of hell culminated with a five-mile timed run. I told Chico, "This is our chance to get out without being hauled outta here on a stretcher. Slooooooow up," and he thought that was a plan.

About a mile into the run, while everyone was screaming and chanting and singing and moving on down the road, I shifted my scheme into first gear by pulling over to the right side of the road and letting others ease on ahead. Chico followed suit. That's when two of the cadre trotted up to our sides, and one of them said, "Look, you guys can make it. If you don't, you've got problems."

Each carried a flashlight that he wielded like a policeman's club. Having heard stories about how skilled they were at using those instruments, Chico and I were freshly motivated.

And there was something more: it dawned on me that the Black Hats, while older than we, were out there running it in their fatigues, setting the pace for the rest of us. Every three weeks, they repeated the same grueling routine they were subjecting us to. If those old guys can do this over and over, I thought, I can do it at least once; gonna stay with 'em and push myself to see what happens.

Chico and I completed the run; however, some didn't—but not for lack of trying. I have no idea where they were sent; I only know they were suddenly no longer at jump school and were never mentioned again.

Monday morning of the third week, we lined up at the jump school assembly area to be bused by platoon and company to a location where we were given numbers before filing into a long warehouse. There, we checked out a main parachute and a reserve parachute. At the far end of the warehouse we suited up to be bused to an airstrip. From the bus, I could see the airplanes, a half-dozen C-119 World War II flying boxcars, which I thought the army had quit using at least by the time of the Korean War. The ancient aircraft didn't bolster my wavering confidence. When the engines cranked, the old plane quivered, and the engine on the left side sputtered. None of the alarming noises seemed to faze the pilot as he taxied into position, and then took off.

As we sat frozen in our squared, meshed canvas, hammock-like seats with our arms folded across our reserve parachutes, I looked across the narrow space between the guys on my side of the plane and those on the other. I could easily see that I wasn't the only one scared, and somehow that made me—if not braver—at least less scared.

When the plane lifted off, we flew in formation with the other planes to a jump site in Alabama. About thirty minutes after we were in the air, the jumpmaster said, "Stand up." The lights in the back of the plane flashed and, as we stood up, he said, "Hook up.... Check equipment.... Stand in the door." When the green light came on, he hollered, "Jump."

That was the moment of truth. I really didn't want to jump, but I knew I had to because I had gone too far to quit. And, if I didn't jump, I had a big, strong suspicion they would live up to the threat of throwing me out. So, when it came my turn, I pushed my static line forward and looked out the door at the parachutes in the air, some opening, some already open. I jumped out, counted to four, felt a tremendous jerk on my harness, and looked up to see my chute spread out above me. With enormous relief I took hold of the static lines and floated to the ground while watching the planes disappear into the distance.

On a cold day, such as that one, you come down much faster than when the air is warm. On hot days, I've seen a current get under a chute and just float it—which isn't something you want to happen if enemy sharpshooters are keeping an eye on the sky.

When I hit the ground I did a virtually perfect parachute-landing fall. I hit the release button on my parachute, ran around behind it, shook the wind out of it, rolled it up, picked up my chute, and walked to the staging area, determined to earn my paratrooper wings.

Tuesday, the second day, I was to be the number-two man to jump, and I was feeling very brave until the plane's navigator slipped out of his berth, grabbed his parachute, and put it on. Even from where I stood waiting to jump, I could hear him over the engine noise: "Every goddamn time I fly in this friggin' airplane, I have to wear my parachute and jump out of the sonofabitch."

I knew he wasn't faking when I looked out the window and saw a billow of smoke the diameter of a fifty-five-gallon drum, which was coming out of one of the engines. I thought, *Well, damn. The second time up for me and the plane's gonna crash.*

Before we reached the drop zone, the jumpmaster hollered, "Everybody stand up. We gotta lighten the airplane now! We have to jump early."

Out the open door, the pine trees below looked like they were an inch tall, and I could see a couple of lakes. I knew everybody in the plane shared the same thought: If we jump and have to land in a lake or in those trees, we're gone; we just aren't experienced enough.

The jumpmaster bellowed, "When the light comes on, stand ready."

The light turned green just as we reached the edge of the jump zone, and we jumped, all landing safely, just shy of the pine trees. That was a long way from where we landed the previous day. I'm sure they let us go as long as they could before ordering us to jump. As I was floating down, I looked up and saw our plane break formation and, I assume, head back to the base. In true airborne style, no one ever spoke of the incident.

Wednesday, the third jump day, was uneventful until someone hollered, "Look! A smoke roll."

Those are words no paratrooper wants to hear. A jumper's main chute had tangled or he had pulled his reserve too quickly. In either case, neither chute had opened to catch the wind. Instead, it streamed behind him like a tube of smoke.

The jumper was dropping from 1,300 feet at breakneck speed. Falling, falling, falling. I could see his legs churning, pumping, as if he was peddling a bicycle, as he frantically tried to untangle his lines. When he hit the ground, his body literally bounced. Neither chute ever fully opened; however, even a tangled chute does slow you down some. Within two minutes, there was a medevac (medical evacuation by helicopter) landing next to him to whisk him away. Afterwards, I heard he had survived, but it was hard to believe that was true.

I really liked that guy because he was always happy; bobbing around like a boxer, joking and yet very serious when it came to his training. He was different. Everybody else was scared to death, trying to concentrate, and worn out. But not him; he was like Mohammad Ali, shadowboxing, jumping, talking; really full of life.

On Thursday, the fourth day, we made the same jump without incident.

On Friday, following our fifth jump, the airborne commander of the training school at Fort Benning came to the jump field and assisted our sergeant and his Black Hats in pinning on our wings, the symbol that said we were airborne.

Two days later, wearing spit-shined boots and dress greens with brand-new airborne patches on them, and with our training complete, we headed for our first military assignments. My destination was Fort Bragg, North Carolina, home of the 82nd Airborne Division.

About three months after arriving at Fort Bragg, I was standing in the chow line at my assigned mess hall. About 300 yards away, at another company's mess hall, a fight broke out, and some of us left our chow line to check out the free entertainment. It was a hellacious slugfest between a huge white guy and a little black guy, both kicking, cussing, and pounding away.

When some soldiers finally got them separated, I couldn't believe my eyes. The little guy whipping up on the big one was the jumper I had seen smoke roll at Fort Benning.

Forget eating; I had to talk to this guy and find out what happened from the time of the smoke roll until the time of the fight, so I waited until things calmed down, then went over and asked him.

"Yeah," he said with a laugh, "hurt my back and arm bad. Had to stay in the hospital for a while, but when I got out, I headed straight back to jump school … and finished. Just wasn't gonna let one screw-up change what I'd set out to do."

It was clear that that plucky little guy regarded the Paratrooper and Airborne Division as military elite; I couldn't have agreed with him more.

———•———

Chapter 4
The Bomb

So, I looked, and behold a pale horse. And the name of him who sat on it was Death, and Hades followed with him. And power was given to them over a fourth of the Earth, to Kill with sword, with Hunger, with Death, and by the Beasts of the Earth.
Revelation 6:8

Shortly after arriving at Fort Bragg, I called home to find my mother highly upset. "Son, have you done something wrong? The FBI was here today and wanted to know all about you." Before I could wedge in a word, she added, "They've talked to your teachers, your sister, even the neighbors. And the whole neighborhood thinks you're in big trouble! Are you?"

I had no idea what was going on until at formation some days after talking to Mother. My name, along with about a dozen others, was called. We were told to stand aside and await further orders. What we eventually learned was we had been handpicked for a special, highly sensitive unit that would be "around" a weapon that required a government security clearance known as Secret. In fact, following a thorough investigation by the FBI, we had been awarded the clearance. Additionally, we were led to believe—and I had no reason to doubt it—that we were the only group within the U.S. Army slated for this yet-unspecified special training. That, however, was not true; the military has a habit of telling grunts only what they want them to believe.

Knowing only that I had received a Secret clearance, I called Mother again to tell her I had been selected, along with a few other soldiers, to handle a special assignment and to tell the nosey neighbors that I wasn't in trouble. In reality, I had just received a Secret security clearance which was necessary for the assignment.

While news of the clearance gave Mother an extra level of comfort, I'm not sure it did much for the neighbors, especially if they stopped to think that some matter of national security was being entrusted to a high school dropout with a highly developed talent for getting into trouble.

When I learned exactly what my training was to involve, I wrote Mother, telling her, "I can't tell you much about the gun because I don't know much yet, and it's also a secret. We're not supposed to tell any of the measurements or range or what type of warhead it fires. Chances are it will never be used, and I really hope so."

That was probably more than I should have said and more than she needed to know, because I didn't want her worrying herself sick. In fact, I didn't tell anyone what I learned. Those of us called out of formation and others, who swelled our number to forty, were given serious talks about the need for secrecy; however, we were never threatened in the event we did slip up and mention "it."

"It" was a tubular metal affair with fins on its rear end and a nuclear warhead on its front. This compact fifty-one-pound bomb (the smallest fission bomb ever deployed by the U.S.) was the size of a large watermelon and was designed to be fired from a 155-mm howitzer, with a range of 1.24 to 2.49 miles. If this description brings to mind what you may have heard referred to as "a suitcase bomb," you have a fairly accurate picture of the weapon. While our baby bomb wouldn't actually fit into any suitcase I've ever owned, it could have been easily stored in a standard plastic beer cooler.

Our band of forty enlisted men and draftees, ranging in age from seventeen to twenty-five, became the Davy Crockett Nuclear Weapons Unit. In other words, "Davy Crockett" was the name of the weapon entrusted to us, and we became known as the Davy Crocketts; however, we were told that no one on our base, except our unit and a select number of the higher-ups, knew what our mission was or what the name Davy Crockett stood for.

We Davy Crocketts were assigned housing in a special section of Fort Bragg and even had trucks dedicated to our use. When we went for field training, we wore special tags and had the area completely to ourselves; all other military personnel were forbidden to be anywhere near us. However, that was our only semblance of separation or quarantine. We were even allowed to take our cameras with us to the field; that's how lax actual security was. When not training or running—our physical fitness was not neglected for a moment—we were free to move about the post and go into town on passes. For all I knew there could have been other units at Fort Bragg with missions just as lethal. It was, after all, wartime, and America was using the Vietnam conflict as a testing ground for technology and weapons, many of which made their official and spectacular debuts in the Persian Gulf.

I had certainly not requested this type of duty, nor was I even qualified for it. My papers said I was trained as a mortarman. The fact that I had absolutely no such training didn't seem to bother anyone, so I was headed on a totally new military path: learning the ins and outs of operating a 155-mm howitzer that launches a nuclear warhead. We, however, practiced only with dummy bombs. The real McCoys, we were told, were stored somewhere underground in Arizona.

Instructions for firing a Davy Crockett were in a manual marked Top Secret, and when not with us in the field, this thick document was kept in a vault at the Fort Bragg Armory. Only the top dogs were cleared to remove the manual from its vault. Each day we trained, the specially assigned sergeant went to the armory, removed the manual from its secure storage, and transported the set of instructions to the field, where we had two setups for equipment: one on wheels, the other mounted on a jeep. With manual in hand, we trained five days a week, learning to set up for launch from the ground and from a jeep.

Our sergeant read page after page of information to us which we were expected to mentally store away. No notes were allowed, and much of what we were taught had to be memorized word for word, especially the firing procedures, which ran nearly three pages in length. No two ways about it, this was a weapon that required a team effort to fire. We could hit the ground and have a nuclear bomb on its way to its target in ten minutes flat. While we were trained to work as an eight-man team, as few as two could discharge the weapon under combat conditions.

Training seemed to be going well until one day the inspector general, some MPs, and the captain of the company, along with some artillery specialists, arrived unexpectedly at our training site. And they were not happy. Somebody had left half of the training manual, which included how the bomb is assembled and fired, lying on the counter in the armory room. Anyone passing by could have picked it up and walked out with it. When the inspector general, who was a one-star general, learned about this bit of carelessness, smoke started coming out his ears, and he was threatening to throw us all in jail—whether we were the culprit or not.

It still amazes me that a weapon of this magnitude was entrusted to a bunch of kids. That small bomb—small in size when compared to traditional bombs—required a team of specialists to fire it. Since there were forty of us in the unit, we were divided into four teams of eight, with the remaining members of the unit in supervisory positions. Although a couple of men could easily pick up the warhead, a total of four was assigned to the loading detail. Our loading routine was: (1) pick the bomb up by its support plate; (2) turn and insert the bomb into the howitzer tube; (3) tighten the screw nuts; (4) loosen the support plate straps, allowing the plate to fall away; and (5) step aside and pick up side arms in order to protect the bomb and the other crew members while they completed the firing process.

After firing, our remaining responsibility was to dismantle the unit and exit the area—assuming that in actual combat we survived the blast.

At one point we were assigned an extra two men, young buck sergeants fresh from Vietnam. As I recall, they were transferred into our unit because they were rangers and had special clearances. They were with us, however, only a matter of days, so I never had the chance to get to know them well. The reason they didn't stay and were moved out so quickly was that everyone in our unit had to memorize several pages of procedures concerning our positions and functions. The new guys seemed unable to memorize anything; one of them couldn't even get the firing commands correct. My personal opinion is both men were so messed up from the time they had spent in Vietnam that their minds were scrambled; they had that thousand-yard stare I soon learned to know so well. At any rate, within a few days, both buck sergeants were transferred and never mentioned again.

Those of us remaining were entrusted with everything there was to know about this bomb, which we were told contained enough firepower to wipe out a small city. Since it was potentially a suicide weapon whose firing crew might not survive, we never practiced with gas masks or seriously talked about the fatality of our mission. A couple of times we joked about a howitzer's relatively short range and shooting a nuclear bomb at a target that was most likely in sight, but serious talk? Never. Even though, down deep, we knew that we would most likely be in the bomb's fallout range and most likely would be hit by its initial blast, we were at that age when you think of yourself as indestructible. So the reality of being part of a suicide squad—American kamikazes, actually—was just not discussed.

While there was nothing really wrong with any of the Davy Crocketts, they weren't my kind of people, and I really didn't want to be in that unit. The others were trained artillery, trained in the mathematics of weaponry; therefore, trajectories and such formed their language. A few were college-student draftees; the rest were airborne, ranging from privates to high-ranking sergeants, as well as one second lieutenant. None of them, however, had any nuclear weapons training prior to the assignment to the Davy Crocketts. On that single account, we were on an even footing.

Where I wanted to be was down the street with the grunts because they got to fly in C-141s, go out west to parachute in the desert, train in Europe, and enjoy the cut-above treatment those airborne recruitment films promised to all, and delivered to some. However, while they were seeing the world, I was stuck at Fort Bragg, where what passed for excitement was going to a Fayetteville, North Carolina, strip joint to drink beer and watch some half-naked girl attempt to dance when she ought to have been home studying high school homework.

I've always been something of a prankster and was then still a kid with his nose out of joint about the series of broken army promises I had been made, so I formed a plan. I would register as a conscientious objector. My thinking was along these lines: This bomb is designed to kill a lot of people, so if they have a conscientious objector in there, they'll get rid of him. Why would they want me? Besides, I didn't ask for a security clearance, and I didn't ask to be in nuclear weapons. In fact, I was infantry and didn't know anything about shooting a cannon.

So, I requested permission to speak to the captain, a lifer from Fort Benning. Permission was granted, and I found myself standing at attention in front of his desk.

"What is it, Hendrix?"

"Sir, I think I'm a conscientious objector and would like to fill out the proper paperwork."

"WHAT?"

"I'd like to fill out the proper paperwork and get transferred somewhere else because I don't want to be killing people with that nuclear bomb we're handling."

He looked me over carefully before speaking again. "Have you talked to the chaplain?"

"No, sir. That's a good idea, and I'll do that next."

"Well, you have to have special forms to be listed as a conscientious objector, and the forms have to be approved by the army. You can't just come in here and tell me something like that. You stay on your duty station, and I'll get the forms for you because I *have to*, once you request them."

About two weeks later, he called me to his office, where he sat holding a pink piece of paper. "Hendrix, have you talked to the chaplain yet?"

When I said that I hadn't but that I had an appointment, he said, "You still go see him." Then he thrust the pink piece of paper at me and added, "Here's your conscientious objector form. Sit down and fill it out."

"Yes, sir!" I took the form, sat down in the closest chair, and started reading.

"Not in MY office, Hendrix. Out in the orderly's office."

After saluting and making a stumbling exit, I gingerly sat down at a table outside, under the watchful eye of the sergeant in charge. He was a career man who wore blue eye shadow and curled his eyelashes. Over time, I learned that, whatever his sexual preference might have been, he was one tough soldier. He had the physical stamina of a Black Hat and jumped every time those of us who were airborne did.

After carefully filling out each and every section of the pink form, I asked permission to see the captain again, submitted the form, and stayed at a frozen parade rest while he carefully read each and every word. "Is all this true?" he asked.

"Yes, sir," I assured him, thinking this was easier than I thought.

"DENIED," he said. "Now, get your ass back to your unit. I'm not sending this out of my office."

Having not breathed a word of my plan to anyone in my unit, I shrugged the whole thing off as another of life's little disappointments, canceled my appointment with the chaplain, and went on with my training. However, that wasn't the end of the matter. Three weeks later, we were getting ready for an I.G. (inspector general) inspection that received the attention and preparation that might have been awarded a visit from the President and all the members of Congress. The woods that constituted our training area were roped off, and guards were positioned along the perimeter. I'm not certain if it was all for show, for the protection of the big dogs, to wrap our project in a cloak of secrecy, or all three; however, we were standing tall when a general and three aides rolled up to see that cannon and how we fired it.

The general got out of his jeep and swaggered over to the ropes that surrounded our mighty cannon. He adjusted the floppy cap he wore, the kind that recruits have to wear, and smiled lovingly at the weapon, pride and admiration oozing from his pores. I was standing close to the rope when he approached, and our eyes met.

"Soldier," he directed at me, "what would you do if the enemy came out of these woods over there and assaulted this position?"

With the most earnest-looking face that I could muster, I said, "Sir, I guess I'd just have to let them go right on through because I'm registered as a conscientious objector."

"WHAT?"

"I don't believe in killing, sir."

"CAPTAIN MAULDIN, come here! COME HERE!"

Our captain and the general moved out of earshot of me, but I could see how red Captain Mauldin's face was. I'm sure he could see prison coming for somebody—at least a mountain of paperwork and a demotion. When the general's aides gravitated toward the two commanders to hear what was being said, their faces turned to solid stone.

To my surprise and disappointment, the whole thing just went away; no one ever confronted me. Furthermore, the conscientious objector forms never appeared in my records. So all I have of my time as a conscientious objector are my memories and the chuckles that go with them.

On July 1, 1968, President Lyndon Johnson signed the Nuclear Non-Proliferation Treaty with the USSR, the UK, and 133 countries without nuclear weapons capabilities in an effort to prevent the spread of nuclear weapons. Although the treaty did not become official for several years, Johnson was serious about it. Wanting to look as earnestly as possible, I assume, he halted certain types of nuclear development on the spot. This meant operations such as Davy Crockett were shelved.

As the ink was drying on the Non-Proliferation Treaty, we were informed that the Davy Crocketts were disbanded, and all of us were given special request forms for transfer. Being a cocky eighteen-year-old, I put on my form that I would like to be transferred someplace with palm trees, clean beaches, blue skies, and weather eighty to eighty-five degrees year round.

When the first sergeant saw what I had written, he said, "Hendrix, you're a wiseass, aren't ya?"

I said, "No, Sarge, I want to go to Hawaii."

He held the form in front of my face. "Well, it doesn't say 'Hawaii' on here."

"Aw, just turn it in like it is," I said.

"Okay," he shrugged. "But don't be surprised if you get *exactly* what you asked for."

—■—

Chapter 5
The Messenger

For he shall give his angels charge over you.
Psalm 91:11

Tweeeeeeeeettt! A shrill whistle rang out, blinding overhead lights came on, and the daily announcement was loudly proclaimed.

"Okay, paratroopers. Hit the flo! You will falls out for our morning run. When you come back, you will sweeps. You will mops. And you will sweeps again the barracks flo. Then you will shine with the buffer—to my preference."

Like clockwork, every morning for seven months, at the exact moment the second hand on his watch hit twelve and the hour hand touched five, Sergeant First Class Willie Franklin appeared in our Fort Bragg barracks bay to loudly remind us of the day's events.

A career soldier, or lifer, is how we thought of him. Sergeant Franklin was our keeper, our guide, and our protector. He had a special concern for the welfare of his troopers, although he would be hard-pressed to ever admit it. This soft-spoken professional flowed with the slow-moving grace of a cat as he moved about. He was maybe six feet three inches tall, a lean 175 pounds, with a dark complexion and the largest hands I have ever seen on any man.

The resume of ribbons and patches he wore over the breast pocket and on the sleeves of his Class A uniform told a story of two tours in Vietnam in which combat, pain, suffering, and heroism were a routine part of life.

At the time, I didn't give much thought to those sewn patches and carefully arranged ribbons; I never really had a reason to concern myself with such details, nor did I have an interest to inquire. It was much later that I came to realize his patches and ribbons were badges of courage earned by this man who spoke little and worked hard. On post the decorations afforded him respect that would never be equalled in any job on the outside—especially in the North Carolina of 1968. There, he could not drink from a "whites only" fountain or use a "whites only" bathroom, but he could risk death or permanent disability on behalf of the very country that forbade him small privileges that we white soldiers took for granted. Outside the barbwire boundaries of this base and dressed in civilian clothes, he became a thing, no longer a human being.

We all lived together, the troopers of the Eighty-second Airborne Division. Our home was a series of three-story cement-block barracks. There were twenty metal-framed single beds, each with upper and lower bunks, and ten on a side, placed at precise intervals down the bay. Forty men to a floor, three floors to a barrack, these barracks stretched into the distance, housing the population of a division that was thousands strong.

The walls were nearly all windows, and at the end of the bay a five-foot-wide fan in a metal-framed wire cage of sorts served to vent the aroma of the sweat of forty bodies of many different nationalities from the barracks bay. Every morning, six days a week without fail, we ran five miles and returned dripping with sweat and vomit. The fan served a very useful purpose.

Having been given orders to disband the Davy Crocketts, we packed our gear and stood by to be transferred within forty-eight hours to new assignments. In one way, it was the end of a good assignment. We had lived in the highest level of comfort the army afforded, not having to go out on maneuvers for long stretches as other units did. On the other hand, we were no longer being trained to execute a form of warfare that would surely bring death to soldiers who carried out our special form of training. So we would no longer be the "Ghost Platoon" that went its separate and secret way—except on payday and late Friday evenings, when, like everyone else, we were looking for a weekend pass.

The bare feet of forty men made a slapping sound as each paratrooper jumped from his bunk and rushed to the showers. Quickly dressing and cleaning our living area, we then headed to the mess hall for a breakfast of cold eggs and warm milk. Following breakfast, we returned to the barracks to pack and prepare for reassignment to a new airborne unit.

But reassignment was not a mass action in our case; we weren't being sent as a unit to continue working as a team. We definitely would have if the nuclear ban hadn't been formalized between the U.S. and the Soviets. Instead, individual assignments dribbled in: several the first day, none the next, a few more a couple of days, and on down the line. So, until it was your turn, you waited, were assigned cleaning details, and waited some more. Some guys were sent to U.S. posts—one lucky dog was sent to a missile base in Hawaii. Others shipped out for European bases, but I don't recall any getting Vietnam assignments.

It was sad, really, seeing an elite group of guys who had bonded into a one-of-a-kind military team being separated, each knowing the chances of ever seeing his buddies again was slim to none. We would shake a guy's hand, slap him on the back, and make empty promises of a reunion we knew, even then, would never happen.

After two weeks of doing little more than sitting around on our footlockers awaiting orders, there were only fifteen of us who hadn't shipped out. With nothing much to do with our time, we mainly watched the clock until we had permission to head for the post bowling alley to drink 3.2 beer at a quarter a can. Each and every day became duller and more frustrating.

On Thursday of the third week of waiting, waiting, waiting, my orders were hand-delivered by Sergeant Franklin. About ten of us were sitting around on our footlockers, playing poker for two bucks a hand, when he walked up to me and gave me the few pieces of official paperwork. As I reached for them, I noticed a sorrowful look on his face. I opened the papers and hurriedly skimmed through, deciphering the army codes.

After reading no more than half a page, I realized Sergeant Franklin was still standing in front of me. When my eyes met his, he said, "I'm sorry, Trooper. Good luck. May God bless you."

I looked around the now tensely quiet room and noticed the dumbfounded faces of my fellow paratroopers. That's when I understood where I was going, where we all were going. Just as I suspected, my destination was Vietnam.

A flood of questions filled my mind. Was this why we were the last to receive our orders? Had the army kept us until last to replace other personnel in Vietnam who had been injured or killed or finished their tours of duty? Had we been culled because we were the best, the worst, or just the unlucky? Why us? Why me?

Once I collected my thoughts enough to continue reading, I saw that the Vietnam express left in thirty-three days. All aboard!

The sergeant continued to stand there. He had surely read my mind and probably knew the answers to my questions, but he didn't offer them. With more than twenty years in service, he was savvy about types of transfers. Resting his huge black hand on my shoulder, he said, "You have a thirty-day pass in the old man's office," then turned and left.

"The old man" was the captain, twenty-seven-years old at most.

Unable to move any part of my body, I watched him go out the door. I thought, *He may be getting old, but he still moves with a practiced grace.* Sergeant Franklin was proud to be airborne, and it showed. Airborne was his reason for being. Although he and I had never been close—after all, he was the boss, and I was the employee—in the months and years that followed, I often remembered him; the training he put me through saved my life more than once.

Someone eventually broke the silence and said we should head for the bowling alley for a going-away-right-before-the-war drinking party. On our way to drown our sorrows, we ran into some others at the bowling alley who had also just received their orders, and our little party turned into a big blowout. Drunken paratroopers got into fights, and the military police were everywhere. I don't remember how we got back to the barracks; I'm just thankful we made it.

The next morning, when the minute hand touched twelve and the hour hand pointed to five, the sergeant quitely opened the door and turned on the lights. Then he moved on. No more whistle. No more proclamation. No more morning runs.

I showered, shaved, dressed, and walked to the orderly room for my thirty-day pass, that thin slip of paper that contained the power to allow me to go home and personally break the news of my transfer to my family.

By this time in my military career, I had a car—actually my second one. It was an old '55 Chevy Bel-Air, a deep blue color with rolled and pleated black Naugahyde upholstering and a three-speed Hurst shift on the floor. It was a real looker, but the rubber boot at the base of the shifter was loose and let fumes from the muffler into the car. Before I got it fixed there were times when I became lightheaded and nauseated from all the carbon monoxide. Nonetheless, that car was mine all mine, fumes and all.

From Fort Bragg to Roswell, Georgia, was 410 miles, a trip I would be making for the last time. My orders were to fly from Atlanta to Fort Lewis, Washington. From there, I'd fly to Vietnam.

That afternoon, when I arrived at my parents' apartment, as usual, Mother and Debbie were as glad to see me as I was to see them. Daddy, I guess, was glad to see me, too, even though he made no show of such feelings. Debbie was, in fact, thrilled when she learned that I planned to leave my car in Roswell for her to drive while I was overseas.

That month at home flew by. I did the usual things soldiers about to head for battle do. I spent time with family, did a lot of drinking with old friends, and took full advantage of the luxury of being able to sleep late. The days whizzed by, and it seemed only a few had passed before it was time to leave for the war.

There was a family get-together on my last day home; my grandparents and a handful of other relatives came over to the apartment for lunch and to wish me well. After hugging and kissing Mother and Debbie and shaking hands with Daddy, I threw my duffle bag into Uncle Deariso Wilbanks's car, and he took me to the airport and dropped me off at the door.

Earlier, there had been a shorter leave that was more important to me than my month at home. Before we were told that we were being reassigned I was given a three-day pass and decided to spend the time at home. The return trip was the truly eventful part of the experience.

Always after a weekend pass, we were expected to be present at 0500 hours on Monday because … we had to "sweeps, mops, and sweeps again the barracks flo, then high shine with the buffer." The only excuse for not being present at that exact moment was to be dead. Even then, as we used to joke, you had to be personally present with a note stating such.

Much of that pass had been spent partying with my friends in Roswell. I just didn't want to spend time speculating with my family over my next assignment. If bad news was waiting for me back at Fort Bragg, which it was, I wanted to wait and deal with it once I knew for sure just how bad it was. After grabbing a few hours of much-needed rest Sunday evening, I was awakened by Mother about ten p.m. I quickly put on my daily uniform and laced my boots, all of which I had brought with me. While I dressed, she made coffee so that we could share a cup before I left. As I drove off, I remember watching her through my rearview mirror, as she waved goodbye through the screen door and fought back tears. We hadn't discussed where I might be transferred to, but the daily headlines were enough to let any thinking person know that the odds were slim that I would get a stateside or European assignment.

As I left Roswell, my thoughts shifted to the road ahead. As usual, I would be cutting it pretty close, but I had faith in my buddy's map saving some time. After all, he was a Specialist Fourth Class, thoroughly trained in reading and drawing maps. But when I got around to unfolding the piece of paper he had given me, one look told me I was in trouble. His "map" was a combination of vague, scribbled instructions, and little sketches. Half the roads weren't identified by either number or name, and his instructions omitted small details, such as whether you turned left or right at dead ends and intersections. *I'll figure it out,* I thought, knowing I still had a long way to go before reaching the start of the shortcut.

At the point where I was to turn off my usual route, something told me to go ahead and put my faith in the guy's map. After all, he claimed to have used this route multiple times. So I exited the freeway and turned onto the two-lane blacktop road, as the piece of paper indicated. Okay, so far, so good.

His notes said the blacktop would end at a stop sign, and it did. But he gave no instructions concerning which way to turn. As I sat at the end of the pavement with the car and my mind idling, I decided to go right, which, by my calculations, would more or less keep me headed north.

The roadbed was so dry it was like powder; even in the dark, I could see the plumes of dust behind me, highlighted by my taillights. As I barreled along, I could hear the grains of dirt embedding themselves in the crevices of my tires and kept thinking how unusually dry this road was. It was also dark and quiet, with not even so much as a house or light of any kind in sight. On both sides, dense pine trees walled the road, thousands of trees. And there was no traffic; I was the sole driver out that night.

For some reason, I was drawn to every detail of this backcountry road. I rolled down my window and held my head out, trying to revive myself with the crisp night air. It was a crystal-clear night with a sky full of brilliantly shining stars.

Perhaps lost and definitely tired, I knew I needed to concentrate, to focus. It was already close to four a.m., and I had to find the post within the next hour or I was in trouble. My thoughts became consumed with what would be waiting for me if I did not make my deadline. The least thing I'd have to worry about would be an Article 15. Being close to the post didn't count. One second late and I would be classified as absent without official leave. An AWOL was something I did not want in my personnel file.

All of a sudden, my headlights picked up a figure standing on the right side of the road. As I got closer, I could see it was a young boy. He was simply standing there, facing in my direction. I slowed down while I did some quick thinking. Was the carbon monoxide leak back and getting to me? Not a sign of life for miles, but now I was looking at what appeared to be a child out in the middle of nowhere in the middle of the night. Did some thugs hiding in the shadows, waiting for a softhearted patsy to come along, put him there?

Risk or no risk, running late or not, I had to stop. As I pulled over, a strange, cool feeling came over me. I leaned over and shoved the door open for him. The old, cracked, and yellowed dome light came on but barely illuminated the interior of the car. Silently, the boy and I studied each other. He appeared to be about four feet tall, maybe nine or ten years old. He was wearing a light-colored, short-sleeved, button-down collared shirt and blue jeans. The really striking things about him were his hair and his features. His closely cropped hair almost glowed, it was so blond, and his eyebrows were the same snowy white. His skin was very pale, as though he had not seen daylight in a very long time, and his thin arms had a clammy, almost wet look. I could not get over how colorless he looked and wondered if he was ill.

After only a few moments, which felt like an eternity, I asked the child, "What are you doing out here by yourself?"

"I'm going to my grandmother's house," he replied.

Perhaps overlaying my own childhood experiences on him, I wondered if he was running away or if his mother and father had been fighting and he was headed to grandma's 'til things cooled off. "How far is your grandmother's?"

He stretched out a slender arm and pointed down the road. "Just down there a piece."

Even if his grandmother's was only a mile or so down the road, I wasn't going to leave the child out in those woods by himself. Where had he come from? And how long had be been walking? "Okay," I said. "If you want me to give you a ride down there, get in."

He climbed into the front seat and just sat there motionless without saying a word as I shifted from neutral and drove off. Trying to be nonchalant about it, I studied him more. He was clean looking, but when I tried to look at his face, I couldn't actually see his eyes. They were there, yet they weren't. *That can't be,* I thought.

A very calm peace surrounded this child, and though confused, I felt relaxed in his presence. Obviously, he was not concerned about getting into a car with a stranger, and if he was running away from something, he had left his fear behind him.

Finally, again after what seemed like forever, though I'm sure only moments had passed, he said, "You're a soldier."

"Yes," I quickly replied. "I'm stationed up at Fort Bragg with the Eighty-second Airborne." Then I asked him, "How far is it to your grandmother's?"

He leaned forward in the seat and craned his neck as though to look over the dashboard and judge the distance. "Just down here a little piece," he answered, then added, "My brother was a soldier."

"Was he stationed at Fort Bragg?"

"He was killed in Vietnam last year."

"Oh, I'm sorry," I said, then added, "I suspect I'm headed for Nam soon."

He turned in the front seat and faced me; nevertheless, whether it was the light or what, I can't say, but I still couldn't see his eyes. "I know," he said. "Don't worry, you'll be all right."

His words startled me. How does he know where I'm going or whether or not I'm going to be all right?

Curiously, I again became fixed on his appearance, wondering why does he have this strange glow about his face, a face I can't clearly see?

The boy showed no emotion, and it dawned on me that he hadn't smiled. Not once. With all these feelings and questions inside, I had a very uneasy feeling about him. The uneasiness came over me out of nowhere, just as he had appeared out of nowhere on the roadside. I wanted to say more to him, but I didn't know what to say.

"Stop." It was the child who broke the silence.

Surprised by his command, I hit the brakes and looked all around. Outside there was no sign of a driveway, mailbox, or light, just trees, trees, trees. Looking behind us and then ahead, it was as though we had gone nowhere at all. I was certain we had been moving and knew my foot had been on the accelerator. "I'd be glad to take you right to your grandmother's door," I offered.

He simply got out of the car, said, "Thanks," and slowly made his way over a small drainage ditch at the edge of the road, then headed toward the pine trees. I watched him, lighted by the spill from my headlights, as he moved.

Moved is the right word—I can't say he walked because it looked as if he floated toward the woods and faded into their darkness. Then he was gone.

Trying to make sense of the entire encounter, I sat there in the middle of the dirt road, confused and bewildered. That pine grove was comprised of thickly planted trees long overdue for thinning.

Yet he seemed to move through them like a mist, not having to bother pushing branches aside.

I slowly drove off, seeing no signs of life anywhere along the dark, empty road. After driving a few miles, my mind abruptly shifted from the child to the fact that the dirt road I was traveling abruptly ended at pavement. Again, guessing which way to turn, in only seconds I knew where I was: at the rear gate of Fort Bragg. With a few minutes to spare I made roll call.

My encounter with the child has remained with me as if it happened yesterday. I questioned myself then and now. Was he a sign, a messenger informing me that I would survive the war? Easy to think that now after I obviously did survive. Nevertheless, my trip down that dusty road has me convinced that the boy I encountered there was a very real angel, one sent to give me courage, comfort, and guidance before I began my journey through the valley of death.

—·—

Chapter 6
The Arrival

The thief does not come except to steal, and to kill, and to destroy.
John 10:10

August 18, 1968, I was given orders to report to Fort Lewis, Washington, in thirty days, for assignment in South Vietnam. In the meantime, I had a month's leave on my hands and headed home to kill time.

My family situation was very much the same as when I first left. My father was still being abusive and squandering most of what he earned, and my mother was still letting him get away with it. My sister Debbie, however, was growing up and was old enough to drive. Wanting to do something special for her, I told her that while I was overseas, I'd leave my car for her to use. She was so excited, I'm sure she counted the days till I would leave.

While not much had changed at my parents' home, the world certainly had, and once outside of my military cocoon, I became very aware of those changes from a civilian perspective. The year 1968 was one of turmoil that has not been equaled since. The U.S. Navy intelligence ship *Pueblo* was captured by North Korea on charges that it had violated North Korean waters ... and the charges were true. Israel, with much prodding from President Lyndon Johnson, had instigated the exchange of prisoners of war with the United Arab Republic. There were protests in Warsaw and Czechoslovakia, and student riots in Paris. Atlanta, which had crossed the treacherous waters of the segregation era, with little more strife than a couple of sit-ins at a Jewish deli that refused to serve blacks, was stunned by the Memphis assassination of civil rights leader Martin Luther King, Jr. Robert Kennedy, who was a shoo-in for the Democratic candidacy for president, was also assassinated, leaving Hubert Humphrey to be selected as the Democratic hopeful during a riot-plagued convention in Chicago. And, of course, in Vietnam we were smack in the middle of that backward little country's never-ending civil war.

But, as I drove through the streets of Atlanta, the biggest difference I noticed was the development of the hippie-peacenik community in the city's drug-infested Tenth Street area, then known as "Tight Squeeze." In their bellbottom jeans, tie-dyed shirts, long hair, flowers, and beads, they were a sorry-looking sight to someone accustomed to military buzz cuts, military discipline, and reverence for our flag. Even more difficult for me to comprehend was their opposition to the United States's efforts to stamp out Communism.

Not everyone shared their point of view, and if you wanted to talk politics with someone supportive of the war effort, it wasn't difficult to find people who strongly believed that Communism was a serious threat and were eager to show their appreciation to military personnel who were risking their lives for the preservation of democracy.

All that aside, I spent most of my time at home, trying to forget about what I imagined was awaiting me in the jungles of a country that we hardly knew existed only a few years earlier. I was home to drink with my buddies and do whatever would keep my path from crossing Daddy's. That was the war I was no longer willing to fight.

On September 15, 1968, I turned over the keys to my car to Debbie, kissed Mother goodbye, and my uncle Deariso Wilbanks drove me to Atlanta's Hartsfield Airport to catch a commercial flight to Seattle. From there, we loaded onto buses for Fort Lewis, Washington.

I arrived at Fort Lewis with my 201 (military personnel file) in hand and went to a transit barracks to receive orders concerning how to in-process for the trip overseas. As I was shuffled from one administrator to the next, each added or subtracted something from my 201, and I was instructed to make a contribution myself: my last will and testament. I was given a series of shots to ward off the scores of diseases prevalent in the Vietnam jungles, and then sent to have my picture made, standing in full uniform next to an American flag. The picture I was to send home, along with a letter we were all required to write: a family keepsake in case we failed to make the return trip.

After about a week of all that, my group boarded an American Airlines plane—complete with stewardesses—and we left Fort Lewis, Washington. After a stop in Anchorage, where I saw my first Eskimos, we headed across the Pacific. Our next stop was Japan, where we were allowed to go to a nearby air force base exchange. With strict orders to stay clear of alcohol, drugs, and contraband, a buddy I had made on arriving at Fort Lewis, Stan Borda, and I figured two out of three wasn't bad and headed straight for the PX (post exchange), bought a quart of liquor, and started swilling it straight from the bottle. Then we hightailed it back to the plane. Next stop: Vietnam.

American Airlines timed our arrival to occur after dark. As soon as our duffle bags were offloaded, that commercial plane was on its way to the safety of the U.S.A.

It didn't take long to learn why they were in such a hurry. Everyone I met seemed to have some horror story to tell about how much the Vietcong zappers itched to take out one of those big commercial planes. Zappers, the people who would run up and throw satchel charges at aircraft or, much like Arabs in Israel, strap themselves with bombs and self-detonate, seemed to have an endless variety of ways to sneak onto military property. They were relentless in their efforts to cripple our aircraft. Looking back, that's understandable; they had no aircraft to use in their defense, while planes and helicopters were our life's blood.

When we transferred from the plane to army buses it was hot and sticky. An open bus window was as good as it got, a window covered with chicken wire to protect passengers from hand grenades or other explosives thrown by Vietcong.

A half hour down the road, we arrived at a huge metal hangar with large doors in each end; the building served as a mass-transit area. In one section of the hangar were rooms with bunks where people could grab some sleep while they waited for what would come next. However, there were more soldiers waiting than bunks, so there were plenty of guys sleeping on the floor, with duffle bags for a pillow. I started out on the floor, too, before snagging a recently vacated bunk.

All of the hundreds of people milling around weren't GIs. There were men, women, and children everywhere you looked, begging for money or attempting to be hired for some menial chore such as shine your boots or bring you a Coke. This chaotic mingling of humanity was my first sight of and experience with the Vietnamese people.

For the three days I waited on my orders, we could only leave the building to go to a nearby mess hall to eat. Each time we did, we hurried back in case our permanent assignments had come through while we were away.

When my orders came through, I was assigned to the 173rd Airborne Brigade, as a replacement in Qui Nhon. On the morning of the third day, via caribou, we took a one-hour flight to an airbase up north, where the cadre there treated us very well.

I particularly remember going to a little makeshift mess hall that overlooked Qui Nhon and a helicopter assault unit that was down in a valley. From the mess hall, I could plainly see maybe eight or nine helicopters, which were tied down on a cement pad that was next to some native hooches. After our meal we were allowed to call it a day because we were dead tired from travel.

But we didn't get to sleep long. About 2200 hours that night, there was a loud explosion. Everybody jumped out of their bunks and looked outside to see four or five additional explosions near our barracks. The few of us greenhorns who wandered outside were told to get back inside, turn our bunks over, pull the small mattresses over ourselves, and lie down. We were under attack by 122-mm rockets, weapons supplied to the Vietcong by the Russian military. As we followed orders I could look through the window and see the explosions down in the valley on the helicopter pad. If an explosion didn't totally destroy a helicopter, it at least turned it over or caused it to buck and strain at the lines anchoring it. The type of rocket they used, I later learned, was notoriously inaccurate, and most of the time it was pure luck if they hit their intended target. Fortunately for us, no U.S. soldiers were killed that night.

The next day we fell out for jungle training, and a sergeant lead us down an eye-opening trail. Along the way, we were shown hidden machine gun nests and booby traps that only a trained eye could spot.

The Vietcong were experts at creating ingenious, lethal weapons out of whatever was at hand. They would nail a tin can to a tree and wedge a hand grenade (minus its pin) into the can. A piece of fishing line ran from the grenade to a tree on the opposite side of a trail. The unlucky person who snagged the line and jerked the grenade from the can was riddled with metal fragments within four seconds.

With even less, they built punji pits, which were holes dug in a trail and filled with forty or fifty sharpened bamboo stakes whose blunt ends were firmly embedded in the earth at the bottom of the pit. Each pit was camouflaged with a layer of thin bamboo strips, topped with dirt and grass. If you stepped onto the covering, you fell into the pit and were impaled on the spikes. They easily pierced legs and bodies, inflicting wounds that were quickly infected. The enemy's homemade weapons were a constant threat in the jungle that awaited us.

We learned the proper way to dig a foxhole with a hand grenade pit inside of it. The pit was there in case you had time to kick a grenade that landed in your foxhole into the pit before it exploded. Those pits saved many lives.

Training of this nature continued for a week, covering a multitude of subjects including how to load, clean, and fire an AK-47; the finer points of throwing hand grenades; and how to fire M-79 grenade launchers. We were shown how to identify North Vietnamese, and even walked through the finer points of the Geneva Convention's Articles of War. After all the official training was covered, we were given unofficial advice, such as to throw away our gas masks because the Vietcong wasn't using gas; therefore, a mask was just extra weight to haul on your back. Seasoned fighters also unofficially taught us that LAWs (light anti-tank weapons), which weighed about five pounds and shot a 66-mm-shaped charge, were great for taking out snipers hidden in trees. These rockets were in a fiberglass tube, which when fully extended to shoot were thirty-five inches long and reminded me of miniature bazookas. They had folding plastic sights and were shoulder-held, one-rocket weapons that you threw away after a single firing.

By the start of our second week we had been issued all our gear and received all our training. As orders came in we headed for the helipad to replace the killed and wounded.

The ten of us going to the First Battalion, 503rd Infantry left on the same day. It was my first helicopter ride, and sitting on the cold metal floor covered with bumpy rivets was a far cry from the commercial plane that had brought us across the ocean.

The trip to our destination, LZ Uplift, was a long one, at least an hour. When we got there we saw that our new home away from home was nothing more than a few buildings, bunkers, and a command post. The hot, sticky, miserable, smelly place had the scent of death about it. For ten or fifteen minutes it would rain so hard you couldn't see your hand in front of your face. Then, almost immediately, the sun would come out, pounding you with ninety-five-degree heat that made your hair and clothes steam as sweat ran down your face and body.

It seemed nearly every man at LZ Uplift had a thousand-yard stare, numb to whatever was surrounding him. Most were combat veterans by then and had experienced extremely heavy enemy contact, and the experience had taken its emotional toll.

Prior to our arrival there were barely enough warm bodies left to go back into the jungle to fight. Our presence would build numbers back up to the point where the survivors could enjoy slightly better odds as they returned to the jungle to test their luck again.

Call it "youth" or "patriotism" or "ignorance," or all three, but I was fairly excited about arriving in Vietnam and anxious to get assigned to a unit and get out into the country and see what it was like. We volunteers believed that we were fighting Communists hell-bent on taking over the world, so we were fighting for our freedom, as well as that of the South Vietnamese people. It was later, much later, that I learned that most Vietnamese people didn't even know what the war was supposed to be about. Nevertheless, we well-trained grunts were ready to turn anyone in our path into a free democrat or dead Communist and awaited our orders to move out.

—▪—

Chapter 7
The Trail

So the Lord said, "I will destroy man whom I have created from the face of the earth, both man and beast, creeping things and birds of the air, for I am sorry that I have made them".
Genesis 6:7

Even though very low on manpower, Charlie Company was already back in the field the day I arrived at LZ Uplift. They had sustained a lot of casualties, so no time was wasted in moving us replacements out in order to fill slots in the ambush patrols that were sweeping the jungle within a sixty-mile radius of our base.

Less than an hour after my arrival, there was a resupply helicopter going out to meet Charlie Company, which we were told was operating to the west of LZ Uplift in the dense jungles of the central highlands, also known as the Suoi Ca Mountains. So a few others and I were loaded on board, along with a fresh supply of ammo and rations. Then it was off to join our company.

As I peered over the side of the airborne helicopter I got my first real look at the jungle. From the air, it seemed so pristine, so thick, lush, and green. The sky above it was brilliant blue and dotted with cotton-ball clusters of puffy white clouds. Because there was no industry in that area to create pollution, the air was so clean it seemed you could see forever. Looking at the apparent serenity below, it was hard to believe those trees concealed men hell-bent on killing one another.

All I knew was what I had been told. There were Communists down there trying to take over this country named Vietnam, a country I can't even remember being mentioned in geography class. For some reason, of all the countries being taken over by the Communists, this was one we had to fight to save; somehow it served as a faraway buffer zone between the evils of Communism and us.

As we approached a clearing just big enough for a helicopter to land, someone in the rear of the chopper took a magazine from his ammo pouch and tapped his helmet with it. I understood: it was time to load our M-16s, so I took a magazine from my bandolier and prepared for whatever awaited us.

We got off the chopper at warp speed, reported to the sergeants, and told them which platoon we were in. "I'm assigned to Second Platoon," I said.

Someone then told me that Second Platoon was in foxholes down at the creek and pointed me in that general direction. So I made my way down and met the sergeant.

He said, "You're going to be in Second Platoon, First Squad," and pointed out their location, where they were manning some makeshift foxholes. As I looked at the machine guns pointed toward the jungle, it was for me a scene out of one of those World War II movies I loved as a kid. I simply couldn't believe I was there.

My first few days weren't to be spent with my squad; my temporary assignment was with Second Squad, where I was assigned to a machine gunner named Small, the blackest man I'd ever seen. His assistant gunner was a young white guy from South Carolina. Like most of us out in the field who actually did the fighting, both were uneducated, sincere, and willing to do whatever had to be done, including risking their lives. So we hunkered down and waited, waited for whatever happened.

Frankly, I needed the rest. Having just come off a thirty-day leave, I was full of beer, tired, hadn't been eating properly, and wasn't as strong as I should have been at the time. Nonetheless, it was my job to carry a 100-pound-plus rucksack on my back, as well as additional ammunition: a 500-round can of ammunition that was quickly added to my back's load, as well as another 500-round can to carry, along with my rifle. That's the glamorous life of an ammo bearer.

But we weren't allowed to sit and wait long. Deciding that we weren't going to encounter any enemy troops at our location, the four platoons that made up Charlie Company were ordered to move out through the jungle, and my fascination with the beauty of that primeval wonderland quickly faded.

Yes, it was beautiful. It was also indescribably hot, humid, and home to the largest mosquitoes I've ever seen. As we trudged along, the alcohol I had guzzled on leave poured out of me, making me look as if I had been hosed down, and I smelled like a beer tap. Kitchens, Second Squad's platoon sergeant, couldn't help but notice and asked if I was okay.

I said, "Everything's fine. It's just that I've been on leave, and I'm a little bit out of shape."

"Don't worry about it," he assured me in his distinct Midwestern accent. "What's more, we're going to bivouac here for the night, so you'll be able to get some rest."

But that didn't happen. It started raining. The bright blue sky turned a dark smoke gray, and the biggest raindrops I had ever seen fell out of those clouds for hours. That particular night I wasn't assigned guard duty; most likely it was Kitchens I had to thank. However, I got little sleep or rest. It rained so hard the water washed over my body, soaking my clothes, my canvas boots, my socks, my long-sleeve military shirt, every scrap of army-issue clothing on me. As I lay on the ground, the water was almost up to my neck, and the only thing keeping my head out of water, as it rushed over me and down into the valley, was my helmet, which served as a pillow. Every time I dozed, my head bobbed and threatened to slide off the helmet's round top and into the torrent of water. All night it rained, not stopping until daybreak.

The next morning's scorching sun caused wisps of steam to rise from our soaked clothes and hair. With no breakfast or sleep, we headed deeper into the jungle, walking about three hours before being allowed to stop on the side of a mountain. With a jungle canopy over us, we dug small pits to lie in, in case we were attacked. Then we each heated a canteen cup of our precious ration of water over the tiny fire of a few Sterno tablets. Once the water came to a boil, we reconstituted some of the rations we carried in our rucksacks, and then dug into the first of our two daily meals.

As I had been taught, we buried everything we left behind, both trash and any sign we had answered a call of nature. When we moved on, no trace of our having been there remained.

My years of watching Tarzan movies had not prepared me for the combination of jungle and mountains. All the many Tarzans who swung across the movie and TV screens had flat land for running. But in Vietnam's jungle, it was a different story. First, running there was not an option with all we carried. Second, the tangle of vines that seemed ever present slowed movement through them to a snail's pace. And third, the mountainous terrain made both uphill and downhill a tough balancing act for anyone hauling between 100 and 150 pounds of gear.

After we had put another five miles behind us, we stopped on the top of a small mountain where a flat spot afforded us an unobstructed view of the rice paddies below. It seemed they went on for miles.

The first squad went down the hill to put out an ambush for the evening while the other squads separated to cover three additional ambush areas. Below our squad was a well-worn trail that the North Vietnamese soldiers supposedly used as their route in and out of the villages in the vicinity. Sergeant Kitchens ordered me to grab a canteen of water, two bandoliers of ammunition, two hand grenades, and one smoke grenade. Then he led his squad and me within fifty yards of the trail. To get there, we had to scramble down an embankment that was steeper than a stepladder, with only rocks, roots, and tangles of vines to keep us from plummeting straight to the bottom where the land planed out. It was about 1600 hours when we left, and the short trip took three-quarters of an hour. I kept thinking that the ones left behind at the night fighting perimeter were a lucky bunch. And that proved to be right.

The trail below was in sharp contrast to the overgrown area we had struggled through. The rich jungle soil had been worn free of grass and bushes, leaving a barren strip of brown mud that twisted through the jungle like a snake.

Sergeant Kitchens assigned me to a far left position near the head of the trail. I didn't know it at the time, but I had been given the most dangerous position. My assumption was he placed me there as an added bit of protection for the men he had built a relationship with and had learned to trust. FNGs (fuckin' new guys) were a dime a dozen, with a constant stream of them flowing in from the U.S. I guess that made my estimated worth, in his mind, less than a penny. He was protecting the men he knew he could count on. If I went down, there would a replacement for me within a few days. That's the way it is when the bullets are flying.

The steep mountainside behind us gave us rear protection, but there were only patches of brush for concealment. About twenty meters to my right was another man, a similar distance to the next and the next, about nine of us positioned at intervals down the trail. Thirty or forty yards to my left the trail disappeared into suddenly dense jungle, while on my right it went down a hill into equally dense jungle. I would have picked a less open spot for an ambush, but my opinions were of no consequence.

The space between us was the only protection we were given. Since a fragmentation hand grenade is designed to burst into hundreds of fragments when detonated, it produces causalities within a range of fifteen meters. So if we were closer, one grenade could take out two men. As green as I was, I knew that our greatest protection was firing first and taking the enemy by surprise.

Once in position, I was about thirty yards from the trail and had a good view of it. After I felt I was positioned the way I had been taught, I laid the hand grenades out in front of a bandolier and me. I also laid out one clip so that I could get to it quickly.

A soldier named Stephens came over and handed me a claymore mine. I knew what it was and how to fire it, but I had never set one out, so I followed him while he positioned it and ran its firing line from the trail back to my position. Although I had been taught to place claymores facing the direction from which the enemy was most likely to come, he placed it facing the area of the trail directly in front of me. Since he wasn't green, I figured he knew something from experience that I hadn't been taught. I just watched. He, however, is the one who should have paid closer attention in class.

After the mine was set and he returned to his position, I settled in. To my right I could see Stephens and Sergeant Kitchens and one more man; the others were blocked from my view by the bushes and vines chosen for our nest. We had a good fire down on this trail and I felt confident we had done a good job of preparing for whatever might travel our way.

After about twenty minutes I heard something to my left. To my unaccustomed ear, it sounded like nasal jibber jabber, my impression of the limited amount of Vietnamese I had heard back at Qui Nhon while waiting for assignment. *Hell*, I thought, *here they come.* A firefight my second day in the jungle!

When I looked to my right to see if anyone else heard what I was hearing, I could see the man to Kitchens's right was passing the time by reading a letter, its white paper like a semaphore, signaling, "Shoot me." Without making a sound, I tried to get the attention of anyone to my right, but those other than the letter reader were concentrating on the view in front of them.

Suddenly, a tree on the hill to my left began to shake. Then it stopped. Then it shook again, and again. What I eventually learned was that all the enemy soldiers coming down the steep part of the trail steadied themselves by grabbing a limb of the tree as they hopped over the small creek that crossed the trail. By grabbing a limb the tree broke their fall.

The sound of voices got closer and closer; yet I was the only one who heard them. Since I had been taught to never talk on the trail or do anything that could reveal my presence, I assumed their brazenness came from there being a large number of men in their party.

Again, I checked the men on my right. Still no one else had heard; no one was ready to fire. I told myself to forget about them and deal with the situation the best I could. First came the point man. I raised my M-16 rifle and, with my thumb, pushed the fire selector to fully automatic. I was afraid the selector's clicking noise might be loud enough to alert the enemy; however, he seemed as absorbed in thought as the members of my squad were. Otherwise, he surely would have spotted me. I let him pass because I had been taught to let as many as possible into the killing zone before firing.

I found myself surprised at how calm I was, watching my first NVA walk by, dressed in his brown khaki uniform that included boots, shorts, and a brown jungle helmet with a big red star on it. I was so close to him—no more than thirty-five feet away—I could see his features. He was sixteen at most; nevertheless, he was hardcore NVA with a thirty-round banana clip extending from the bottom of his AK-47 Russian assault rifle. The remainder of his military issue was in a backpack that seemed more an extension of him than a burden to be carried.

I glanced to my right and saw that the rest of the unit had finally spotted him, and this time the rest did as I had been taught. All of us laid back and waited for more to enter our killing zone before announcing our presence. In a matter of seconds, the novelty of seeing my first NVA was over because about ten more had come into view, all dressed in NVA brown and fully equipped with assault rifles, and jabbering nonstop. I placed the front iron sight on the M-16 on the man who had just moved directly in front of me, then looked at him through my rear peephole sight, lining them both up, as I had been taught to do, in order to assure I got the kill with my first burst of fire.

The man at the far end of our line kicked things off with an initial blast, and I followed suit. The NVA I had selected as a target received two automatic bursts of fire from my weapon. I saw his face fill with fright and tormenting pain as the full-metal-jacketed M-16 bullets tore through his chest. He half spun as the velocity of the impact shook his dying body. Blood immediately oozed from his brown shirt, and he fell to the ground like a sack of potatoes.

The hailstorm of hot-red lead we were pouring down on that trail was so fierce it seemed impossible that anyone within our killing zone could survive. But at least one NVA had. I watched with confusion and amazement, as if watching a slow-motion shot in a war epic movie, while this lone soldier ran back to the man I had shot, straddled the fallen body, and reached down to check his neck for a pulse. When he looked up, he seemed so young to me. In retrospect, he and I were about the same age, but he was experiencing something that still lay ahead for me. His eyes were full of grief and rage over the loss of a friend.

Then he spotted me. And before I could snap out of my trancelike state, he raised his AK-47 Russian assault rifle and sprayed the jungle all around me. I saw the smoke and fire coming from the end of the weapon as the projectiles left the red-hot barrel and hurdled in my direction. The air was cut and burned as the bullets passed within inches of my ear. Lying there, holding my M-16 stock tightly against my side and tightly gripping the forearm with my left hand, I aimed as best I could at the enemy soldier and pulled the trigger. A quick burst of .223-caliber ammo rocketed through the chamber of the rifle; then the kid crumpled and fell beside his friend.

The NVAs not in our killing zone scattered in their retreat, some firing as they went. I looked to my right and saw our unit was pulling back and heading up the hill. As far as I was concerned, they started a little too quickly, because I was at the far end with a fight from the NVA diehards on my hands. When I started to run I realized I hadn't fired my claymore; so, wisely or stupidly, I doubled back and squeezed the firing device so hard I broke the handle. But it still activated the mine. When the smoke and dust cleared I looked to see if the survivors—and there were quite a few of them—were going to come into the jungle after us. They did not, probably thinking there were more of us than there actually were.

But the shooting wasn't over for the day. After firing the claymore and starting to run in order to catch up with the rest, I slammed into some vines, and my empty rifle became entangled. As I struggled to pull it free some NVAs spotted me and started firing. I dropped the rifle, took the hand grenade I had left on my belt—my other grenade remained on the ground where I had set it out—pulled the pin and went crawling on hands and knees back up the jungle. About fifty yards to my right I spotted Sergeant Kitchens and worked my way over to him. Once I reached the sergeant I realized a ricocheting bullet had hit his head.

"Hey, Sarge, you okay? Where is everybody?"

"It looks worse than it is," he assured me as he pressed the wound, trying to keep it from bleeding. "Go on up the hill with the rest. We're going to get some artillery in here."

"No, you're hurt. I'm going to stay here with you," I said and started digging in my pockets to see if I had anything that could serve as a bandage. "Besides," I admitted, "my rifle's down there, tangled up in the bushes."

He gave me a wry smile and said, "We call 'em catch-me vines."

I showed him the hand grenade I was holding and assured him, "I'm gonna stay here with you till help comes."

"Okay." He looked at the grenade in my hand and said, "Hold onto that tight till you just gotta throw it."

I'm not certain if the group on the top of the mountain was called by radio or heard the fire or got notified by messenger; somehow, they learned what had happened, and a couple of sergeants led two squads down to us.

By the time they arrived the NVA had apparently moved on; so the new arrivals wanted to go down to the trail, see what sort of damage we had inflicted, and search the bodies for intelligence information. After turning Sergeant Kitchens over to a medic, I told one of the other sergeants I wanted to go, too—in fact, I had to go back and get my rifle. He noticed the hand grenade I had been holding for at least half an hour, wrinkled his brow, and asked, "You got a pin for that thing?"

"I think I dropped it on the ground when I pulled it," I admitted.

"Well, hold on to it, and just don't throw it."

While I struggled to free my weapon from the vines, using only my free hand, I kept looking around for that damned pin. With a lot of luck, I found it, stuck it back into the handle of the grenade, and bent the cotter pin so that it would again be safe to put the grenade away.

While I flexed my hand, which was by then numb from having gripped the grenade for so long, I collected the other grenade I had laid out, then joined the thrill seekers down on the trail.

By the time I reached them guards had been posted at the extreme ends of the trail to assure our safety while we searched the bodies. The distinct odors of rotten fish and scorched flesh came from the battle wounds, which were already drawing flies. I wanted to throw up as I watched their blood soak into the fertile soil of Vietnam. Body parts were strewn across the jungle floor, a leg here, a foot there. When my claymore had blown, it had reduced one soldier to hamburger from the knees down. While it worked out to my advantage that Stephens had set the mine facing an incorrect direction, he had also aimed it too low, failing to compensate for the slope of the ground. Nonetheless, it had served us well.

All in all, it had been a textbook assault. As I looked around at the carnage, I became acutely aware of the quarter-size mosquitoes that were buzzing around me like small, black attack helicopters. The repellent I had doused myself in before leaving for the jungle had long ago been washed away by the preceding evening's downpour, and those oversized bloodsuckers tried to drain me dry.

There were a total of four NVA bodies. The one that interested everyone the most was my initial hit. He was a major, something I frankly didn't know until I was told. On him he had a Geneva Convention card, family pictures, maps of the area, orders in Vietnamese, and a major's belt. One of the guys quickly took the belt as a souvenir. When I picked up the officer's AK-47, one of the men told me that if I took it back to the rear and had the barrels plugged, I could send it home. So I lugged it for a full day before deciding that it was not a souvenir I really wanted to keep and tossed it into the bushes.

The second body to receive a thorough searching was that of the NVA who had stood over the major. One of the men reached into the right-side pocket of his uniform and removed a plastic bag filled with a greenish, gray-brown, grasslike substance that was completely foreign to me.

"What's that?" I asked.

"You don't know?" said the medic as he came down to join us.

"No. Never seen anything like that."

"Well," he said, "it's what they use to season their food. Personally I kinda like the stuff, so I think I'll take it."

"You're welcome to it," I said, moving on to see what had been found on the other bodies.

That evening when we were in a night fighting position, that medic had gone out on a listening post with some of his buddies. The rest of us could see and smell the smoke coming from the marijuana I had not recognized. In short order, one of the sergeants was at the medic's listening post straightening the guy out. Drugs simply weren't tolerated in our platoon. And I'm glad they weren't. In a crisis, no one wants to have to depend on somebody who is stoned out of his mind.

After we finished searching the NVAs and returned to base camp, I found someone had polished off both quarts of water in the bladders that I had hauled from LZ Uplift. Every drop of it was gone.

More bad luck: just because I had put down half of the NVAs killed that day it didn't get me out of pulling guard duty that night. So I returned to my lowly ammo-bearer position and was reunited with the machine gunner named Small and his assistant gunner.

At midnight, it was my turn at the gun, and I could hear something off in the jungle, about 500 yards down at the bottom of the hill. So when they called me on the radio for my sit rep, I told them I was hearing something. A platoon sergeant that was on his third tour of duty came over and listened. He said that it was probably the VC or NVA moving out under cover of darkness because they had no idea how many of us were there. I didn't hear anything else the rest of the night and was glad of it. I had had about as much excitement as anyone needed for one day.

After returning to the States I began dreaming about that specific turn at guard duty. It was the same dream over and over and over. In it, I was in the same position as that night, taking my turn while Small and his assistant slept. In the dream, the North Vietnamese started coming down the trail and I started firing the machine gun. To the left, I could see the gun, taking bullet after bullet from the belt, and on the right, I could see it spitting out the empty shells. As the NVA came down the trail, I kept shooting and shooting them, until they piled up like cordwood. There was a high hill of bodies, and the blood was flowing like the rain had the night before. Blood was up to my throat, flowing over my shoulders, while the assistant kept feeding the bullets into my machine gun.

Eventually I would wake up. I never again had that dream while in the service, but I revisited it time and time again after returning home. Each time, the details were exactly the same, no variation whatsoever. The dream persisted for three years, and then never returned. It was my only war dream, and I remember it now as clearly as if I had just awakened.

The next day we traveled about four or five more miles into the jungle before being called back. The entire unit was picked up by helicopters, and Charlie Company was transported back to LZ Uplift. On the way back Sergeant Kitchens told me he was going to have me transferred to his squad because I was the kind of soldier he wanted fighting with him. But my transfer didn't take place; he was transferred before the paperwork got approved.

After a few days of food and rest we saddled up again and headed back into the Suoi Ca Mountains to spend Thanksgiving there while on our next mission.

—•—

A platoon medic and Hendrix

Chapter 8
The Priest

And I say to you, my friends, do not be afraid of those who kill the
body, and after that have no more that they can do.
Luke 12:14

I didn't realize it at the time, but when we returned to LZ Uplift and turned in our gear, my military education was just beginning. It was an education that covered more subjects than how to kill while avoiding being killed.

A bunch of us decided to go into Phu Cat, a nearby town, and let off a little steam. There was army transportation for us in the form of a deuce-and-a-half open truck headed that way; so, with visions of whores, booze, and wild and wooly times, we moved out.

En route, we drove by a Vietnamese marketplace, where the locals sold vegetables, Coca-Colas, and anything they could steal from the U.S. operations. Apparently, no one cared about the stealing. Markets such as this one were where American soldiers went for the supplies they couldn't get issued to them. If you needed a poncho, a helmet, a blanket, or other item, it was there and for sale on the black market.

Security of government supplies was notoriously lax. For example, one of the men aboard the truck had stolen a case of CS grenades, which look very much like regular hand grenades but are used to suppress riots and to smoke the enemy out of buildings, caves, and tunnels. The fumes from one cause your eyes to burn, your nose to run, and your skin to sting all over. While CS grenades can't kill you, they can certainly make you wish you were dead.

When we got caught in traffic at the marketplace somebody started throwing candy over the side of the truck as if we were on a float in a Fourth of July parade. When it started raining candy the children and elderly came running. After the candy throwers had attracted a crowd they switched from sweets to CS grenades. As about twenty grenades popped in rapid succession, clouds of the pain-inflicting gas floated through the crowd, and the mean-as-hell bunch on the truck were having a ball until the wind shifted and brought some of the gas back toward the truck. That's when those of us not involved in the cruel trick started threatening the throwers.

As the people fled, we rolled on into Phu Cat, which was nothing more than a primitive village. If, for example, a woman walking down the street felt the urge to relieve her kidneys, she simply stepped into an alley and took care of business in full view of passersby. For more serious calls of nature, there were foul-smelling networks of trenches behind the settlement's rows of huts. The trenches led to putrid cesspools placed here and there, which were easily located by just following your nose.

The children of the town, like the dogs, had huge hunks of hair missing. There was no running water and hygiene was clearly of little concern.

Most U.S. soldiers looked upon these people as prehistoric, as subhuman; therefore, there was little in the way of relationships formed between the Vietnamese and the American forces. For that matter, I was soon to realize also that friendly relations were seldom formed between the U.S. troops and ARVNs (the South Vietnamese troops) who were supposed to be our allies. Fair or not, they were viewed as untrustworthy cowards. So the soldiers I joined held total disregard for the people we were there supposedly to help. And new recruits found the thuggish and disrespectful attitude of seasoned soldiers highly contagious.

For these and other reasons, it was dangerous to stay in Phu Cat overnight. The Vietcong came into the villages after dark to get what food, money, and information the locals had to give them. Unprotected soldiers were fair game. Nevertheless, the guys I went to town with decided to spend the night at a hotel of sorts, nothing more than a village hut with rows of cots. But in Phu Cat, it was four-star accommodations. The mama-san in charge collected five dollars a piece from each of us, promising, "No beaucoup VC … no VC come here … I take care of you … love GI."

I guess she was as good as her word, because we had an uneventful night, as far as safety was concerned. She not only "loved GI," she sold love to them, since she reigned over a flock of young girls who had a price for everything a GI could imagine.

While the hospitality was nothing to complain about, the food was another matter. I could not force down the local "cuisine." On subsequent leaves I always took dehydrated rations with me. In the corner of the hut where we stayed was a charcoal fire pit and a large black kettle that contained a soupy stew of fish. When I eventually saw the preparation process it didn't improve my appetite. They scaled the fish, lopped off the head and threw it into the pot. Next, they ran a knife down the backbone of the fish to remove the little fillets from each side. Then they ripped the inside of the fish out and added it and the fillets to the pot, along with some water. This was stirred and cooked for hours. The foul-smelling concoction was then ready to eat or drink.

There was never any question as to who had eaten the stuff because the odor of it seeped from their pores. Later, I learned that the smell often exposed the presence of enemy soldiers in the jungle long before we could see them.

The next day, on our return to LZ Uplift, we learned we were being sent back into the Suoi Ca Mountains on ambush patrol. We had hoped that they would keep us at LZ Uplift through Thanksgiving, but that was not to be. Other troops in the field had earned a rest. Since only one of the four companies serving out of LZ Uplift could be bunked and fed there at any given time, rotation was inevitable. Besides, four companies of soldiers together at the same time would be a magnet for enemy attacks. So we prepared to leave the simple luxuries of cold showers and sleeping on cots under a tent.

The time remaining at the firebase was spent cleaning our weapons, sleeping, eating, and drinking, drinking as much water and beer as we could hold. I was never into liquor—much less drugs. But that didn't mean some of the guys weren't or that heroin wasn't readily available. Most users were black, and all of the druggies stayed in a clique … and in trouble. The rest of us much preferred seeing them left behind on sick call or a work detail, rather than having to depend on them in field situations. In fact, once hooked, very few were not culled out and kept away from the field for the safety of all.

While the food at LZ Uplift was nothing to write home about, at least it was hot. Powdered milk and eggs were staples in our diet. It didn't take me long to realize that the craziest, toughest guys always made it to the front of the chow line. When I asked someone who had been stationed there a month or so how they pulled it off, he said, "Because they've got the most ears."

What I learned was that the mess sergeant was a lifer who had been in airborne for years. If you could show him ears of the gooks you had killed while you were in the boonies, he'd let you eat first and eat as much as you wanted. So these guys were going to him and showing him the string of ears they wore around their necks, under their shirts.

While I don't know what preservation process the Old Testament's David may have used on the head of Goliath, which he dragged around in a sack after killing and decapitating him, I do know the ear-curing process because it was something I soon saw firsthand. A freshly harvested ear was usually stuck inside an empty foil bag that originally held crackers. Then it was covered with salt donated to the cause by other soldiers who hadn't used all the salt in their rations. At rest breaks ears were removed from the salt to dry in the sun. About ten days of this process produced a black, leathery ear ready to join others on a man's neck chain.

After getting a chance to talk to the mess sergeant, I decided that he was crazy as a buzzy bee. Anytime someone said something about killing a gook, his eyes would light up like a Christmas tree. He just loved it. I was surrounded by a lot of tough people, but I don't think any were as crazy as he was. And at first, I was not as brutal as they were, but you get sucked up into the system.

While you didn't have to be at this war game long to be loony some of the guys arrived that way. For example, one of the replacements waiting to join us on our return was a kid named Danny, a fresh assignment in Second Platoon. Danny was about the size of a twelve-year-old and still had peach fuzz on his upper lip and cheeks. He strutted around, bragging about how many gooks he was going to wipe out and how tough he was. When he first tried to talk to me, I looked into that baby face and asked, "How old are you?"

He stammered, "I'm eighteen. Whadda ya talkin' about?" I knew he was lying. "My daddy's been in the army all his life and I'm gonna make a career of it, too. I loooove the army—grew up with it."

I figured he had a lot more growing to do before he was old enough to be in the army, but I let it go and got busy doing something until he wandered away to swap his daddy's war stories with someone else more interested in listening.

About 1200 hours, an alarm call came in from a unit that had made some heavy contact from North Vietnamese soldiers at a spot near the Ho Chi Min Trail, in the Suoi Ca Mountains. Some of our sister companies were in some heavy contact and wanted support to perform a blocking action while they assaulted. Our job would be to set up ambushes and block the enemy retreat to the south. So we prepared to go support them.

The helicopters came thump-thump-thumping in across the clear blue sky of a beautiful day. Great weather or not, I had an intensely bad feeling about this mission. Maybe it was because I had had a taste of the reality of war and killing three men. Maybe it was because I was disappointed over not being transferred to Sergeant Kitchens's outfit. Maybe it was because I had gotten a better understanding of the mindset of the people around me. Or maybe it was all these things. But premonitions don't stop missions, so we loaded into the choppers and headed for our dropoff point.

As we neared our destination I could see large towers of gray-black smoke rising into the sky from our artillery rounds. There were also sudden leaps of dirt clods and grass that sprang into the air and then showered to the ground. When we got close, the firing stopped, and the first wave moved in toward a small clearing. I could see the men jumping from the choppers while they hovered four or five feet off the ground—no easy task with a full rucksack on your back and a supply of ammunition. They started running to the tree line and disappearing into the foliage.

As my chopper moved in for our turn I saw the green tracers from the enemy fire coming our way. There were pluses and minuses that came with using tracers. While they helped you walk your fire in on your target—even with small arms—they also were expensive and clearly told the other side exactly where you were. So our side had chosen not to use them, and I could see why.

During the entire process of offloading our troops, only one man was wounded. Considering the volume of fire coming our way, I think we were very lucky. Another piece of luck was having the NVA fire go away long enough for us to take our night fighting position. As we were cutting our lanes of fire I noticed the terrified look on little Danny's face. But I didn't have the time or inclination to stop and deal with him. So I continued cutting down the jungle undergrowth in a forty-five-degree arc in front of me in order to better see any signs of movement.

A listening post was sent out and, for some reason, that's where the lieutenant wanted the firepower; so the machine gunner, his assistant, and the ammo bearer manned the post, which was facing the hillside we thought the NVA might come from.

We settled in, ate, and tried to get some rest. Since I didn't wear a watch it was hard to ever have an accurate concept of time; our days simply went from light to dark to light. However, I was awake, just having returned from guard duty, when someone started screaming, "Gooks in the perimeter! Gooks in the perimeter!"

I turned to look and saw the shape of a GI in the middle of the perimeter, throwing a hand grenade. I spun around to look in the direction he threw, expecting to see signs of the enemy there, but saw no one. What I did see, however, was the hand grenade hit a tree, bounce back into our perimeter, and explode. The hot, jagged pieces of shrapnel from that M-35 Super Frag decorated the night air like a volley from a Roman candle. "Gooks in the perimeter! I'm hit, I'm hit!"

We all started pouring lead down our lanes of fire. But we weren't getting any return fire, so we stopped, and the only sound was the continued screams of a single voice: "I'm hit! I'm hit!"

By the time things calmed down, I saw that the medic was tending the screamer. It was Danny, who had had a dream that gooks were overrunning our perimeter. Before he could separate his fears from the facts, he had thrown the grenade that bounced back and wounded him. He had filled his leg and side with shrapnel from his own hand grenade. Fortunately, he was the only one hurt as a result of his actions.

By the time I saw who had been hit, the medic had him patched up as best he could and ready for the medevac that had been called. Since there was no clearing for it to land, the chopper hovered over the jungle and lowered a metal cable with a device that looked like a big fishhook. On the hook was a padded seat to which Danny was strapped for liftoff and a trip to the nearest military hospital.

When word spread as to what had happened, there were a lot of angry Americans in that jungle. The helicopter's presence gave every North Vietnamese soldier in the area indisputable information as to our precise location. Knowing that there were wounded could only bring more heat on us, which infuriated everyone.

Normally, for a stunt like that, the others beat a man to a pulp. But Danny's wounds saved the rest of his hide. However, when we returned to LZ Uplift and learned the rest of the story, everyone wanted to take their frustration out on his him *and* his father. Danny's dad, a master sergeant in the recruiting division, had falsified the kid's records, saying he was seventeen when in truth the boy had just turned sixteen. Little Danny was sent back to the U.S., but I never learned what disciplinary action his father faced, if any.

When the sun rose, we were allowed to heat some rations and eat before moving toward a new destination about three klicks up into the mountains. About a third of the way there we started taking heavy fire from an ambush above us.

In the military, you are taught that your best chance of surviving an ambush is to run directly at the enemy, firing away as you go. But that was impossible in this situation because of all the tree limbs and vines that had to be pushed aside as you went. About all we could do was stop, kneel, fire, and try to take cover. The CO (commanding officer) called in some artillery with 175-mm guns, but it took about fifteen minutes for help to arrive. Fifteen minutes may not seem like long under normal conditions, but it can seem like a lifetime in a combat situation. I reloaded four times during that unending quarter of an hour. Finally, the artillery arrived: some Cobra gunships with Gatling guns, 2.75-inch rocket launchers, and 40-mm grenade launchers. They raked the area, 2,400 rounds per minute.

We also called in two wounded, but before the medevac arrived, we had to move about a quarter of a mile to a clearing that was adequate for the chopper to set down. The jungle hoist cable wasn't appropriate because a hovering chopper would have been a prime target for the NVA in the area. Luckily, we only had wounded; no one was killed.

When we eventually reached our destination we were allowed to take time to eat. During our break word came that we were to move to a nearby village and search it for NVA. We took four squads. One platoon set up an L-shaped ambush within sight of the village to catch anyone who tried to get by us or came back in retreat. My squad and another walked the path up to the village. Soon, we could see the huts surrounding the courtyard and the pigs rooting about in the area, and the villagers going about their farming activities. However, when the people spotted us, they scurried away, running in every direction except toward us.

Inside the village, we came upon a back row of hooches, six or seven of them. I didn't know it at the time, but one of those structures was a Buddhist house of worship. About the time we spotted the back row we started taking some fire from some black-pajamaed VC to our left and more on our right. I went down on one knee, firing at the movement right beside the huts, and saw somebody run out of one of the huts. We fired and moved, fired and moved, driving forward. Green tracers burned through the air, and everybody was firing in all directions, firing at anything that moved.

When the firing stopped I looked around the side of that Buddhist house of worship and saw a fairly young Vietnamese lying on a pile of firewood that was next to a little porch-like area on the side of the building. He was lying across a two-and-a-half-foot-high stack of little round sticks of cooking wood, lying with his stomach on the stack. His elbows were propped up on the woodpile, his two hands were together in a position of prayer, his chin was propped up on his hands, and he was chanting. When I noticed his head was shaved and he wore a white robe that was freshly stained with blood, I knew we had shot the village priest.

I hollered for a medic. The medics were positioned in a safe rear area because you always take care of them; after all, they take care of you.

I went over and pulled up the robe. In his back, the priest had taken some bursts of fire in the area of his waist and the meat had been literally ripped away, leaving bone and flesh hanging out. His muscles throbbed and thumped as blood ran down his kneeling body. The flies came swarming, so I lowered the robe to protect the wounds as best I could.

A sergeant from another platoon came up and demanded, "Whacha got?"

"We've shot the priest," I stammered. "A priest."

"Aaah, fuck him."

"No, no. I've called for a medic."

And that's when the medic appeared. As he reached out to touch the young priest, the sergeant bellowed at the medic, "Get the fuck back there where it's safe."

"But, Sarge," I insisted, "this is a priest!"

At that point, the gooks started shooting at us again from the left, and our men in that direction began returning fire. I threw my rifle up and added a burst of fire at the gooks' position. When I did, I heard a long stream of fire behind me and spun around, certain that they were coming at us from the rear.

But that's not where the fire came from. I saw the sergeant lower his weapon and walk over to the priest who was freshly riddled with M-16 bullets. He put his foot on the priest's shoulder and kicked him off the woodpile.

"What the hell are you doing?" I yelled. "We can't be killing priests!"

The sergeant's face screwed up into a livid rage. "Get the fuck outta here before I shoot you," he ordered.

"Sarge, we can't be killing the priests. We just can't. We're pissing everybody off; we just can't do that."

"Look soldier," he bellowed, "if you think I'm calling for an airlift for some goddamn gook and taking the chance of getting a medevac shot down for that baldheaded piece of shit, you're crazy as you look. Now, I'm giving you an order. You move your ass out and go after the NVA, or I'm gonna shoot you, too!"

The look in his eyes told me he was serious, deadly serious. So I moved out, repeatedly telling myself that I may not have been in Vietnam long, but I knew what had been done was not right. We weren't—at least I wasn't there to kill church people. Even though at the time I didn't consider myself a religious guy, I knew how I would feel if somebody started killing ministers and priests back home.

Moreover, I knew when we left the area that we weren't going to take time to bury him. We never buried enemy dead; just left them for the animals. So when the NVA and the Vietcong returned, they would see we had killed a priest, and would hate us three times as much as they already did.

We went on to fight in the mountains for the next two days, and then rested on a hill to eat a Thanksgiving dinner that was flown in; a meal kept warm in hot boxes. Everybody got a slice of turkey and some dressing. The food was welcome, but what came with it was not.

Along with the food came a Catholic priest who administered communion. At first, I couldn't understand the exasperation of the seasoned soldiers, but I soon did. From that day on, I also dreaded the sight of some hotdog chaplain in the field because chaplains and snipers came in a package deal. The priests and ministers always arrived in a helicopter, which had to have a place to land because most of the chaplains were too old to jump while a chopper hovered. Furthermore, when they came, they wandered from foxhole to foxhole in an attempt to chat with the men. A patient Vietcong could know the exact position of every foxhole before a chaplain left. We always got fire into any area one of them roamed. And they drew fire to the helicopter as well. But the chaplains seemed oblivious to the danger they brought us. Anytime you saw one of them coming toward you, you wanted to plead, "Sir, please, for the love of God, squat down and quit endangering all our lives."

Unfortunately, you couldn't talk to them like that. In fact, we were heavily lectured about not cursing around the chaplains and always showing them the utmost respect. But each time I heard that be-nice lecture, I thought of the very different way in which we had treated that Buddhist priest: savage and deliberate murder.

—•—

Chapter 9
The Knife

He shall judge between the nations, and rebuke many people:
they shall beat their swords into plowshares, and their spears
into pruning hooks: Nation shall not lift up sword against nation,
neither shall they learn war anymore.
Isaiah 2:4

Being a machine gunner has its pluses and minuses. You have an M-60 that's capable of firing 750 rounds per minute, but you're positioned at the front of your unit, which makes you a prime enemy target.

I had quickly moved up from ammo bearer to assistant machine gunner to gunner; so there I lay that April morning in 1969, flat on my belly with nothing between me and the thick jungle undergrowth but my utility shirt. As the sun rose, so did the white-hot steam from the ground beneath me. On my right shoulder was the stock of my M-60 aimed at a jungle trail that reached into the mountains. In the other direction the trail led to a valley that we grunts called the

"Valley of Death." That's where, on an average day, we witnessed more pain, suffering, and death than most people ever see. I don't know what military importance that patch of jungle had, if any. It was just one of many routes enemy soldiers traveled to a village in the valley, where they stole food, raped, and beat any local villagers whom they suspected of being sympathetic to the Americans. Even so, none of that made that particular village or trail unique.

While watching the mountain trail, I wondered if they would come that morning, or if it would be a good day for us. I got my answer when I saw a tree approximately fifty meters up the trail move and heard the muffled sound of voices. Then here they came: North Vietnamese soldiers, looking very professional, very determined, in their brown uniforms. They were carrying Russian AK-47 machine guns and had other weapons strapped to their bodies. Once a number of them were in my killing zone, I squeezed the trigger of my M-60 and watched the front lead scouts fall into the deep jungle grass. They were dead, but the rest were not. The remaining North Vietnamese troops took cover, and a vicious firefight began. For what was probably only a few minutes—but seemed like an eternity—American boys in their late teens and early twenties fought valiantly for their lives against Asian boys close to the same age, each ignorant of why they were fighting and only wanting to live, to go home, to be safe again.

While my mother had taken me to church off and on during my childhood, I can't say I was ever a religious person. But during that firefight I felt the acute need for more protection than I could muster on my own. As I reloaded, I looked up and called out, "God, this is Denny Hendrix from Roswell, Georgia, down here. And I need some help."

The rain of metal continued. When it was time to reload, I looked up again and called, "I said I need some help down here. Please save my unworthy hide."

That may not seem much of a conversion to you, but it was for me because, despite what the boy on the road to Fort Bragg told me and despite all the sermons I had dozed through as a boy, this was the all-important moment when I first acknowledged the existence of a supreme being, and the first time I ever asked for help from God or man.

And help came. The enemy fire stopped when American helicopters appeared over us, attacking the unit that we were fighting. So our sergeant ordered us to pull back and let the gunships finish the job. We crawled back a distance into the jungle, passing the bodies of a few of our buddies, our medic among them.

When the firing stopped, a strange, eerie quiet fell, along with a thick, heavy morning fog that mixed with the smell and sight of gunpowder, making it almost impossible to see more than thirty meters in any direction.

As the humid, smoky air cleared, we began attending to the wounded and dead. Since our medic was killed in the first two minutes of the firefight, those of us who had field bandage dressings helped the wounded. The dead we could do nothing for so we covered them with their ponchos and left them alone. Then it was time to wait, wait for the helicopters to pick up the wounded and the dead, a time to check our weapons and get ready for whatever came next.

This seems so incongruous now, but while we waited, most of us put our headphones on and listened to the Armed Forces Radio station from Da Nang play the Top 20 hits from back in the States.

Those radios were important to us. They were a link with home, and a reminder that the whole world wasn't at war. As I lay there in the jungle, I heard for the first time the song "Magic Carpet Ride" by Steppenwolf. I thought, as I listened, that it sounded like drug music to me, and I would have much preferred something by George Jones. But we rarely heard country music on Armed Forces Radio.

While I listened I realized I was one weapon shy. Apparently, as I was crawling around on my belly, my belt had come unbuckled and a sheathed hunting knife had slipped off my belt. Although I had never used that knife in direct combat, it had served me well in other ways. I used it to clear my line of fire of grass and vines, to prepare my rations, to cut and clean my nails, and as a warning to anyone who was toying with the idea of messing with me. For me, it was more versatile than a Swiss Army knife, and I felt naked without it. So, cussing and grumbling, I rebuckled my belt and began searching the undergrowth for that knife.

It was not standard issue; I had brought the knife with me from the States. Prior to leaving for Fort Lewis, Washington, when relatives gathered to wish me good luck (all thinking it would be the last time they ever saw me alive), a cousin's husband, Roger Bullard, gave me that Old Timer. It was a classic buckskinner knife with a highly polished rosewood grip handle, a stainless steel blade, and a leather sheath cut to fit on a belt. Two silver metal plates that read "Old Timer" were imbedded in the handle, one on each side. The knife was like a piece of wood and steel sculpture, a perfectly balanced instrument, a work of art. The sheath included a strap with a buckle that held the knife in the sheath when not in use.

Roger told me, "Take it with you to the war. You might need it."

So I stowed it in my duffle bag and that knife traveled with me to Vietnam, where I wore it on every combat mission. In some ways, I guess I looked on it as a good luck charm. Having been the only gift I received before leaving for duty, it most certainly was a tie with home. Others in our company had similar knives they carried, and that was just fine, as far as our commanding officers were concerned. Anything that improved our personal arsenal of weapons was viewed as a plus.

But there I was on my hands and knees in the jungle, feeling around in the grass and vines for my lost knife; however, no amount of searching uncovered it. I traced and retraced my paths in the area. No luck. It was gone.

A few days afterwards, while I was still steamed about the loss, we were in another jungle rumble with what I assumed were the Vietcong survivors of the skirmish in which I lost my knife. Again there were casualties on both sides. When the Vietcong disappeared into the jungle, we cared for our wounded and dead, and then searched the bodies of the enemy soldiers we had killed.

The ground was muddy, so one of the more brutal guys in my squad sat on a dead gook while he stopped for a drink of water. He immediately jumped up and started cussing. When the full weight of his body had landed on the gook's chest, the corpse's lungs exhaled an astonishing amount of putrid gas.

While cussing nonstop he rolled the body over to claim its ears as his trophy and ticket to the front of the chow line. I laid claim to a different, more prized trophy: my knife. There it was on the gook's belt. Both of us recognized it as not one similar, not one like it. No.

It was my knife! Happy as could be, like being reunited with an old buddy, I took it and reattached my Old Timer to my belt.

In a day or so, we were sent back to LZ Uplift, and I was really looking forward to the chance to scrub down with soap and water. I stripped, wrapped a towel around me, laid out my belongings on my bunk, and headed for the showers, which were located by a holding pond at the far end of the firebase.

There was always a man assigned to guard duty at our tent. His job—whether he did it or not—was to make certain that no one bothered anyone else's possessions. Since we had no way of securing anything under lock and key, the guard was our only protection.

When I returned from the showers I noticed that my knife was gone. The guard swore he knew nothing about it and that no one had been near my bunk. Frankly, I believe that he never saw anyone go near it because he had turned guard duty into naptime.

I was pissed. Not only was my knife gone again, we had no clean clothes, so I had to put my dirty, stinking jungle uniform back on, everything except my socks, which I had thrown away because their heels had worn away, leaving giant blisters on my feet. The socks, I knew, would be replaced the next day—whether or not I got other clean clothes.

Dressed in my filthy uniform and boots, I headed for the mess hall, figuring some chow might improve my disposition. When I walked in and looked up the line, I saw it: my knife. It was on the belt of a guy from another platoon.

I stepped up and got in his face. "Hey, you sonofabitch," I greeted him through clenched teeth, "you stole my knife!"

"No, no, not yours," he stammered. "I bought this knife off a gook."

"Uh-uh. No. Hell, no! You stole it while I was in the shower. Stole it off my bunk. Gimme my knife back now. RIGHT NOW!"

Although none of his buddies backed him up, just looked the other way, the guy continued insisting, "It's my knife. I paid for it."

Still sticking to his story that he bought it off a kid gook, repeating it over and over, he removed the knife and sheath from his belt and handed them to me. There was no fight; the look on my face won the argument for me. With the look and the reputation I had built for being a tough soldier with a string of enemy kills to my credit, I was known as a guy who didn't run, stood my ground, blew my hand grenades, and set an example for other soldiers to follow. There was no way I was going to back down from a fight with him, even if he was armed with *my* knife.

And it definitely was mine; you get to know the little nicks and scratches on something you carry with you day and night. But the knife wasn't with me long. The next month, on a subsequent return to LZ Uplift, I stretched out on my bunk for a nap, laying my stuff on the floor under where I slept. When I awoke, the knife was gone again, this time gone for good.

The knife, of course, was replaceable. You could buy knives from the black market thieves just outside the base; some as nice as the one Roger had given me. But I didn't replace it because it was, in my mind, irreplaceable. It had been my one tangible link with home.

—•—

Denny Hendrix in the jungle with his M-60 machine gun preparing for ambush patrol

Chapter 10
Blessed Are the Children

Whoever receives one little child like this in my name receives me.
Matthew 10:42

The sun was hot, and the central highlands air of Vietnam hung thick as maple syrup around your head and mouth. It was hard to breathe—much less hump through the jungle with a full rucksack on your back.

We carried all we needed to live and fight for days in those rucksacks, pouches constructed on steel frames that fit the contour of your body from your shoulders to your waist. The canvas attached to the frame in such a way that the pouch set high on your shoulders in order not to throw you off balance. Even so, the steel frames dug into our backs and sides as we trudged and pulled our way up the mountain trails, trails that severely tested even the toughest among us.

On this particular mission, we were told we had the latest and greatest in army technology to help us sniff out the enemy: a Kit Carson Scout *and* a scout dog.

The K-9 was a German shepherd, and with him came an American scout dog handler who was mighty proud of his pooch. The dog trotted ahead of us as we moved out, sniffing everything in sight. He covered the area ahead of us, sweeping first left, then right, then left again, then right again. Even though he wasn't finding anything it was interesting watching his hunting ritual as we trudged along with our 100-pound-plus loads on our backs.

Midday, we were still humping but the dog was not. He collapsed with exhaustion. The handler was certain he was going to either have a dead dog on his hands or have to carry that German shepherd the rest of the way. The dog was literally too tired to stand—much less trot along on his merry way, sniffing out the enemy.

Our medic didn't have a clue as to what he could do for the dog, and the handler wasn't about to allow the animal to be put down. So, in exasperation, our platoon leader called for a medevac. One came and away the German shepherd and handler flew for medical observation and rest while we moved ahead under the weight of our heavy loads.

That was the first and last time we enjoyed the assistance of a scout dog, and I wish it had been the last time we enjoyed the assistance of a Kit Carson Scout as well.

We had been on the move since daylight and there were plenty of signs that Charlie (nickname for the VC and NVA) had been in the area. We didn't have to wait for the Vietnamese scouts who had defected to our side to tell us how to read the signs.

"Kit Carson Scouts" is what we called them because they tried to present themselves as bold, brave frontiersmen who knew the terrain intimately; guides who would see you safely through dangerous territory.

Well, the territory was dangerous, and to my mind, so were those scouts. They were, at best, a necessary evil; North Vietnamese defectors who turned to the Americans' side because they were hungry, because we paid them, and because they thought their side was going to lose. When they came to us, offering their services, the U.S. sent them to an indoctrination camp in a secure area. In contrast to the front lines, the indoctrination camp must have seemed like a spa to them. Three hot meals a day and all they had to do was sit there and listen to someone tell them what nice guys we Americans are.

When their camp days were over, in theory, their minds were turned around and they just loved us for being there to help. In gratitude, they were supposed to show us where enemy units were. But their indoctrination didn't always take. Some were infiltrators sent to purposely steer us into traps. When we would happen upon an abandoned campsite, it was always the same mix of broken French and English: "Beaucoup VC. Maybe one, maybe three days ago."

Yeah, lots of VC recently; it didn't take a self-proclaimed Kit Carson to figure that out. Those scouts were lazy, and I didn't like that. On top of that, they were always nervous, which, in turn, made me nervous. I still believe they led American units into ambushes as often as they steered them clear of danger.

We were moving along the foothills northeast of Bong Son on a "search-and-destroy" mission. That was the new name for our maneuvers; in the past, the high-ranking brass had called these spots where all hell could break out any second "free-fire zones." The finer points of terminology were wasted on those of us standing in harm's way. We knew we were there to kill, and that was the bottom line.

A search-and-destroy mission was good in some ways and not so good in others. American aircraft would fly over the area targeted for an operation and drop leaflets, telling the people to leave the area immediately. The leaflets also said that anyone found in the target area after a certain date and time would be considered a Communist enemy soldier and that they would be attacked by the American forces that were operating in the area. Perhaps this made some general back in Washington sleep better at nights, but when we arrived in one of these areas where written warnings had rained down, we found those leaflets all over the ground. Technically, they had been warned, and it was too bad that only one in about a thousand peasants could read. I sure didn't see any institutions of higher learning out there in the jungle in 1968. But I did see paper, ink, and aircraft fuel wasted. Most of the locals used the paper leaflets to help start their cooking fires.

On this particular day my platoon was looking for a trail that recon had reported to intelligence earlier in the month, a trail leading from the jungle-covered mountains to small villages located in the low-lying areas. As we moved silently through the thick undergrowth, I could see the brown straw huts of one village below, all arranged in a circle with a courtyard in the center.

There was very little movement down there, which was not surprising. The Vietcong and the North Vietnamese troops hid in the mountain jungles during the day then moved into the villages at night for food and new recruits.

Our assignment was to find the nearby mountain trail that intelligence had told us existed, and ambush any enemy soldiers using it. It was getting late. We had found the villages, but not the trail. I couldn't help but think it was likely another trick pulled by our Kit Carson Scouts.

The platoon leader held up his closed hand first, indicating he wanted to stop and take his bearings. This was a great time to fall straight on your ass and let the rucksack break the fall. After you did, you just sat there, sweat running into your eyes and into your mouth like you were drinking water from a glass. Miserable weather, insects, disease, and nothing resembling creature comforts: that about sums up the most appealing characteristics of the area.

While the platoon leader read his map and was on the radio, I watched our Communist-turned-American scout. He was jumpy. His slanted eyes and small head turned in every direction, continually glancing all around us as if he knew something we didn't yet know.

After fifteen minutes or so, word came back through the long green line of men stretched out on the wet jungle floor: remove your packs, stash them alongside the trail, and cover them with grass and branches. The only ammo we were to bring were two bandoleers of ammunition, two hand grenades, and one smoke grenade. The platoon leader then asked for all the squad leaders to meet at the head of the column.

Great! That, I figured, would give us another fifteen minutes to rest before we moved out on this mission. Just as I guessed, in about a quarter of an hour our squad leader, Hernandez, returned with instructions. He was a good guy, a native of Puerto Rico who spoke with a heavy accent. Sometimes I wondered if he understood English very well. The platoon leader was also from Puerto Rico and virtually impossible to understand—especially when he shouted orders.

We were to move forward about one klick, where we should find the trail that the North Vietnamese Army was reported to be traveling under the cover of darkness as they moved to and from the mountains. Each squad of our platoon was to move into a different area, except our squad; we were to set up right on the trail, giving us more of a chance to kill the enemy. The rest of the company was to move to other positions to cut off any escape of the enemy after we sprang our ambush; we would all work together as a total killing machine.

I was excited. I loved ambushes because they were, more often than not, productive. We, on most occasions, killed more of them than they killed of us.

Move out! Charlie Company of the First Battalion, 503rd Infantry, 173rd Airborne Brigade was on the job. We held more enemy kills than any other unit in our battalion.

All the squad leaders had worked over their maps together to minimize the risk of shooting each other. I always hated it when one of us got lost and almost killed a buddy, thinking he was the Cong coming through the jungle. Yep, that happened on more than one occasion. We were then a solidly united company with a great company commander. He was a "lifer" from Columbus, Georgia, older and army-smart. His lean, long, pointed face would have been right at home on a recruiting poster. While he was probably no more than thirty-seven, when you are nineteen that seems very old.

We moved out on our assigned mission; Fletcher took point, and I took the slack man position right behind him. The Communist traitor of a guide went with another squad and I was glad to see him go. I became progressively distrustful of those guides and was not the only American who wanted them gone. I knew for a fact that some of the scouts were killed in the line of duty. Apparently the army high-ups became very creative when explaining why so many of the guides died of gunshots to the backs of their heads.

It was quiet as we slipped through the thick, green growth. No one spoke or even dared to make a sound. We used eye contact to signal when we needed to communicate. The enemy was near, and we knew it.

When we got to "the trail," I was stunned. We hadn't been prepared for what we saw. There was no little trail; it was a rigging road large enough to drive a jeep down. Bad sign. The Ho Chi Minh sandal prints in the trail told us that the local Vietcong had teamed with the NVA in the area, definitely bad news. When the two came together to fight as one unit, it meant they were looking for someone to hurt and hurt bad.

We scouted for an advantage point overlooking the trail, a place to set up our ambush. The sergeant chose a small, flat piece of property farther up the trail and we moved into position. Each man took his place in a line about ten meters apart. Once we had our position, we moved down to the trail and each placed the claymore mine he carried so that it faced the direction from which the enemy was expected to approach. Once in place, we armed them with a blasting cap that fit into a slot in the mine. With mines in position, we returned to our posts and lay flat on the ground, facing down, with a good field of fire on the trail. I laid out two hand grenades on the ground in front of me as well as one bandoleer of ammunition. I kept a second bandoleer on me in case I had to move out fast and lost the other one. I looked down the line, and everyone was ready. We lay motionless, watching and listening for any enemy movement.

I had been on many such ambushes before. Your legs and arms always got cramped because you get tense just waiting to kill as many enemy soldiers as you can when the time does come. Usually in addition to cramps, I got a bad headache from the tense waiting time. Occasionally no one came at all, and sometimes there were more than you wanted right there in front of you. But I felt good about this ambush. All the classic signs were here: the well-used trail, the NVA bootprints and Vietcong sandal prints in the trail's mud—signs that said at least a company of enemy soldiers was in the area, and that they probably came this way often.

But nothing happened.

After about two hours I gave up on the ambush, thinking we would pull out soon. I looked down the line to our sergeant, hoping for some kind of signal. He was turned the other way, looking back up the trail. Suddenly I saw the far end of the line raise their rifles to their shoulders and knew this was it. What a rush that was! In short order, I would be in a firefight. That's how you think when you're nineteen and naively convinced you are indestructible.

We each allowed eight or nine enemy troops to enter our killing zone before we opened fire. I don't know who fired first; it didn't matter. We blew the claymore mines, and I threw my two grenades right away. Then I picked individual targets.

The firefight was vicious, the noise deafening, as the air hung thick with the burnt gunpowder. We were firing twenty rounds of ammo with a single pull of the trigger.

Several North Vietnamese lay dead before me on the muddy trail as the survivors overcame the initial shock of the ambush and began fighting back. Their AK-47 rifles were talking, making a sound different from the American M-16 rifle. It was a pop-pop-pop sound, while the M-16 makes a crack-crack-crack noise.

This ambush was already the longest one I had ever been involved in. The NVA were actually assaulting our position. In a matter of minutes, they were in our perimeter. It was total chaos.

We had hurt them on the initial blast, but they were soon everywhere! I rolled to my side to reload and saw a group of black pajamas coming up from behind us, firing. I turned to return fire as one NVA soldier ran over me. To my surprise he didn't shoot me. So I emptied a clip into his back before he realized what he had done and turned to fire on me.

The sergeant was on the radio; I heard him shouting into the phone receiver. It sounded like Spanish to me. I didn't care what it was as long as it got us some help!

We had hit the point element of a large unit of gooks, and they were kicking our asses. I could hear my buddies shout for help or ask for the medic after getting hit.

There was no time to help. I was just trying to stay alive. Those gooks must have been on drugs because they were running throughout the ambush line as if it wasn't there. Eager to die for Uncle Ho, I guess.

After ten minutes or so, the jungle floor was covered with the dead and wounded from both sides. We could not pull back because there was a hill behind us. We had no cover, and the gooks had worked their way behind us anyway. I got down to my last six clips when the first mortar shell hit the ground. *Oh hell,* I thought, *those gooks have mortar support!* I hoped help was on the way, but feared that the rest of the company had hit gooks, too.

We continued firing at the brown uniforms with all the marksmanship we could muster. No matter how frightened I rightfully become, to this day, when I sight down the barrel of a weapon, my hands and arms become steady, dependable.

It was not until the mortar rounds started hitting with a more frequent thud that I realized they were ours. Ours! To the northeast of the village I could see the forward observer talking on the radio, calling in support. That relieved me some, but not much, for he was calling the rounds right into our position. They were falling all over the place, and we took some casualties from our own rounds. It seemed like years, but shortly after the mortar rounds started coming in, the NVA and their cronies, the Vietcong, moved out, leaving their dead.

We formed a small fighting perimeter and took count of our wounded and dead. The plan was already in place to move the wounded back down the trail to a clearing so that dust-off, the medevac helicopters and their crews, could pick them up. Once you've stood under one of those birds as it descends, you understand why the soldiers tagged them dust-offs.

Our sergeant had called for dust-off and told them we had disengaged the firefight and would be at the clearing in twenty minutes with four wounded and two KIAs.

We were all rattled; being jumped was not supposed to happen. This many gooks in one place was a rarity in our zone. The sergeant had told us that we would be met at the clearing by other units and that we would secure a perimeter for the night. Not until the next morning would we move out to look for the NVA.

Our packs, which were back in the location where we had been ordered to leave them, were to be picked up by a squad coming from that direction and brought to us at the dust-off location. So we gathered our wounded and dead and made it to the rendezvous location to meet the choppers and the rest of our company. This trip was nerve-racking. Dangerous. We were almost out of ammo of any kind. I hoped the NVA were off licking their wounds and that we would have no further mixing it up that night.

The dust-offs made their approach and dropped in like a rock. We loaded our buddies on the chopper, and they were off in what seemed like seconds. I loved those medevac pilots; they were both brave and crazy. They would come in after the wounded anytime you called them. Of course, they preferred that you were not in heavy contact because the gooks would stop shooting at you and shoot at them, since there was a bounty on helicopters. Rumor was any gook who downed one earned three days of rest and recreation because the choppers were so mobile and such an advantage for our side.

Before midnight our company had joined together at the edge of the clearing in the jungle. We were all on perimeter guard alert. The gooks were still in the area, and as strong a group as they appeared to be; they might attack again without any warning. We were so battered that the nightly observation post did not go out. Without lookouts, we could get no warning prior to an attack. We just hunkered down during the night and prayed for morning. We always preferred fighting in the light, if possible. The air strikes were more accurate, and you could see the little bastards. But that night seemed to last forever, and I was much older when the sun came up the next morning.

The captain called for all the lieutenants to meet him in the center of our formation for a briefing. The brass, back in the rear, was excited about our ambush on the trail, and they wanted a body count. What's more, they wanted it "today."

That's the way it was; you put your life on the line, killing the enemy, and some pompous jerk safely stationed at the rear gets promoted for doing a good job. I never could nor will I ever be able to figure that one out.

After an hour of planning and discussion, the platoon leaders came back to give us our marching orders. My platoon was to move along the bottom of the hill, just inside the jungle canopy, and to the right of the nearby village. We were not to engage the enemy, if possible, until the other platoons were in place to set up a blocking wedge. We were going after these North Vietnamese soldiers who were working in the area. The rear brass wanted a high body count at all costs!

At 0630 hours, the order came to move out. The platoon leader, Lieutenant Rodriguez, moved closer to the front of the column than usual. I volunteered to pull point for Second Platoon that morning. Having lost some friends the evening before, I wanted some payback!

I moved slowly, first up the mountain incline and then leveling off to put us just inside the brush.

We could see the village to our left, about ninety meters away, the usual circle of dirt-floor huts. Between the settlement and us was a rice paddy. On the village side of the paddy was a dike that was topped by a path. There was some movement in the village that morning, and I could hear voices, sometimes shouting, sometimes sounding like a fight. My hand shook from tension, and sweat ran down my face like a river. I had deep cuts on my arms and hands from all the movement through the jungle. Each time I glanced behind me, I could see the tension on the faces of my friends. They were pissed off about the losses we had suffered. Once they found the gooks, it was going to be bad for somebody.

As we came to an area that would expose our position, our column tightened up, much tighter than usual when on a combat patrol. I had just turned to motion "let's move forward" when, from the village, I heard a loud noise. It sounded like a platoon of gooks coming our way, but it was difficult to see what was on the other side of the foliage that grew along the edge of the dike. Across the village's small rice paddy pond, I saw people running out of the village and down the path next to the rice paddy. Some wore sampans, all wore black pajamas. Rodriguez shouted at the top of his lungs, "Get 'em! Get 'em!"

Every man in my platoon either fell to the ground in the prone firing position or kneeled and opened fire on the shadows as they ran from us. The fire was heavy; each man unloaded his magazine, then reloaded and fired more.

Originally, I had seen more than a dozen people running; when the firing stopped, I saw only a few standing.

The lieutenant was frantic, running around shouting, "No, no, no, don't shoot them; go get 'em, *catch* them, *capture* them!" So we moved out to where the people were laying on the ground.

The long run across the rice paddy tired me some, but I was among the first to arrive at the location. What I found knotted my gut. There wasn't a soldier among the dead and wounded. No adults either. But the water that we waded through was red with blood, and so was the normally black soil.

We found only a bunch of kids, all between the ages of six and twelve. Seven had been killed by our burst of fire. Some of the children had their arms nearly torn off by the impact of the M-16 bullets; others had large, gaping holes in their bodies. Blood was everywhere. The children were crying and screaming, and some platoon members started to cry. The ones who were not hit probably thought we were going to kill them next. One little guy was lying face down, not moving. I rolled him over to check for wounds and wished I hadn't. His face was completely gone; it stayed on the ground, and all I saw was a hole the size of my fist where his little face should have been. A girl about twelve years old was holding her stomach and crying as she sat on the ground. The medic from our platoon was working at a frantic pace, but he was only one man. He moved the little girl's hands from her stomach and her intestines fell out onto her legs, and then spilled onto the ground.

I have never seen such death and destruction inflicted upon those so young. The high-powered M-16 rifle bullet is one of the most effective military projectiles because of its speed and the shock it creates when it comes in contact with the body. The physical damage it did to those children is seared in my mind's eye.

Rodriguez was devastated and called for medevacs to take the surviving kids to the hospital. They replied that they could only come for wounded or dead soldiers because of the activity in progress. For the next ten minutes Rodriguez helped us do what we could for the wounded, using what little medical supplies we each carried with us. Our efforts may have been laudable, but we were getting nowhere. He called again for the medevacs, this time telling them we had wounded in action. Within twenty minutes, here they came, flying in at about fifteen feet off the ground, 100 miles an hour. When they landed and saw what we were dealing with, we didn't catch hell for having lied about the wounded being civilians instead of soldiers. Instead, the children were loaded into the helicopter and whisked away to the nearest American field hospital.

During all this time, the parents who lived in the village would not come out to claim their children for fear of being killed, too. Who could blame them?

This incident was investigated by the army and logged as "an accident." At least that's what I was told. The lieutenant was transferred back to the rear, and I never saw him again.

To this day, I believe Lieutenant Rodriguez did not mean for us to shoot those children, only wanting us to round them up to be questioned. It was all a mistake, a misunderstanding of his order. *"Catch 'em,"* he meant to say … not, *"Get 'em."*

It's my belief that children always pay the ultimate price in war.

We moved to another location late that afternoon, one close to the village, and dug in for the night. Just after sunset, the forward listening post, our first line of defense, had no more than moved into position when we received three M-79 grenade shells inside our perimeter—our own grenades. No one saw where they came from and no one was hurt when they exploded.

We called an M-79 a "thumper" for the sound it made when launched. These were U.S. weapons, so that raised interesting and unanswered questions. Had the Vietcong or a villager taken these weapons off U.S. soldiers? I assume that was the case because they had no choppers flying in supplies. Were the shots specifically in retaliation for the deplorable deaths of the children? Again, I can only speculate. If enemy troops were retaliating, it would be characteristic for them to really let loose, not just launch a couple of grenades. However, only a couple of grenades might be all the firepower a villager possessed.

I believe it was someone with a connection to the village sending us a warning. Was it one of the Kit Carsons, or a parent from the village? During war, accurate answers to questions such as those are hard to come by.

As I lay on the ground, thinking about the day's events, my perspective on war was forever changed. From that day forward, I did not hold a personal grudge against the enemy that I had to fight. If anyone had killed my children, I would have fought back, too. I would have fought back with all my might.

The next day at dawn, we were up and preparing to move out to the mountains and get the generals their body count. I had many more days in Vietnam to serve, but fighting the Communists was never the same after that incident. I was young and dumb when I arrived in Vietnam; I was 100 years old when I left that country.

—■—

Chapter 11
Dead Man Hubbard

Honor your Father and your Mother, that your days may be long
upon the land which the Lord your God is giving you.
Exodus 20:12

I had been "in country" for almost three months and was already an "old timer" in the ways of Nam. We had been in the boonies for about two weeks when word came to make ready to be "extracted out," army mumbo jumbo for being hauled back to our main base for a few days of rest before moving on to another jungle hell hole. Where to next? We didn't know, and I hated those surprise moves.

"Uncle Ho" had his forces hidden very well. That mission we abandoned had been just a lot of humping and looking for someone to kill, but no luck. We assumed our next visit to the jungle would be to a fresh area where the brass believed we could find a lot of gooks. Our brass needed a body count, needed one in the worst sort of way, because no body count meant no promotions for the undeserving.

We checked all our gear, and then humped about two klicks to a rice paddy that was considered a safe area; but there were no gooks out working their crops that morning. Unseen gooks usually weren't a good sign. It could mean that the villagers knew the area was crawling with NVA and had fled to avoid being caught in the crossfire of a fight. So if farmers saw you coming but didn't run and hide, that usually meant there were no enemy soldiers in the area. On the other hand, people in the fields and rice paddies could be soldiers who had taken time off from killing Americans to work their crops, weapons stashed nearby. Vietnam was not a place where you should take anything on face value.

The entire company lined up along the rice paddy, and we leaned back on our rucksacks for a break. Situations could change in an instant, so there was no telling how long it would be until the next chance to sit and catch your breath. We knew to rest every chance we got.

I looked down the long line of men, all dressed in their camouflage green, and wondered if I looked as young as most of the other airborne troopers did. That line was long and very impressive—just kids, really, but true-blue airborne. Out there in the jungle, we were military to the core; inwardly, we all dreamed of getting to the rear to rest, eat, and drink beer until we passed out. That was about as good as it got in Vietnam. And we were so tired, so tired from the past few weeks of humping the thick jungle trails, discouraged that no security was sent out to listen for Charlie. I guess everyone thought we were secure. Besides, if any NVA were in the area, they would have ordered us to hunt them down—not come in for a new assignment. Nevertheless, not sending out security was a mistake.

Since the village directly behind us appeared deserted that day, we sat facing the flooded rice paddy. From that spot, we could see hundreds of yards to our front, which was unusual in that part of the world. The sergeant came by and told us that enough choppers were en route to carry the entire unit back to LZ Uplift. My entire squad welcomed this news with a great big thumbs-up.

Uplift was somewhat safe, and we could at least get hot food there. As we sat waiting on choppers we shot the breeze about what we were going to do once we reached the rear. Every man among us was going for a shower and hot chow; that was a given. It seemed like hours waiting on our ride, but in reality, it must have been no more than forty-five minutes before I heard someone say, "Make ready, here they come!"

There was no need to alert me; it seemed I could hear a chopper long before anyone else was aware of that one-of-a-kind thump-thud, thump-thud sound they repeated and repeated as their blades sliced through the air. Even after returning to the States, when helicopters were no longer a life-or-death issue for me, I could always hear one long before anyone else was aware there was a helicopter somewhere nearby.

The first wave was to arrive from the south, set down just long enough for us to jump on board, then zip over the treetops until we were safely back at Uplift. That was the plan, but plans out in the jungle were always in pencil and could easily be erased by an order or an attack.

When they appeared, the helicopters made a large circle, passing us far to the east. The heavily armed Cobra gunships were already on station, giving cover to the slicks, UH-1 transport helicopters, which usually only had M-60 machines guns mounted just inside the door area. The flight went south far enough to form a straight line, and then … here they came, like great, green grasshoppers, leaping across the sky.

As the aircraft approached, we kept low and were ready to load. I happened to glance down the line of troops and notice our radiotelephone operator (RTO) stand up, his radio antenna waving in the air. This was not SOP for operators. The NVA always targeted the radio operator when they could. This was their thought pattern: kill the head of the snake and you kill the snake. U.S. soldiers without a radio to call in air support or artillery presented the gooks with a much more level playing field.

Just as the young operator got to his feet and turned around to pick up his weapon, I heard a loud firecracker-like noise: a Communist AK-47 rifle doing its thing. The radio operator spun around—but minus half his face—then fell onto the rice paddy dike like a brick. The squad medics were on him in seconds, and the entire line turned toward the small village behind us and opened fire with everything we had. While we sat there, thinking we were safe, thinking we were in a deserted area, the gooks had been patiently waiting in spider holes (one-man, camouflaged fighting positions) that we hadn't uncovered on a previous sweep of the village. All that time, they had been waiting for the choppers to enter their fire zone.

At the first shot the choppers were out of there, but the gunships stayed and started to work on the village. The flight group had some slicks with them that reported spotting movement of NVA troops to the north of our location. My squad, along with another, moved into the rice paddy and set up an M-60 machine gun on one of the dikes.

We were firing to the north of the village when the chopper reported enemy movement to the other squad's RTO.

In a flash, the gunships were all over the place, firing every kind of ordinance in their arsenal. After about fifteen minutes, the gooks burrowed into the jungle, probably figuring that with that much firepower raining down on them, it would be smarter to leave, live, and fight another day. A medevac made a dive out of nowhere to whisk the dying RTO and another wounded trooper to a hospital.

What I heard next was tough to believe. We were going to be pulled out immediately, even after that incident. The aircraft made their move to pick us up, and we boarded without further incident. Once in the air, the flight was less than an hour to Uplift. There, we were offloaded onto the hot, dusty ground in flight waves, very orderly, very professional. We formed up to make sure we didn't leave anyone behind, and then headed to the tents to store our equipment. Next stop, the outdoor showers. One hundred naked men standing in line, waiting to wash the grime of war off their hides must have been a sight to the gooks who worked on the firebase. After showering, we headed to our supplier of beer, a tiny store outside the firebase perimeter, which was run by a little old Vietnamese man we called papa-san.

For a couple of days, we just pulled perimeter guard, ate hot food, and drank beer. And on the third day of our stand-down at Uplift, some members of my squad and I were sitting on a bunker, just killing time, when the sergeant walked up with a boney, fair-haired, pale-skinned guy with powerful yet sad green eyes. The sergeant told us that the new man was assigned to our squad and that we were to get him settled in. Then, without ever telling us the fellow's name, the sergeant left.

We introduced ourselves to the FNG, but not a word came out of his mouth. He just parked his butt on a sandbag and stared at the ground. Finally, Brodi asked him what was written on his helmet headband. I really hadn't paid attention to the writing till Brodi mentioned it. For the first time, the guy spoke in his slow, deliberate way. "Hubbard," he replied. "It says 'Dead Man Hubbard.'"

Brodi, who up until then held the unchallenged title of weirdo in our unit, looked at him as if he was crazy and didn't say another word. I said, "Then come on, Hubbard, let's get you settled and all go grab a beer."

He gave me an expressionless look, picked up his equipment, and followed us to the tent where we slept. After his gear was stashed and a few beers had been downed, I asked Hubbard what he meant by the writing on his helmet, especially since he had just arrived in the country and hadn't even been out into the boonies.

Hubbard looked straight into our half-drunk eyes, gave us a cold, penetrating look, and said, "My family needs the money. If I get myself killed over here, they'll get $20,000 in insurance money."

When I asked him why they needed the money so badly, he replied, "They could buy a trailer home with all that money, and a real home's somethin' my mama's never had. A home of her own would be like a dream come true."

Both drunk and nosey, I plowed on, asking questions, probing, and not minding my own business. In a matter-of-fact manner, Hubbard spelled it out for us. Number one, his entire family back in Mississippi was dirt poor. Number two, he figured that his getting killed in Nam was a given. So, number three, for his folks, his death would be a good thing.

He seemed to mean what he said, and I sized him as being a nice guy—if not overloaded with intelligence. After hearing him out, I got right to the point. "Hubbard, a guy who thinks like you do is dangerous. You stay clear of me."

With that, I left and went to see some buddies of mine across the firebase, and frankly didn't think about Hubbard much for some time.

Three days after his arrival, we got word to prepare to move out to the boonies the following day. So we stopped our drinking, got our ammo and weapons together, and loaded our packs with enough supplies to last us at least three days in the jungle. The rumor was we were moving about twenty-five miles away into a hot landing zone where a large unit of North Vietnamese Army regulars was reported to be located. We needed rest for what was ahead, so everyone turned in early.

The next morning a hot, crimson sun peaked over the horizon as the four platoons that comprised our company were formed up in the dust, as we had so many times before. Our platoon leader gave us a quick briefing about the landing zone, then an even quicker inspection of our gear and weapons before we moved to the end of the firebase to load onto the choppers that would transport us to the jungle. I guess it was a compliment that he expected us to be properly equipped and prepared for whatever we might soon face.

I didn't see Hubbard that morning, nor did I think about him. Frankly, I had other thoughts on my mind. By that point in my trips to the jungle, I knew that the guys who got mentally prepared were the most likely to come back in one piece. So my thoughts were about survival: my survival and the survival of all my buddies.

In that morning's briefing, we learned recon patrols had located a large number of NVA and Vietcong in the general area of our destination. These troops were reported to be hardcore, seasoned killers, tougher than any we had ever fought. So we weren't in for a picnic if we located them.

Two squads from my platoon were to exit our choppers just east of a specific village area. Our other two squads, along with the entire remaining platoons of Charlie Company, were to land in the rice paddies just outside of the same village and make their way into the settlement. That would put them in the open for a short but dangerous time. I was glad I wasn't with them because I knew they were going to catch the worst of it if the gooks were hiding there.

With all this roiling and boiling in my brain, we got on board and the blades started to turn. In a matter of minutes, we were airborne. The whirling dust of the firebase was below us now as we moved high into a clear blue sky that was tinged around the eastern edge with the remnants of the sunrise. I sat back and waited with anticipation as we moved toward our destination, hoping that the gooks would be gone, and at the same time hoping they would be there because I was ready for some action.

After a short time in the air we were told to make ready to leave the chopper. The pilot came in fast and literally bounced off the soft, moist ground below us. I was jarred somewhat and lost my footing but managed to get out with everyone else before the pilot took off.

We hit the ground running 'til we reached a high bank area in the jungle. There we set up our ambush, and I thought that we had found a great place. It was so thick I was sure nobody could see us.

To our left front the advancing platoons landed and moved toward the village. In less than two minutes after the choppers dropped them off the firing started. We could tell that both platoons that had inserted themselves into the edge of the rice paddies were in heavy contact.

Our sergeant radioed one of the platoon leaders and asked for instructions, which were: We were to hold on because there was a large movement coming our way. So I laid out my two frag grenades in front of me, waited, and listened to the steady firing near the village. Over our radio, I could hear the platoon leader calling for dust-off right away. They had two KIAs and six WIA. Initials took less time to say than *killed in action* and *wounded in action*. What's more, it made the horror of it all less personal, less painful to the lucky ones.

The day wore on but the enemy soldiers did not make it to our position. Later I learned that they had a system of underground tunnels that led them away from the village so that they could escape any ambush that might be set for them in the rice paddies. After several hours, contact was broken off, and we controlled the area completely.

That evening, after meeting with those who had been doing the hard work that day, I asked Stevens, a buddy in Second Platoon, to tell me who got zapped, and he said, "I didn't catch both names, but one was some new guy named Hubbard."

I went numb for a moment as everything Hubbard had told me rushed through my head.

Stevens said Hubbard had only taken about ten steps before the NVA opened up from the tree line and he was the first man to get hit and fall. "He was killed instantly; never knew what hit him, poor bastard."

I said nothing, but inside I was freaking out. His body had been hauled away when the dust-off took place, so I never saw him again, alive or dead. But I certainly remembered his words and wondered if it was just his time, or had he run the clock forward?

One thing was certain: a family back in Mississippi was headed for a graveside service in some country church cemetery, then on to the mobile home lot down the road.

——•——

Chapter 12
Wounded In Action

*And war broke out in heaven: Michael and his angels fought with
the dragon; and the dragon and his angels fought, but they did not
prevail, nor was a place found for them in heaven any longer.*
Revelation 12:7-8

The telegram my parents received read:

A WA388 XV GOVT PDB 3 EXTRA=FAX WASHINGTON DC
10 1024 EST=

MR AND MRS IRA H HENDRIX,

756 MIMOSA BLVD ROSEWELL, GA=

THE SECRETARY OF THE ARMY HAS ASKED ME TO INFORM
YOU THAT YOUR SON, PRIVATE FIRST CLASS DENNIS L
HENDRIX, WAS SLIGHTLY WOUNDED IN VIETNAM ON 7
JAN 69 AS A RESULT OF HOSTILE ACTION. HE RECEIVED
A FRAGMENT WOUND TO THE LEFT KNEE. HE WAS ON A

COMBAT OPERATION WHEN HIT BY A FRAGMENT FROM A HOSTILE BULLET THAT RICOCHETED OFF ACOCK.

HE WAS TREATED AND RETURNED TO DUTY. SINCE HE IS NOT REPEAT NOT SERIOUSLY WOUNDED NO FURTHER REPORTS WILL BE FURNISHED;

KENNETH G WICKHAM MAJOR GENERAL USA C-1190

THE ADJUTANT GENERAL=

Typographical errors aside, that telegram message was not accurate. We were out in the central highlands of the Suoi Ca Mountains, combing a fifty-square-mile area, looking for a group of NVA and Vietcong that had been ambushing some local patrols and killing villagers they suspected of being sympathetic to the Americans. So our job was to locate them and make them "neutral," which is army talk for *kill every damn one of them.*

During our search, we came upon a cave complex. When a small number of us ventured inside, we found a large, underground stream of sparkling clean water that flowed through the cave. Over the centuries that stream of water had carved an underground chamber large enough to comfortably conceal about thirty-five or forty people. It had definitely been used a short time before as a field hospital, likely a stopover point en route to bigger, better-equipped medical facilities elsewhere in the jungle. Empty penicillin bottles, syringes, bloody gauze, and scraps of printed paper littered the cave's floor. I picked up one of the pieces of printed pages and mailed it home. I still have it, but haven't learned what it says.

By the time we finished exploring the cave it was getting late. Our lieutenant decided we should put up a night fighting position near the cave and set up an ambush, in order to capture anyone coming to the cave in search of medical care. I had no expectation of ambushing anyone; the other way around was more likely. Obviously they had vacated the cave because they knew we were in the area. So they knew where we were, but we didn't know where they were.

Somewhat to my surprise, the night passed without incident. I even had plenty of time to clean my weapon and get in a reasonable amount of sleep. The next morning we packed and headed on up the mountain to see if there might be other caves in use as hospitals or storage facilities for weapons and food. I pulled slack man, and the point man was about forty yards ahead of me.

We had been humping along for about three-quarters of an hour, moving slowly as we went, when I noticed a clearing up and to my left. And I spotted something else: a brown helmet barely visible in the clearing's tall grass. Quickly raising my rifle and aiming just below the helmet, I pulled the trigger ... but only heard a click. I was shocked. The weapon had just been cleaned the night before, and if there's one thing I knew how to do properly, it was how to clean a rifle.

My patrol buddies behind me, having seen me aim and pull the trigger, searched out the brown helmet and started firing. I hit the ground and pulled the injector rod on my rifle back to remove the unfired cartridge, but there wasn't one in the chamber. I couldn't believe I had done something so careless. When I cleaned my weapon the previous night, I had put off inserting a live cartridge in order not to make noise, then entirely forgot to do it. So for nearly three-quarters of an hour, I had plodded through the jungle with an empty rifle.

After loading, I did my best to make up for my mistake. As we started firing back and forth, we worked our way toward the grass where I had spotted the helmet; however, they weren't holding their ground. The soldiers in the grass kept moving, too, firing and retreating. It was not heavy fire; there were maybe three or four of them on the ground, and they were just popping caps at us.

When we reached a wide, deep stream, the kind Southerners call *creeks*, and started across, well-hidden snipers—I never actually got a look at them—joined the party and began firing at us. From the rhythm of their firing, it was obvious that the snipers had bolt-action rifles. It was also obvious that they did not have much training because they couldn't seem to zero in on any of us. As their bullets zipped by their intended targets you could see the water rise up, boil, and bubble each time a stray piece of lead pierced the creek's surface.

Finally, three of us got across to the far bank and headed up the side of the creek, traveling steadily in the snipers' direction. Moving through some thick, bamboo-like jungle grass, I tripped on something and went down on my right knee. At first it felt as if someone had grabbed my ankle, but it was just a tangle of vines.

The couple of seconds I spent struggling to free my foot of that vine made all the difference for the sniper. While he couldn't hit a moving target, he proved he could hit a still one. I heard a shot and felt a sharp sting on my left knee: a bullet had grazed it deeply enough to cause the blood to flow. There was no ricochet, as the telegram my family received stated, nor was there a fragment imbedded in my knee. But there was a deep cut and my knee was swelling rapidly. Despite everything our medic had at his disposal, the situation kept accelerating, and the fear of a serious infection was a realistic one in that disease-infested jungle.

As quickly as the rest of the unit could get the situation under control a medevac was called in. I was taken to the hospital because the cut kept gushing blood no matter how tightly the medic wrapped it.

While I was in flight to the U.S. hospital in Quin Yan, my unit moved on to destroy another Vietcong field hospital, one far larger than the cave operation we had located the day before.

I stayed at the hospital almost a week before they released me to return to LZ Uplift and reunite with my unit. Just before we returned to the jungle to continue the fight, my company submitted paperwork for me to receive a Purple Heart; however, I didn't receive the medal until I was presented with my second Purple Heart more than four months afterwards.

During the week I lay in that hospital bed I had plenty of time to think. So I had qualified for a Purple Heart, killed more North Vietnamese soldiers than I care to count, witnessed a murder, participated in the grimy pleasures of Sin City, grown to hate the Vietnamese people, and had become highly suspicious of the U.S. government. It was clear we were fighting a white man's war, a war we couldn't win, and a war that was causing a fatal split in our cause and in our country. Nevertheless, I felt rotten for having left my buddies in the jungle to fight that pointless war without me. The bond between people who fight side by side is thicker and more binding than blood.

—■—

Chapter 13
The Saint Valentine's Day Heart

Be careful—watch out for attacks from Satan, your great enemy;
he prowls around like a hungry lion, looking for some victim to
tear apart.
1 Peter 5:8

February 14, 1969. I found myself at Firebase Uplift Pony. My unit was there on a three-day stand-down. A little rest, a fresh supply of ammo and food, and then we were to head back to the jungle. The rain had slacked off, the beer flowed freely, and there were the luxuries of hot food and warm baths. We lived for these breaks.

But they did not come around often. We had been in the boonies for about three weeks, and Charlie had kicked hell out of us. On three occasions we had been ambushed. One of our best men had been wounded and two had been killed; all were my friends.

The locals did not warn us of our enemy's presence on any of the occasions, even though they had to have known exactly when and where we were to be attacked. Their refusal to help us defend them further assured me that we were fighting a pointless war.

I had wandered around the firebase for nearly two days when I got word to meet my squad at the first sergeant's hooch. When I got near, I saw my whole squad standing in a circle. Even at a distance I could tell from the tone of my buddies' voices that they were pissed. As I neared the circle I could see the lieutenant and company commander standing in the middle of it. Not a good sign. Seeing both of our leaders in one place could only mean one thing: a mission.

I moved in close to hear the details of the mission being explained and couldn't believe my ears. With only two days' rest, we were being sent back. Those idiots were going to send only a squad, just ten men, back into the jungle alone. We had just come from there in company strength and still got the hell knocked out of us. *What*, I thought, *could a single squad do? Something's wrong with this picture*, I thought. And why send one squad—*my* squad? Why not the entire company?

My buddies were doing enough griping for three squads; so, not being able to do anything about it, I resigned myself to the fact that we were going, and that was that.

The time was late morning, and we didn't like going out late. More often than not, when you went out late in the day it meant you stayed in the jungle overnight. But staying overnight wasn't part of the plan—at least not according to the sergeant's quick briefing. When he added that there would be no choppers to transport us, I was about to ask why when he said, "Get saddled up and meet at the north end of the firebase for more instructions. That is all," and walked away. So I got my gear together and moved to the staging area of the firebase.

We were to move out about five klicks to a village that we had not entered in our earlier search-and-destroy mission. Intelligence had informed our command that the local Vietcong and NVA were using this village as a stopover point and food-gathering area. That meant the locals in this village either gave food or helped gather food for the enemy. Who could blame them? If they didn't, they would have been shot. So their choice was simple.

I dreaded going back out there. The Cong were in control of this part of the world, and they knew it. I didn't give a damn how much information the villagers had for us to extract. I didn't want to hump five kilometers through the jungle to coerce information out of them that could be false or could be true—assuming we could even find someone who spoke English and was willing to be of help. We certainly didn't speak more than a phrase or two of their language. More importantly, five klicks presented too much of a chance for ambush. However, what made sense to me or what I wanted didn't matter; we were moving out.

The war was back on.

We were at least moving light this time. Each man took only twenty clips of ammo, two hand grenades, one smoke grenade, one canteen of water, and one ready-to-eat meal. Just add water and stir.

I felt I could run with this small amount of gear. Compared to the usual weight of our rucksacks this was like hauling a bag of feathers. No, sir; no fuss from me about the weight.

I looked around the firebase as we prepared to move out. There were people ambling around in an I-don't-give-a-damn manner, gooks and American soldiers alike. The men not going on a mission often just pretended that a mission was not happening at all; it was easier that way. When your buddies got killed, you didn't feel like you could have helped them. Hell, you didn't even acknowledge that they were out on patrol. What could you do if they were in a jam? That attitude made surviving easier. I could see some choppers coming in from the south; probably needed fuel or something like that. They weren't concerned about me; I wasn't concerned about them.

We were almost at the barbwire perimeter when the lieutenant popped up again. For a moment, I thought he might be going with us, but I should have known better. As we semi-circled about him, he said, "For every man who brings me a Vietcong heart for Valentine's Day, I'll give him a three-day R&R."

Figuring he would have to be out of his mind to be serious, I took it as his newest twist on delivering a pep talk. So, armed with all the bullshit I could take in one day, I was ready to move out. One soldier, however, suddenly ran back for something he had left. His name was Brodi.

It seems I have always been a magnet for crazies and weirdos. That's the only explanation I can give for Brodi following me around like a puppy. I didn't even like the man and made an effort to be wherever he wasn't. Nevertheless, he seemed determined to be my shadow.

Brodi was about twenty and short. His complexion was an eerie white, and his features seemed rounded out of shape. Despite his stature, he could hump with the best of them. He didn't talk much; just sat around sharpening a bowie knife much of the time. Spooky. He held a whetstone firmly in his left hand and the handle of that long-bladed knife in his right, making small, circular motions. With every stroke of the blade on the stone, his whole right shoulder rotated. Each time the knife blade made contact with the stone, it screeched a sound that's impossible to forget, a grinding sound almost like sandpaper against a cement block, yet high pitched and shrill.

And there was that smile, that evil smile he wore as he made those rounding motions with his body. At the conclusion of each sharpening ritual, he took the knife in his right hand, raised his jungle fatigue sleeve, and shaved the hair from his arm in one long, swift, swiping movement. He gave me the willies, and I believed he would kill at the drop of a hat, no matter who you were.

One time he was on guard duty with a guy who said something he didn't like. In a flash, Brodi was all over that soldier, pounding him, breaking the guy's glasses, and beating shards of glass into his eyes. They had to ship the poor bastard to the U.S. for surgery.

They should have shipped Brodi to a funny farm somewhere, but the war needed crazy killers, and Brodi fit the bill.

When he came running back to join us, he flashed a plastic bag and an evil grin at me. As best I could tell, the bag was empty. We had waited on him for that.

When we moved out, Donohue was point man and I was slack man, second in line. I didn't know what position Brodi had taken up and didn't care, as long as I didn't have to put up with him during our five-klick hike through the jungle.

163

We moved silently when out in that tangle of vines and trees. Silence meant living; anyone who violated the code paid dearly for it. I've seen men beaten so severely by their comrades for making noise that they had to be medevaced to the hospital. On a combat operation—especially one in the jungle—there is no room for a screw-up. Silence is serious business; the lack of it could and did cost lives.

Afternoons were the hottest time of day in the jungle. The humidity there was so great it was like trying to breathe underwater. Even though we moved slowly and carried lighter-than-usual loads, sweat poured out of our bodies, and with it our energy; nothing new about that.

The march was routine until Donohue abruptly halted and went to one knee. I gave the signal to stop the forward movement and joined him. There in the wet, muddy trail were Ho Chi Minh sandal prints. Lots of them. Apparently the gooks had moved in from the west through thick jungle so as not to be detected. Then they entered the trail and continued in the direction of the village that was our destination. Just our luck, they were ahead of us. But our luck could have been worse. If we had accidentally met them head-on, only God knows what might have been the outcome.

Donohue's discovery changed the whole mission, and the sergeant called back to the firebase to get instructions concerning what we should do next.

I was glad for the break. All of us were already worn-out, even though we were only halfway to our destination. A perimeter guard was set up while the sergeant called back for new orders. When he received them he passed the word along in a low, choked whisper: we were to continue to the village and check it out for NVA.

Donohue the New Yorker let his feelings be known in a stream of slurred, rapid-fire words. Though mostly unintelligible to my ears, his feelings were easily understood. His anger and frustration amounted to nothing more than wasted energy, and we silently pushed on. By then it was getting late. If we were to make it back to the firebase before dark we had to move out on the quick step.

Finally we reached the village and moved in close enough to see that it appeared to be abandoned. Not even a pig in sight. This was bad news; it meant the civilians knew we were coming, which meant that the gooks did, too.

But where were the gooks? I thought. Where were the ones who made all those footprints on the trail? Had they already been here and gone? It didn't seem likely.

We eased around the village, not entering but looking for signs of an ambush. It was possible—again not likely—that the gooks who made the footprints in the trail turned off and headed in another direction before they got to the village. This could mean they had been diverted to another area to help a sister unit in a fight or were planning to attack something big. Either way, the village being deserted suited me just fine.

It hadn't been deserted for long. I could smell the sickening odor of the fish head and guts stew that had been boiling in the village's communal kettle earlier that day. One whiff of that stuff and it was easy to understand why the U.S. troops dubbed the natives "fish heads". I never did learn the source of the collective derogatory term "gook" for Vietcong and the North Vietnamese Army.

165

We entered the village, searching the huts for anyone who might be hiding. I was poking around in one of the filthy little huts when in walked Brodi with that shit-eating, evil grin on his face.

"You should be on the other side of the village, Brodi," I told him. "What are you doing in here?"

"Looking for my three-day R&R leave, Hendrix."

"Whacha mean by that?"

"You know, the Valentine's Day heart from a Vietcong. The lieutenant, he promised me. Promised if I bring him a real heart, I can go on R&R for three days. He promised. You heard him."

I knew he was dumb, but I didn't realize he was that dumb. I also knew what a mean little bastard he was and didn't want him to turn on me for being the messenger who delivered bad news.

"Brodi," I said carefully, "the lieutenant, he wasn't talking just to you, man. He was bullshitting all of us. Bullshitting us, man. He really didn't actually mean what he said."

Brodi looked at me for a second, but it seemed like an hour. The evil grin transformed into seething sternness.

"The lieutenant was not lying, and I'm gonna find me a gook and get his heart. You wait and see. Just wait and see."

He wheeled around and stormed out of the hooch. When he did, I made tracks for the other side of the village, wanting to be as far away as possible until what I said sunk in and was believed.

My dislike for this reeking collection of hovels grew by the minute. Whoever left got out of here in a hurry and without making a sound. I had the feeling that at any second we would be hit and wiped out. But we kept searching.

It wasn't long before a commotion at the other end of the village brought our individual searches to a stop. It was Brodi. He was shouting and cursing at a squad member named Baker. When I looked inside the hovel where they stood nose to nose, there was Baker, trying to push Brodi away from a pathetic old gook who lay at Brodi's feet. The man was ancient, looked sick, and probably had TB, which was rampant in that part of the country.

The sergeant rushed up and asked what the problem was. Baker said he entered the hooch and caught Brodi about to stab the old man with his knife. When Baker stopped Brodi, Baker became the one being attacked.

The poor old bastard on the ground was babbling and coughing. Since we didn't understand his language and he didn't understand ours, the two things I did understand were he was really sick and that I didn't want to get near him.

The sergeant ordered Brodi and Baker to separate and get back to work, and with a lot of gestures and a word or two the old man might have understood, the sergeant tried to assure the villager that no one would hurt him. Figuring he had done his best to get his message across, the sergeant ordered all of us to get back to work and left the hovel.

Except for the old man, we had come up empty-handed. Since it was getting late and we needed to move out if we were to get back to the firebase that night, the sergeant formed up the squad. We were more than ready to go and knew we had been lucky on this recon mission.

I pulled point on the way back, with Donohue as my slack man. The men behind us moved out in single file, almost stepping in each other's tracks. Once the village was about ten minutes behind us the sergeant took a routine head count to make sure we hadn't left anybody.

But, we had; the count came up one short of the full squad. Number one, this had never happened to me before. Number two, I knew as sure as I was wearing army green that the missing person had to be Brodi. And it was.

When the sergeant turned to go back to find him, I looked up at the sky, hoping not to hear my name.

"Hendrix, Donohue, let's go."

The three of us headed back to the village, while the rest of the unit waited to see if we would find Brodi.

A swarm of questions swirled in my brain. Had a hidden Vietcong soldier caught him and killed him, then made an escape into the jungle? Had Brodi stepped on a booby trap somewhere in the village? Had he? But nothing I imagined proved to be correct.

As we entered the village Brodi was coming out of the hooch where we had left the old man.

"Where the fuck have you been?" the sergeant exploded. "We moved out twenty minutes ago."

Then the sergeant saw what froze Donohue and me in our tracks. That crazy bastard Brodi had blood on his fatigue shirt and all the way down his trousers to his boots, blood that had coagulated into dark red glue. The slaughterhouse stench that clung to him already had flies swarming around him in a frenzy. But he didn't care because he was one happy guy. In his right hand, he held his unfired M-16, and in his left, he clutched the clear plastic bag he brought with him. The bag was dripping blood and held a silent human heart. Even through the blood and body fluids that had seeped out of the lifeless organ partially filled the bag, you could see the heart clearly: the membranes, the tissue, and the remnants of arteries.

"You crazy motherfucker," the sergeant sputtered, "what in the hell have you done to that old man?"

"Go look for yourself," Brodi snickered, "if ya got the balls."

When the three of us looked into the hooch, we faced the most gruesome sight I've ever seen. People blown apart by hand grenades are no rival for what we faced. The defenseless old Vietnamese lay on his back, reduced to a hacked-up slab of meat. What was left of him was sprawled across the dirt floor. He had been stabbed and slit open like a hog on hog-killing day. Ribs were broken, intestines were spilled across the dirt floor, and there was so much blood it looked as if a truckload of livestock had been butchered, instead of one poor old geezer.

From what I saw, I assume that, after slashing him open, Brodi had put his foot on the man's rib cage to hold it open while he went for his prize: the man's heart. The one thing Brodi hadn't mutilated was the man's face. I think the sight would have been easier to take if that twisted, tormented face had also been peeled away, leaving the man looking like nothing more than a pit bull's dinner. A tub of guts and bones was what we stared at, not an enemy soldier; he was too ancient, too sick. He was a victim, like many others in that war, both American and Vietnamese.

What do you say to a snickering, feral creep who stands holding a weapon in one hand and a human heart in the other? I guess the sergeant was equally at a loss for words. He just bellowed, "MOVE OUT," and we backtracked to where the remainder of the squad lay resting and waiting.

"Did you find Brodi?" "What happened?" "Is Brodi okay?" We were pelted with question after question.

I gave the same reply to everybody who asked: "Yes, we found him. And I'm sorry that we did."

We moved slowly back to the firebase, looking for the enemy soldiers that we knew operated in the area. During one of the few breaks we took on our trek home Brodi came to my position and wanted me to admire his prize. He waved his plastic bag and boasted that he had cut the heart out while the gook was still trying to fight him off, and he went on and on in excruciating detail about how the man cried as he slid the razor-sharp Bowie knife down his chest; about how the blood squirted out the man's mouth; about how it gushed from the two-foot incision he slashed down the man's chest and belly. Detail by gagging detail, he went on until I just looked at him and said, "Get fucked, Brodi, just get fucked!"

Because it was getting dark and the perimeter guards would be getting trigger-happy, our RTO called the firebase and told them we were coming in. So-called "friendly fire" was the last thing we needed. The proper password was given and we entered the compound, where everyone there was already preparing for the night.

When the lieutenant approached us from a dug-in bunker on the perimeter and asked the sergeant to come in to report and be debriefed, like a child with a new toy, Brodi ran up to the officer.

"I got my R&R in the bag. Here's your heart, Lieutenant," said Brodi as he proudly held up the plastic bag for the officer to see and admire.

In a voice that was level and calm, showing no trace of whatever he might have felt, the officer simply said to Brodi, "Come on in and tell me about how you got this Vietcong."

I watched as the lieutenant, the sergeant, and Brodi walked away into the night. The heart was never mentioned again in my presence.

What was mentioned a lot by Brodi was the three days of R&R in country that suddenly came his way. There was seemingly endless bragging about all the whores he had, the great food he enjoyed, and the volume of booze he put away.

Shortly after his R&R, he received a transfer he wanted so much he positively drooled when he talked about it. He was transferred to a LRRP, Long Range Reconnaissance Patrol. The last I saw of him he was running across a hilltop through a growth of elephant grass to climb on board a chopper that took him away to his new assignment. I can still see the shit-eating grin on his face as he took one final look back at the rest of us hunkered down in our foxholes.

—•—

Part of Hendrix's squad on combat patrol in the jungle near Qui Nhon, Vietnam

Chapter 14
Shoot the Prisoner

Thou shall not kill.
Exodus 20:13

It was a white man's war. The blacks knew it, and so did I. They didn't want to be a part of it, and I was getting a belly full as well. My last two or three months in Vietnam were rife with racism. When I first arrived, however, we all pulled together; but by March of 1969, it was slowly and surely becoming a "they" and "we" situation. And one particular incident at LZ Uplift shifted the racial issue into high gear.

A black soldier up on drug charges was being sent to the brig at Long Binh, the official army jail in Vietnam. The first sergeant brought him up on charges because he stayed wasted on heroin and kept going AWOL to escape being sent to the jungle with the rest of us.

It would be a lie to say that the majority of us were anything less than delighted to be rid of him. No sane person wants to be in a jungle firefight and have to depend on someone strung-out on drugs to save his life. Being happy to see him sent away had nothing to do with race, as far as I was concerned; I'd have been just as happy to see all the heroin addicts removed from our midst, white and black. No, he wasn't the only one.

The guards transferring this particular druggie were just a couple of grunts who happened to be white. As I heard it, the first sergeant told them, "Don't let that prisoner escape. If he tries to escape, shoot him."

That sergeant may or may not have been serious, but when the man did try to escape, one of the guards shot and wounded him in the leg, which was within military guidelines. (However, a warning shot first certainly would not have been out of line.)

When word spread of the man's attempt at fleeing, few were surprised because everyone knew he stayed strung-out on heroin and would do anything to get more. The shot was, however, a shock. Still, I figured it would be a forgotten issue by the next day because, over there, what was hot news in the morning was ancient history by night; things changed so fast.

But this shooting was an incident that grew into retaliation and a racial divide that became permanent. The blacks, as part of a violent protest over the shooting, burned our mess hall to the ground. It wasn't much of a mess hall, but it kept the rain off your head, and you had wooden tables and benches. Of course, the rioters were as inconvenienced as the rest of us, but to them the sacrifice must have seemed worth the statement their act of arson made.

The arson was also conveniently "forgotten," and no disciplinary action was taken. It took several weeks for the construction workers to receive supplies and rebuild the chicken barn of a building that had been burned. During the wait, we ate hunkered down near our assigned bunkers, and the platoon started dividing up. Whites ate at one place; blacks ate at another. The segregation became even more intense on night guard. Whites and blacks were no longer assigned shared bunkers. They had theirs; we had ours. Both factions fired their weapons sporadically throughout the night, almost never at each other's bunkers—but very close.

As the intimidation and threats became more and more elevated the higher command just looked the other way. They clearly knew what was going on because they stopped driving their jeeps around the perimeter at night, knowing full well that the Vietcong and NVAs were not their only enemies; "friendly fire" could easily come their way, and there are no fingerprints on grenade shrapnel.

Even through all of this I still had some black friends in our platoon. Being from a dirt-poor family, I had grown up in an area of town where whites and blacks lived close together. So I really didn't have an "us against them" mentality, and I guess it showed. Still, all of us were getting mean and insensitive. Fighting was simply what we did, whether we were turning on the Vietcong or one another.

Early one morning in February 1969, we were standing in formation at the firebase, preparing to be inserted into the jungle west of LZ Uplift. A new hotshot lieutenant named Grant was checking our equipment, paying close attention to the cleanliness of our weapons. He made no secret of how pleased he was with his military manner—even though he had started on the wrong end of the formation for a protocol inspection.

Lt. Grant, just a kid in his early twenties, was one of the products that Officers Candidate School was turning out faster than Ford Motor Company was turning out Thunderbirds. And I guess that was a necessary thing, because we ran through junior officers at a rapid clip; if they weren't killed, they were promoted.

During his "reverse" inspection, Lt. Grant suddenly stepped back and threw an M-16 rifle into the air. It landed barrel first in the red dirt of the firebase floor. That little maneuver may have seemed cute at Candidate School, but not out in the real world of combat. Clearly this was one officer who wasn't going to make it in the boonies along with our group of seasoned troopers. You do not abuse your rifle—or anyone else's—for any reason; a semi-dirty weapon is better than no weapon at all.

Any confidence or respect he had after starting the inspection backwards also hit the dirt. The trooper silently retrieved his M-16 and the lieutenant continued his inspection, ignoring the disgust and hatred of the men he faced.

I watched out of the corner of my eye as he reached out to take another weapon for inspection. After performing a textbook perfect receive, he looked down the rifle barrel and took two steps backward; it was clear he was planning to toss another rifle. As Lt. Grant lowered the weapon to gain some momentum before slinging it over his shoulder and skyward, the owner moved forward to within an inch of the officer's face. As they stood there, nose to nose, the rest of us held our breath and waited.

Finally, the lieutenant handed the rifle back to its owner, much like a little kid returning candy to the candy jar after his mother caught him with a fistful. The lieutenant may not have known it at the time but he probably saved his own life.

The inspection was completed without further incident, and choppers appeared from the west. I thought, *How in the world could we be losing this war with all these machines and all the bullets we can shoot?*

The birds came in low and slow, touched down in the fog of dust they spewed upwards and outwards, and the thump-thump-bumping sound of the rotors subsided as they slowed. We boarded while the helicopters crouched like large monsters swallowing up humans as fast as they could enter their gaping bellies.

The FNGs boarded first so that they could secure a seat deep inside the chopper; the veterans sat on the edge with legs hanging out, making the skids their footrest. I took my place on the edge of the chopper's belly and leaned backwards to ease the weight of my rucksack from my shoulders and back, then watched LZ Uplift shrink to the size of a kids' playground as we lifted up.

As sick and tired of that place as I was and as much as I had grown to hate the Vietnamese, I never failed to be touched by the primeval beauty of their land. My appreciation of the view was interrupted by the sight of the co-pilot tapping the pilot on the arm, a sure sign that some army bullshit was about to go down. The entire flight, all the troop-filled helicopters, started circling to the right. The man closest to the co-pilot leaned up, and I could see some hand signals. There was also shouting, but the racket of the engine was too much for me to understand the words. Later I learned that a large unit of NVA had hit a recon team in the area, and to save their hides, they had called in red leg (a term for artillery, derived from a uniform worn by artillerymen during the Civil War). The choppers had to exit the area quickly so the artillery could do a fire mission. We made a large sweeping circle to stall for time while the artillery put enough rounds into the area for the recon to get out. Next, the sergeant sitting closest to the pilot made the most dreaded motion of all: He held up an M-16 clip for all to see, tapped his steel pot with the clip, and then shoved the magazine into his weapon. We all knew this meant we were near and were going ahead with the mission.

And we came in fast. Way too fast, which meant the chopper pilot wanted us off the chopper double time so that he and his crew could get out before the gooks zeroed in and blew his chopper to hell. As we descended, I saw puffs of grayish white smoke rising from a small green valley, the aftermath of 175 artillery rounds called in to cover the recon soldiers' exit from the area.

Our chopper's door gunner stopped firing so that he wouldn't hit any of us as we exited the chopper. I looked one more time at the door gunner, and his M-60 barrel was smoking, red hot from firing all those bullets into the jungle below. My body turned numb as we lowered into the valley; I knew the red legs had stopped firing, and show time was here.

The first wave hit the ground and moved out in the direction of the tree line. I was on the second wave, and our chopper was about five feet from the ground when we were told to de-ass the ship. Five feet is mighty high when you're jumping with a hundred pounds of gear on your back. Nonetheless, we were eager to jump because white and green tracers were hitting the chopper, making that ding-ding sound as they tore through the skin of the ship.

With all the military intelligence at the U.S.'s command, you would think we could sneak up on them. But no, we had to attack them head-on. I hit the ground with a hard thump, thinking that if I were lucky, I'd break an arm or leg. I immediately went down to the ground, rolled over, and to my dismay, stood up uninjured. My squad quickly moved out to the south end of the valley, advancing in a spread-out tactical maneuver we had been taught at Fort Bragg before our departure to the live-fire exercise across the big water. As we approached the tree line there was a blast of machine gun fire, and our point man fell dead.

We all flattened immediately. The sergeant moved forward and told me to take point. I was about to protest being on point more often than anyone else, when he cut me off, pointing to an indentation in the tree line and telling me to make for that area. I looked back, and for the first time realized why the hurry. We were in real trouble: the gooks were suddenly all around us.

Assuming the company commander must know we have moved into a company- or battalion-size area of gook operations, I couldn't understand why we hadn't been sent more red legs or gunships? *Hell*, I thought, *we're all in this together, aren't we?*

While firing and cursing, we moved all the way to the point Sergeant Hernandez wanted us to reach. Results: one dead, two wounded, and the rest of us scared to death; but we fought on and held our area. As I was reloading my M-16, I heard the familiar thump of a chopper's motor blade and assumed they were coming to get us out of there. I was wrong.

I was near the entrance of the jungle and did not have a 360-degree visual; therefore, I could not see the choppers. I then realized that they had not come to extract us; instead, they had come to rake the jungle with bullets. When he realized the choppers weren't for us, the sergeant asked for the radio, but the RTO was to the left, lying on his stomach. In our rush for the tree line he had fallen back! That is a mortal sin; the RTO always stays with the platoon leader.

After getting his attention, the RTO crawled over to the squad leader, Sergeant Hernandez, who made contact with the platoon leader and gave him a report. The platoon leader said to hold our position and be ready to protect a medevac that would be landing for the wounded. That was a good thing for the wounded but not for the rest of us, because a chopper was like a magnet when it came to drawing enemy fire.

We waited about forty-five minutes, and word was passed that the choppers were near. The volume of fire had decreased from the jungle tree line, and that was fine with me. But, with the arrival of the choppers, I knew it would surely pick up again.

But for the time being, the gooks had almost stopped firing; only an occasional burst or two from a machine gun was heard. This was alarming. Downright suspicious. Why did they stop the fight? Where did they go? The choppers were en route and the wounded had been relocated in one area to make it easier to remove them from the battlefield. I was ready for the heavy volume of fire to begin as the grunts were loading the KIAs and WIAs onto the chopper, but it did not happen. What in the hell was up?

The first chopper lifted under the strain of the American bodies placed in the belly of the ship. I could tell it was overloaded, but that's what you did when a chopper arrived to extract the dead and wounded. You never knew if another one was coming in or not, so all the dead and wounded had been taken care of. Still, it was all too quiet.

The squad leaders met with the platoon leader and we got our marching orders. My squad and Second Squad were to move into the jungle, locate a small path marked on the map, and follow it to the village about six klicks from where we were then located. The other two squads would hook up with the second platoon and do an end recon. Then they were to meet us at a location near the village.

We made our way up from the low ground and into the jungle. Thankfully, this time I was not on point. Some other unlucky grunt got the privilege of leading us into that humid hell. We moved slowly through the thick underbrush into the direction of the trail on the map. The artillery had done its gruesome job. Along our path there were mounds of human flesh, legs, heads, arms, feet. Reassembled, they would add up to about twenty-five dead NVA soldiers that their surviving comrades left behind when they pulled out.

The big question was why did they pull out? Had they run out of ammo? Maybe this was another trick, or had they just lost their taste for killing Americans that day? I didn't know the answers but that's ok. What really mattered most to me at the time was I could live one more minute.

After several hours, we found ourselves near the village on the trail that was marked on the map. The sergeant placed one squad in position to cover my squad's back as we went into the settlement to search for any evidence of the NVA or the Vietcong. And once again, the sergeant put me back on point. I had grown to hate being point man; in my mind, the added danger more than eclipsed the honor. Nonetheless, Sergeant Hernandez chose me to be lead point again because we had worked together before, and I knew he trusted me in a pinch.

I moved like a shadow in the cover of the jungle, trying not to disturb the pigs and chickens that were foraging in the dense foliage. I didn't want them announcing our arrival. With one eye on the village and the other on the trail leading into it, we moved forward, darting from cover to cover. When we approached a village we never knew if there would be booby traps in our path or if the villagers were friendly to the Communist cause. If so, they would stop at nothing to please the local NVA commander.

We worked as a seasoned team, one in which the new guys could never enter, depending on each other's experience and determination to survive this pointless war. I motioned for Servantez to move to the right, and for two more to work with him. I took the left side with the remaining grunts, and we moved from cover to cover, finding no one there; but we still had to clear the huts, which was the really dangerous part.

Throughout that treacherous jungle the gooks had bomb shelters dug into the earth with makeshift board coverings. The shelters could hold five to six people, an entire family. If the village were friendly to the American cause they would hide in the holes when the NVA came; if they were friendly to the Communists they would hide in the holes when the Americans arrived. In any case, it was dangerous to clear these holes, and it was common practice to assume that anyone hiding from us was our enemy. Standard procedure with any shelter discovered was to remove a frag grenade from our web gear, pull the pin, lift the cover, and take no chances.

It was spooky; not a gook in sight, not even the old or the sick. Sergeant Hernandez moved up and said the lieutenant had radioed, saying they would be waiting near a clearing about one klick from us. The sergeant reported that we located no weapons or people in the village. Oh, they had been there, all right. The signs were everywhere that it had recently been a heavily populated village. The natives had to know we had been hit at the landing zone. They probably thought we would accuse them of helping NVA, which was likely.

I was ready to move out of that area because it had enough gooks in the surrounding jungles to make a war movie. We pulled back to the edge of the village to rest for a while and to eat some of our dried rations. We had not eaten all day and were getting hungry. I took a seat on a stump near the entrance to the village, where I could see if anything moved or didn't look right. The rest of the guys took similar positions as we prepared to chow down. We were getting ready to move out when the RTO pointed at a village hut. There, just as big as life, standing in the opening to the hut was a gook in his early twenties. He was dressed in black silk pajamas and had jet-black hair. Next to that, his skin seemed milk white. Hell, he looked healthier than I did. The RTO raised his rifle to shoot the gook but the sergeant stopped him. We needed a prisoner; we needed information on the unit we had fought that morning. We were running across that courtyard like high school players on a Friday night. When the gook saw us, he let out a scream, a loud, deafening shrill, and the look on his face was pure fright. He froze in panic when this gang of grunts approached him and tackled him to the ground.

The RTO turned his ankle during the capture and could barely walk. I thought, *Why didn't I think of that?* But it was too late.

Hernandez told me to carry the radio. I reminded him that I had never operated a radio before, but when he shrugged off the information, I thought, *Well, at least I'm not point man, too.*

The sergeant told me to report in and tell our lieutenant that we had captured a Vietcong suspect and to ask if he wanted us to bring the prisoner in for questioning. So I figured out how to operate the radio and said into the mike, "Head Hunter One Kilo to Head Hunter One, we have captured a Vietcong suspect dressed in black pajamas, about twenty-three or twenty-four years old. Healthy; well fed; has bruises on his shoulders, back, and hips that indicate he's been humping ammunition or food supplies for the enemy."

"Head Hunter One to Head Hunter One Kilo, good work! Bring him down for interrogation."

"Head Hunter One Kilo, received."

I relayed the message to the sergeant, and he gave orders to tie the man up. Using strips of his shirt for rope, we tied his hands behind his back and made a hangman's noose to place around his neck so he could be guided or forced to the ground if he tried to escape.

I was glad we had that prisoner; the information we could get from him might, in the long run, help save some lives. The jungle was thick in the area where we were moving; we needed to find a trail or at least move to a little higher elevation and hope that the undergrowth would not be as thick up there. The radio was heavy on my back, as I was not accustomed to carrying it. The phone mike got caught on twigs that continually pulled it off my shoulder. In short, I wasn't enjoying my new assignment.

The new point man moved on toward our destination, and everyone was very quiet as we made our way through the tangle of vines. I remember being impressed with our noise control. No canteens were clanking; no new guy fell down a steep hill or dropped his rifle. Everything was going well as we kept traveling into the jungle like a long, green, poisonous snake, twisting this way and that. As we moved on, the radio handset made a buzzing noise, signaling an incoming call. I pushed the side button on the handset and spoke quietly into the mouthpiece, almost in a whisper. "This is Head Hunter One Kilo, go ahead."

"This is Head Hunter One. Head Hunter One Kilo, do you still have the prisoner?"

"Head Hunter One Kilo, affirmative. We're en route to your location."

"Head Hunter One. If the prisoner tries to escape ... *shoot him.*"

The last two words of the message were said slowly, distinctly, like a separate command. "Do you mean 'shoot him'?" I asked.

"That's what I said."

"Head Hunter One, received."

I quickly stepped up to the sergeant, punched him on the arm, and in a low voice said, "Psst. Hey, Sarge, the lieutenant just called and said, 'Shoot the prisoner.'"

"What?"

"That's what he said: 'Shoot the prisoner.'"

He took the mike and radioed, "Head Hunter One Kilo to Head Hunter One. Head Hunter One, repeat message."

While I could no longer hear what the lieutenant actually said, I saw and heard the sergeant: "Yes. Understood. Yes, sir."

He handed me back the mike, and I asked, "So what did he say?"

With a glazed look in his eyes, the sergeant told me, "He said, 'Shoot the prisoner.'"

For a time, we continued moving in silence. "So whacha gonna do?" I asked.

"I'm gonna shoot the prisoner."

The sergeant called us to a halt and lined us up like a firing squad in an old Zorro movie. He stood the Vietcong about thirty yards in front of us, in a little clearing, and then announced, "We're going to shoot him firing-squad style."

The look on the men's faces were of horror. We just stood there, not believing what we had just heard. A big, heavyset black guy named Wilson said, "Look guys, this ain't right. I ain't gettin' involved in nothin' like this. This is murder!"

He walked around to the end of the firing line behind us, and then back to his position, and repeated, "I ain't gettin' involved in this. This is wrong."

Someone hollered, "You shut your mouth up, or we'll shoot your ass, too. We got orders."

186

Some bickering started among the troops. Yeah, it was wrong, but it was an order: sentiments to that effect. The sergeant stopped the chatter with his instructions. "We're gonna do this on 'ready, aim, fire.'" So the sergeant stood at the end of the line and repeated the words as a command: "Ready. Aim. Fire!"

But not one person pulled a trigger.

The gook started grinning, and stuck his chest out in mockery and defiance.

The sergeant said, "Look, this is it. Everybody ... ready, aim, fire!"

We all aimed. Some fired, while some of us didn't. Frankly, I'm not sure why I didn't fire, because I had become mean enough. However, I didn't.

I was looking down my rifle barrel when the three or four shots went off. I jumped in shock as I saw the bullets hit the man in the stomach. His guts fell out as if he had been ripped from the groin to the chest with a knife. Even so, he didn't fall instantly; it took a moment. When he did fall it wasn't like in the combat movies. He did not get blown backwards so that you saw the soles of his feet. Instead, when his guts fell to his feet, he collapsed like a rag doll into the pile of his intestines.

I stood there listening to the total silence and smelling the gunpowder. The only thing I recall saying after that was, "Let's get saddled up and outta here."

When we got inside the perimeter and were met by the lieutenant, he asked, "Where's the prisoner?"

The sergeant said, "You said to shoot the prisoner."

"Well, I didn't really mean for you to shoot the prisoner."

"But, you said…."

They moved out of earshot, and I shook my head and thought, *This is the most screwed-up mess I've ever been in. I don't think any of us are going to get out of here alive.* Then I washed my hands of it and walked off.

Humans in that jungle war, whether military or civilian, were dispensable. It seemed it didn't matter whether they were on your side or the enemy's side. When I look back on the Vietnamese man's execution, I think that the only honorable man among us was Wilson, the one trooper among us who stood up for what he believed. Sure, a lot of us didn't fire our weapons, but we didn't speak out like Wilson had.

I've often wondered if he was also one of the men who torched our mess hall as an earlier expression of his indignation concerning the disregard for human life, be it wrapped in white, black, or yellow skin.

—■—

Hendrix and squad buddy burning down village hut after receiving fire
from the village

Chapter 15
Poor Man/Rich Man

*But those who desire to be rich fall into temptation and a snare,
and into many foolish and harmful lusts, which drown men in
destruction and perdition.*
1 Timothy 6:9

I awoke that March morning just like most mornings in
Vietnam, wet, tired, hungry, and broke. When I joined the army I
was financially burdened, and that's the way I stayed. I was thirteen
thousand miles from home in the jungle, feeling like a loser. Fate,
however, was going to fill my pockets with more money than I had
ever seen before in one place. And best of all, I would live to tell the
story.

The listening-post patrol was returning from its night position.
Each evening, a three- or four-man patrol went beyond the fighting
position of the platoon or company and set up in an area where,
it was assumed, they would be able to give advance warning of
approaching NVA soldiers. I hated that duty; it was dangerous and

frightening. Nearly every time I had to go out someone fell asleep, leaving our location open to Charlie. On many occasions, we were more than lucky that Charlie had been asleep as well.

As a precaution, we counted the troops as they reentered our circle. There were occasions when an NVA would just fall right in line and try to get into a perimeter to blow a grenade. Those little tag-along NVA were called zappers. Kill as many Americans as you can and get yourself blown up for your trouble. It was the NVA equivalent of the Japanese kamikaze pilots that crashed their planes into American ships during World War II.

When our listening post returned, I knew they had been asleep all night; you could tell by the lack of chatter and the look in their eyes. On the positive side, they all looked refreshed and ready to go. I knew the look because I had been there. When patrol had evolved to uninterrupted sleep no one ever said a word.

So, after a lucky night, we ate and prepared for whatever surprises the day had in store for us. As we loaded up, I thought, *What the hell, another day will soon be over, and I'll be one day closer to going back to the world!*

Why we called the United States "the world," I don't know; we just did. It was part of the army lingo that was passed from soldier to soldier. I guess sharing a common language was part of the bond, the esprit de corps that's necessary to maintain a fighting unit.

I grabbed my rucksack strap with my right hand, lifted it up, and slid it into the harness before it had time to fall back to the wet, mossy jungle floor. After securing both arms and pulling the tension straps tight—so tight it would sometimes cut off the blood circulation—the rucksack was then properly secured to my back.

Feeling like a dumb pack mule about to plod through the jungle again, I slapped on my steel-pot helmet, picked up my rifle, and propped against a rock to await the time to go kill somebody and make America proud.

As usual, Head Hunter Platoon was to take the lead, and as usual, I was appointed point man. I had learned too late that doing something well in the army means you get to do it over and over again while some goof-off watches you. "I like the way you move us through this thick jungle," is what the sergeant said.

He also knew that my intuition—gut hunches, E.S.P., or whatever you want to label those watch-your-step feelings—was usually dead-on.

Seeing as I had lost the battle, I made my way to the radio telephone operator and told him to keep on his toes because I just didn't feel right about the area that was our destination. After putting heads together with the platoon leader and the squad leader to study the map and see just where in hell we were going, I took the lead into the undergrowth.

After about three hours, the hair on the back of my neck suddenly stood straight up—just like a dog's hair does when he senses danger and prepares for an attack. I raised my arm and made a fist with my left hand, while clutching my M-16 in my right hand. The men behind me froze. The guys all knew that when I felt and acted that way I meant business. Something was out there; I just couldn't see it yet. I looked back at the makeshift path we had created while coming up that hillside and could see the long green line of American uniforms, white and black hands clutching weapons, ready for anything that came our way; they had come to trust my instincts.

After we stood there motionless and silent for at least half a minute, I motioned for the others to stay while I crawled slowly through the thick, tall grass and troublesome catch-me vines. Those vines made the tops of the bushes shake, and that shaking could give your position away.

Never before had I gone more than fifty meters from the unit when pulling point, but this time my instincts carried me deeper and deeper into the jungle and away from the main element. I felt I needed to return but continued inching forward. After crawling about 150 yards, I realized I was at the edge of an unmapped trail—a well-used trail at that. The map did not show any villages in this area. This was disconcerting because even though people who had never set foot in the jungle drew our maps, those maps were usually amazingly accurate.

Armed with this unexpected information, I turned around and tried to retrace my every step because, if this trail was a local VC or NVA area of operation, there were surely booby traps everywhere. And I didn't want a punji stake up my butt.

Once I made it back to our fresh-from-training-school platoon leader and told him about the trail, he looked like a kid who just found a pony tied to his Christmas tree. "Great!" the second lieutenant said. Then he had to call to battalion to find out what to do next.

After talking to someone on the other end of the phone for a solid ten minutes, he gathered all the squad leaders in a huddle. The instructions he passed on were to move forward to the newly discovered trail and follow it to the lowlands. This educated idiot said that he and the educated idiot he had been talking to believed that we might have found a new movement route for the NVA in the area.

Any of us high school dropouts could have told them that! I had encountered a similar trail a couple of months earlier in the same mountain range. When we followed that one we encountered beaucoup NVA and took a heavy casualty rate. I thought that if we follow this trail to the valley, all I can say is they better start getting black rubber body bags ready in the rear. My feelings about that trail, that jungle, that war, that butter bar lieutenant and his orders were all bad.

I started looking up at the sky, hoping, hoping, and hoping that I would not be picked to pull point again. You know, like when the teacher calls on you when you didn't know the answer and you try to be invisible? it didn't work when I was in school, and it didn't work that day in the jungle.

"Hendrix, take point. Move to the trail and head south. Move slowly, now," he said, as if he had to tell me not to sprint into an enemy ambush.

Earlier, I was alone; this time I had a group of about forty men—young boys, actually, many of whom were still virgins. Yes, we even had some of those there, too. We were all so young then.

As I moved forward I looked back for just an instant. All I could see was my slack man, the sergeant, and his radiotelephone operator with him. That meant the rest of the unit was putting distance between them and us, which was a good tactical move.

I reached the trail and moved onto it cautiously, M-16 raised at the ready. Nothing moved. It was daytime, but dim in the jungle.

Occasionally, the jungle canopy opened and the light rushed in, startling you with its brightness. I could tell that many men had been traveling this path. It was beaten down good, like a cow path to the water trough back home. My bad feeling about this search-and-destroy mission grew with every step. I didn't want to walk my buddies or myself into an ambush, but I could smell one coming. Literally. This time, it was not the stench of the sour, homemade rice wine that the NVA and Vietcong drank, which you could smell from a mile away when it came out their pores. This time it was a freshly dug latrine, complete with maggots and flies, located about ten feet off the trail. We were practically in their backyard.

I turned back. As I passed my slack man, I pointed down the trail, and he nodded affirmatively to show he understood that I had to move back with some information. I got to the sergeant, and the second lieutenant came forward. When I told them what I had found and that we were in a lot of trouble because it was likely a large unit of NVA—not just a scout team—the young officer reacted with the bravery of the dumb. That twenty-four-year-old, fresh-from-school wonder wanted to make a name for himself, so he told me to go back and continue moving down the trail. I just knelt there on one knee, looking the lieutenant squarely in the eyes. He spit out the words, "Did you hear me?"

Without answering, I pushed myself up and retraced my steps. This time, as I moved beyond the latrine, I noticed another smell, one that reminded me of when my grandfather butchered a hog and would build a large fire underneath a huge iron kettle to boil the hog in to help scrape the hair off the skin. Hog killing had a distinct odor of fire and death, and that smell had stayed with me always.

I motioned for my slack man to come up and for the rest of the unit to stay put. We eased down the path and around the bend. Bingo! It was a village with about nine grass huts. We froze for a moment and just looked to see if anything moved. The real reason we stayed still was we were scared shitless. I never expected to see a village in that area. But there it was, looking almost identical to the last dozen villages I had seen. The big difference was there were no signs of life other than some chickens and pigs wandering about. Whatever animal had been recently butchered had vanished along with the people, and that was not a good sign. It meant they knew we were coming, which could only mean we had walked into the makings of an ambush.

The slack man and I moved back up the path to the main unit, and the lieutenant and squad leaders met me for a quick briefing. I was for moving out east, finding a clearing, and calling in the evac choppers before dark. The lieutenant was, however, not so easily intimidated. He sent five of us back to the village to check it out, which meant we had a twenty-four-year-old John Wayne in charge who was sending five grunts to possibly fight a company of NVA. No seasoned officer would have ever done that.

When he turned his back for a second, I motioned to the squad leader that I thought the man was crazy. The squad leader nodded in agreement, then slipped over to my side and told me that was precisely why I was going to be one of the five to go back and play Army Man.

The word was passed to drop rucksacks and take only ammo and hand grenades. The rest of the unit would circle up in case the bad guys came home. Then five of us moved toward the village.

I pulled point. Baker was my slack man, and a Hawaiian guy we called Pineapple was third in line, while Donohue and Servantez brought up the rear.

We rounded the bend, and to my left at the village's edge, I could see a small pond of water, clear and cool-looking. To my right, just outside the village perimeter, were neatly stacked bales of hay. But I saw no large animals that would eat the hay. Moving past the bales, we made our entrance into the village and began searching the huts.

That village was as uptown as the others we had come to know. Mud floors, no windows, no doors, pig shit everywhere—even on the rolled-up straw mats used for sleeping. I felt like hollering out to the jungle, "We're here to free you from all this filth. How about letting us make little Americans out of all of you?"

We moved to the pond area to have a look. As we turned from the water, an automatic weapon fired so close to me I thought it might have burst my eardrum. I turned just in time to see Donohue firing at a treetop on the edge of the water. Almost instantly, a blob of black in the top of the tree fell like a bear that had been shot by some hunters in the Georgia woods.

We all moved to the edge of the point and could see a small man dressed in black silky pajamas, lying on the edge of the pond, his lower torso dangling in the water while his upper half was anchored on the bank. Donohue gave him another twenty rounds in his upper body just to make sure he was not going to vote next year.

We were all at the ready level now. The radio blared, begging someone to answer it. When our RTO did, it was the sergeant calling. He had heard the gunfire and wanted to know if he and the rest needed to move in, but our fearless lieutenant decided they would hold their position until further notice. Instead, he and a handful of men would join us.

One Victor Charlie doesn't make an army, but where there is one there are more, more probably on their way the second they also heard the shots. Just after hearing that the lieutenant was on his way, Servantez opened up with his M-16. We all looked surprised to see several NVA crawling out of the lake. If it had not been so serious, the sight of those gooks coming up wet would have been funny. But I was not back at Sun Valley Lake in Roswell, Georgia, horsing around with my high school pals. I was half a world away from home, and we were fighting for our lives. Everyone opened up on the gooks as they swam to the edge of the water and tried to get a foothold on the bank so they could get out and fight. Using move-and-fire tactics, we advanced toward the pond, killing all in sight. When the bullets stopped, the pond was crimson red, and five more bodies lay dead on the bank and in the immediate area.

But the job wasn't finished. One of the guys said he saw movement in the water. What he had seen were some live NVAs in the pond; however, they disappeared into what appeared to be a cave half filled with water. We took up guard positions while Pineapple moved to the edge of the pond and threw a grenade into the opening. You could hear the water splash, then a terrific explosion. After he threw three more grenades into the opening, we heard some trashing around inside the cave for just a short time, then complete silence.

Pineapple, a gung ho, tough, six-foot-two surfer type with an appetite for danger, volunteered to go inside the cave while the rest of us stood guard. He slipped off the bank and into the bloody water, and then moved toward the opening of the cave like an alligator easing up on its prey. For a brief moment he gave us a lopsided grin before disappearing through the cave entrance.

He was gone about a minute when we heard automatic weapons fire from within the cave. Before we could decide what to do next, Pineapple came slithering out of the cave, still wearing that grin he had on his face when he went in. As he reached the bank, he held up a sizeable leather pouch and his rifle, and one of the guys met him at the water's edge to take them from him.

As we pulled Pineapple out, he reported seeing at least two more dead NVA in the cave. Then he explained the shots we heard. He had moved to the rear of the cave, but it was too dark to see much, so he turned to leave. As he turned, he felt movement to his front right and sprayed the area with his rifle. That was when he saw a small-framed person throw something toward the opening. As the man made the throw, he collapsed into the water. Pineapple groped around and found what the man had thrown: a leather pouch. He grabbed it and got the hell out of there, figuring the pouch might contain valuable military information.

As Pineapple emerged from the water, the lieutenant and his RTO crept into the village, leaving the rest who came with them on perimeter guard.

Pineapple proudly handed the pouch to the lieutenant, who cut the wet leather strap with his knife and opened the pouch. We couldn't believe our eyes. There were no military documents inside. The full bag was packed with South Vietnamese currency, all large bills. It was getting late, and we had to make a decision on how to handle the money because none of us, not even the lieutenant, had ever seen anything like this before.

The lieutenant wanted to turn in the money, but we talked to him about it at length. Finally, he assigned Servantez to count the money. There was more than $130,000 dollars in the case. We had stumbled onto a North Vietnamese paymaster. He and the others were in the area, paying the Vietcong and the NVA that fought the Americans for them. They must not have been paid for some time, considering the amount of money in the bag.

We continued talking about what to do with the loot. Finally, the lieutenant agreed to divide it up equally, if we would leave enough to turn into First Battalion, enough to make him a hero. He got no argument from us. Each man counted out 12,000 Vietnamese dollars. The lieutenant did not take a share. The more he turned in, the better he looked to the higher-ups.

Sworn to secrecy by the lieutenant—and that included the RTO, who wasn't cut in on the deal—we stuffed our pockets with the bills, planning one hell of a blowout when we got to the rear! My side pocket hung heavy with the weight of my cut of the money, and I was now "rich" beyond my dreams. We had to work fast or the rest of the guys might find out about our secret and want in on the deal. But we fought for it and deserved it, we told ourselves; nobody was getting in on our money. Nobody. The war was finally going our way.

The lieutenant radioed for the rest of the unit to come to our location to set up perimeter guard, and when the commanding officer of First Battalion heard the report, he said he was coming out in a chopper to personally take charge of the cash and thank the lieutenant for doing such a fine job of capturing the paymaster and recovering the money … as if the lieutenant had picked off all those enemy soldiers and had bravely breast-stroked into the dark cave.

While we waited for the lieutenant's moment of glory, we set fire to the ring of huts and piles of hay bales. Shortly before dark, as the fires burned out, a chopper flew in what I would call a giant, accompanied by some first sergeant from the rear. The lieutenant proudly showed his superior the cave, the dead gooks, and the leather pouch of money. The big guy took the pouch and looked inside. That's when I saw that smile of victory drain from his face. "Is this all you got?" he snarled. "I can't believe you called me out here for this shit!"

While he chewed the second lieutenant's ear and stomped about, the first sergeant who came with him said he wanted us to write up the lieutenant for a Silver Star. I looked at the squad leader, and he looked at me. By that time, Servantez and one of the others who had been involved in the actual fight had come over to see what was going on. One member of the group spoke up, saying that the lieutenant wasn't even there until afterwards. But that didn't faze the sergeant.

"Look, we want to promote the lieutenant and bring him to the rear. So he needs a Silver Star before he leaves the field."

I said, "Hell, no. That ain't right. He was in the rear, almost a mile away."

The squad leader whispered to me, "Hendrix, if we don't do something, he's gonna get real pissed off with us and make trouble. Don't forget what we've got in our pockets."

That didn't change my mind or anyone else's, so we walked off, leaving the first sergeant to write up the lieutenant himself. That done, he and the furious rear commanding officer flew away.

Too bad they left mad, because right after they lifted off, while I was taking some pictures with the little 101 Kodak that I sometimes took with me in a plastic bag, Pineapple started poking around in the straw that we had burned earlier. Under it, he found a trap door. When he lifted the wooden plank door, we found 100 AK-47 rifles in the hole. They were still wrapped in gun-oil grease, having never been used.

We went to all the straw bales and found three more trap doors. Beneath each we uncovered an additional 100 AK-47 rifles. Four hundred in all—what a haul! This village must have been a resupply stop for the gooks on their way south.

The lieutenant, seeing a second shot at glory, put out the word. The captain of our company was now within humping distance of us. When he was advised of what had taken place, he was mad as hell, demanding to know who gave the lieutenant permission to call First Battalion and have a superior sent out without the captain being involved.

The lieutenant was in for it. Our captain was a lifer from Fort Benning, and he didn't play games. When he arrived on the scene, it was back to army regs, as usual. We put up a defensive night fighting position and stayed up almost all night. I was rich and too excited to sleep. Not one of the squad members told our secret, not even the lieutenant. I was a little nervous about some of the guys, but they held tight. The next morning, First Battalion sent out some tunnel rats to blow the dam on the pond and clear the cave to see if there was anything else in there. The pond was drained, and it was clear that the cave had been emptied by Pineapple. All were finally happy with the mission. But it wasn't back to LZ Uplift for us yet.

Our company loaded onto choppers and headed to the lowlands near some rice paddies. We were slogging through the water when we received fire from the other side. I, along with my buddies, fell into the hot, slimy, stinking water, returned fire, and crawled to the nearest dike. We spent the next four days in the rain, in the rice paddies, and wet with sweat just trying to survive in that area. But hell, we were rich. It had been worth it. I could pay off my car that I had left behind and buy myself one helluva wardrobe to wear on that glorious day when I would exchange my military duds for civvies.

Finally, the word came in that choppers would pick us up at 1300 hours about one mile from where we were originally inserted into the jungle. That meant I was, at last, going to the rear to count my money and figure out how to exchange it for U.S. dollars.

While we waited on the extraction choppers, our group of thousandaires got together and agreed to meet behind the shower tent as soon as we got to the firebase. The plan was to talk about what we were going to do with our loot and to renew our oath of silence. Everyone agreed, scattered, and waited.

The big green birds were right on time and we headed out, but it was a ragged ride. Our chopper maneuvered with the grace of a flying cow and landed hard on the dirt at the firebase. As I hopped out of the door, I got a look at the pilot, not old enough to shave yet. Despite his lack of piloting skills, we were back and I was rich.

Not bothering to change out of the stinking clothes we had been wearing for days, we all headed for our rendezvous point behind the shower tent. Even before the last guy arrived, we were already arguing about what we should do with all our money. I felt like a Chicago gangster who had just knocked over a pool hall.

You could feel the distrust building. It was like being at a poker table with Doc Holiday in Tombstone, wondering who might be holding five aces. One of the guys raised a question that was already floating around in the back of my head. Did anyone take more than the rest of us?

After a lot of arguing and name-calling we agreed on a plan. We would all, on the count of three, empty our bulging side utility pockets into a pile, them deal out the money, a hundred for me, a hundred for you, a hundred for him, and so on. We'd keep dealing out the bills till the huge pile was divided equally into six smaller piles. So we formed a circle and, in unison, counted, "One, two, three, go!"

We all dug into our still-soggy pockets and pulled out wads of wet paper strips. To our absolute horror, what had been multicolored money now looked like a kindergarten finger-painting project. The many colors of ink had bled and smeared. You could no longer even make out the picture of whatever damn gook was on the bills.

Some of us just sat there for a while; others went off to get drunk. Dead broke, again, we were feeling like a bunch of losers. But looking back, I realize I still came out of the situation a winner, "rich" in the most important sense. I lived to return to the U.S. and tell the tale. Not all of those guys did.

Our brave second lieutenant, however, came out of the adventure with something of great value. The discovery of the stash of weapons—which he was also not involved in—was added to the first sergeant's request for the second lieutenant to be awarded a Silver Star. The lieutenant received it, a promotion to first lieutenant, and a position in the rear.

Little more than a month after that, on April 22, 1969, I earned my second Purple Heart, but you already know about that because that's where my story began.

Some years after returning from the war, I read a statement made by Ho Chi Minh. In one paragraph he encapsulates the Vietnam War, its participants, and outcome.

If the tiger ever stands still, the elephant will crush him with his mighty tusks. But the tiger will not stand still. He will leap upon the back of the elephant, tearing huge chunks from his side, and then he will leap back into the dark jungle. And slowly the elephant will bleed to death. Such will be the war in Indochina.

—•—

Joseph Anthony Servantez-My friend killed in action September 1969
(He loved to chew bubble gum and his mother always sent him "Joe
Bazooka" bubble gum)

Chapter 16
Killed In Action

Thoughts by a Young Veteran.
The years others knew as youth,
I spent learning the meaning of death.
The times others spent learning to love,
I passed away, hoping to live through endless nights.
The moments others remembered as laughs in classrooms,
I remember as forgotten hopes, long ago crushed by the reality of war.
The unfulfilled dreams of others are yet to be thought by me,
Since I am in search of my elusive youth,
Looking for years lost in combat, which are no more.
And will never be.
Author Unknown

—•—

During the Vietnam War, there were 8,744,000 Americans in the military; 2,700,000 of that number served in Vietnam. Of those serving in Vietnam, fifty-four died in captivity; 47,072 were killed in combat; and an additional 313,616 were wounded. In other words, one out of every ten Americans serving in Vietnam was killed or wounded. An additional eighty-one U.S. servicemen were killed in Laos and Cambodia.

The following 1,748 members of the 173rd Airborne Brigade were killed in action during the Vietnam War. Another 8,747 unit members were wounded during the same period.

NAME	DIED	CITY	STATE	RANK	AGE
HICKS, RANDOLPH TRUMAN	1965-05-28	MC EWEN	TN	PVT	18
ANDERS, EDWARD JAMES	1965-06-18	LOS ANGELES	CA	PFC	18
VAN CAMPEN, THOMAS CHARLES	1965-06-24	OROVILLE	CA	PFC	19
PIERSON, DENNIS LEROY	1965-06-26	MINNEAPOLIS	MN	PFC	21
BUSTOS, MIKE GARCIA	1965-06-28	HUNTINGTON	IN	SP4	23
CAMPBELL, JERRY RAY	1965-06-28	GRAHAM	NC	PVT	20
HILL, MAURICE RICHARD	1965-06-29	LOS ANGELES	CA	PVT	18
HOWARD, DAVID LAFATE	1965-07-07	FOUNTAIN INN	SC	SSG	22
MEEHAN, RAYMOND PATRICK	1965-07-07	ROCKVILLE CENTRE	NY	PFC	23
RAY, DURWARD FRANK	1965-07-07	COLUMBUS	GA	SGT	21
RICE, JOHNIE EDWARD JR	1965-07-07	FREEBURN	KY	PFC	21
ZINN, RONALD LLOYD	1965-07-07	ORLAND PARK	IL	CPT	26
JOHNSON, ALLEN ISAAC	1965-07-07	CLOQUET	MN	PVT	18
SHAW, JOHN DILLINGER	1965-07-07	SUMMIT	MS	PVT	22
JOHNSON, MCARTHUR	1965-07-07	WILMINGTON	NC	SGT	25
HERNANDEZ, RUDOLPH VILLALPANE	1965-07-07	SAN ANTONIO	TX	PVT	20
ALMEIDA, EDWARD JOSEPH	1965-07-08	NEW BEDFORD	MA	PVT	18
KOHLER, LUDWIG PETER	1965-07-26	SAN FRANCISCO	CA	PFC	39
HATCHETT, KYLE HENRY	1965-08-23	NEW YORK	NY	PFC	20
BRONSON, THOMAS CARL	1965-08-31	FAYETTEVILLE	NC	PFC	21
MARQUEZ, PAUL JOSEPH	1965-09-09	SAN PEDRO	CA	SP4	22
CAMARENA-SALAZAR, EDUARDO	1965-09-17	EL CENTRO	CA	PFC	21
ANDERSON, LEE E	1965-09-19	PHOENIX	AZ	SGT	21
EMBREY, GRADY KEITH	1965-09-19	LA GRANGE	GA	PFC	19
PIERCE, LARRY STANLEY	1965-09-20	TAFT	CA	SSG	24

211

FLETCHER, LON M	1965-10-05	ALBUQUERQUE	NM	PVT	18
HAINES, ADHERENE LOUIS	1965-10-05	SUMTER	SC	SP4	20
HEATH, RUSSELL M	1965-10-05	PHILADELPHIA	PA	PFC	20
HUGHES, JESSE RAY JR	1965-10-05	BLOOMFIELD	MO	SP4	20
HYETT, KENNETH MONROE	1965-10-05	ALLEGAN	MI	SP4	21
SCHINDLER, THOMAS JAMES	1965-10-05	BALTIMORE	MD	SGT	25
MOSES, ABELL	1965-10-05	NATCHITOCHES	LA	PFC	20
BURGANS, RICHARD	1965-10-05	NEWARK	NJ	PFC	21
LAKE, LARRY VERNON	1965-10-06	INGLEWOOD	CA	PFC	19
TARKINGTON, CURTIS RAY	1965-10-06	SCOTTSDALE	AZ	PFC	19
GULLEY, RONALD WALTER	1965-10-08	FRANKLIN	IL	SP4	21
BRANCATO, MICHAEL GEORGE	1965-10-08	LOS ANGELES	CA	PFC	21
RIZOR, DAVID LEE	1965-10-09	WASHINGTON	PA	PVT	21
HIMMELREICH, HARRY EDWARD	1965-10-10	UNION BEACH	NJ	PFC	19
RICK, EUGENE MERLYN	1965-10-10	COON RAPIDS	MN	SFC	32
BERRY, JAMES GRAYSON	1965-10-10	BARBOURS VILLE	WV	SP4	20
FRANKLIN, LAWRENCE ANDRE	1965-10-10	WENATCHEE	WA	SGT	23
PRESIDENT, ERNEST	1965-10-10	FORT PIERCE	FL	SP4	24
ROBILLARD, WILFRED ROLAND	1965-10-10	MANCHESTER	NH	PFC	18
SCHUKAR, RONALD KEITH	1965-10-10	VANDALIA	IL	PFC	21
WILLIAMS, VAN	1965-10-10	NEW YORK	NY	PFC	19
NELSON, DUANE MICHAEL	1965-10-10	SIOUX CITY	IA	PFC	22
REILLY, JAMES JOSEPH JR	1965-10-10	WASHINGTON	PA	SFC	39
FLOYD, JAMES WALTER	1965-10-10	WINSTON-SALEM	NC	PFC	19
DUNCAN, RONNIE MARSHALL	1965-10-10	WAKE FOREST	NC	PFC	23
MINCKS, JIMMIE LEE	1965-10-11	NEW CASTLE	IN	SGT	35
STEWART, EDWARD LARRY	1965-10-12	BLUEFIELD	WV	SGT	26
STARKES, JOHN MILTON JR	1965-10-12	NEW YORK	NY	PFC	23

MINNIX, LEROY FRANKLIN	1965-10-12	LUCKEY	OH	PFC	19
DAVIS, WILBERT CLAUDE	1965-10-12	SPRINGFIELD	MO	SGT	25
LUIS, GEORGE GREGORIO	1965-10-22	PAHOA	HI	SP4	20
OLIVE, MILTON LEE III	1965-10-22	CHICAGO	IL	PFC	18
JONES, THEODORE R JR	1965-11-08	AUBURN	NE	SGT	33
RUSSO, MICHAEL PHILLIP	1965-11-08	NEW YORK	NY	PFC	21
BELTON, JAMES	1965-11-08	STATE PARK	SC	SP4	22
FOSTER, BYRON JAMES	1965-11-08	DETROIT	MI	PFC	23
GOIAS, EVERETT WILLIAM	1965-11-08	SAN FRANCISCO	CA	SP4	20
GREENE, LLOYD V INCENT	1965-11-08	PATERSON	NJ	SGT	29
HOLCOMB, REBEL LEE	1965-11-08	WICHITA	KS	SGT	38
HOWARD, LAWRENCE PAIGE JR	1965-11-08	PHILADELPHIA	PA	SGT	26
HUGHLETT, JOHN ALBERT	1965-11-08	BRIGHTON	TN	SGT	23
LOCKETT, CLEO	1965-11-08	BIRMINGHAM	AL	CPL	22
ORRIS, STEVE III	1965-11-08	WAYNE	MI	PFC	19
SPENCER, CORDELL	1965-11-08	BESSEMER	AL	SP4	24
TATE, SCIP	1965-11-08	NEWARK	NJ	SP4	19
THURSTON, CLAIR HALL JR	1965-11-08	THORNDIKE	ME	2LT	22
TURNAGE, THOMAS ALFRED	1965-11-08	TEXARKANA	AR	SP4	21
VINCENT, GEORGE	1965-11-08	LOS ANGELES	CA	SP4	23
NATHAN, JOHN ARTHUR	1965-11-08	SAN FRANCISCO	CA	SP4	19
UGLAND, DAVID LEONARD	1965-11-08	MINNEAPOLIS	MN	2LT	23
WILLIAMS, TROY BYRON	1965-11-08	MOUNT HOPE	WV	SGT	29
HAMILTON, JOSEPH THOMAS	1965-11-08	PHILADELPHIA	PA	PFC	20
SOBOTA, DANIEL JAMES	1965-11-08	PEORIA	IL	PFC	18
SMITH, HAROLD MCRAE	1965-11-08	SUMTER	SC	PFC	19
UPTAIN, DAVIS	1965-11-08	FAYETTE	AL	PFC	21
GOLDMAN, HAROLD	1965-11-08	OCALA	FL	PFC	17
RUTOWSKI, DENNIS DAVID	1965-11-08	WATERFORD	WI	PFC	22
CAMPOS, MAGNO	1965-11-08	LAHAINA	HI	SSG	32

TOLLIVER, SAMUEL STANLEY	1965-11-08	RICHMOND	VA	PFC	18
BROWN, HERMAN	1965-11-08	RICHLANDS	VA	PFC	18
CARLTON, LAVALLE ERNEST	1965-11-08	CLEVELAND	OH	PFC	18
HUMPHRIES, WAYNE WARREN	1965-11-08	SHAWNEE	OK	SP4	21
HARRINGTON, CLIFTON WILLIAM	1965-11-08	ABERDEEN	NC	SSG	34
HILL, LEROY	1965-11-08	WASHINGTON	DC	PSGT	34
KEEL, DAVID LATTIMORE	1965-11-08	HOUSTON	TX	SFT	26
CANNON, HENRY TUCKER	1965-11-08	JACKSONVILLE	FL	SFC	31
WHITAKER, KELLY EUGENE	1965-11-08	MEMPHIS	TN	PFC	18
HARDEN, ROBERT WESLEY JR	1965-11-08	WAYCROSS	GA	SP4	21
MITCHELL, CHARLES LEROY JR	1965-11-08	NEW YORK	NY	PVT	22
MARQUEZ, VALENTINE	1965-11-08	WILEY	CO	PFC	21
MATHISON, MICHAEL K	1965-11-08	EAST ST LOUIS	IL	PFC	19
POTTER, JERRY LEE	1965-11-08	ENGLEWOOD	CO	PFC	18
HANNIGAN, JOHN EDWARD III	1965-11-08	ANTIOCH	CA	PFC	20
MEDLEY, MICHAEL MILTON	1965-11-08	JACKSON	MI	PFC	18
AGUILAR, RUDOLPH RENE	1965-11-08	LOS ANGELES	CA	PFC	19
GRAHAM, KENNETH ERROL	1965-11-08	DEFIANCE	OH	PFC	21
WARD, DANNY RUSSELL	1965-11-08	BEAUTY	KY	PFC	19
BRAYBOY, BRYANT JR	1965-11-08	PHILADELPHIA	PA	SFC	33
EIDSON, SAMUEL ARLEN	1965-11-08	NORTH BIRMINGHAM	AL	SSG	32
ELMORE, GARY LEWIS	1965-11-08	GARDEN CITY	MI	PFC	23
SHAMBLINE, THEODORE	1965-11-11	FAYETTEVILLE	WV	SSG	29
PARTEE, WARDLOW WESLEY	1965-11-12	FLINT	MI	PFC	19
MOODY, FRANCIS	1965-11-14	NEW YORK	NY	PFC	19

HOLMAN, SAMUEL L	1965-11-17	BALTIMORE	MD	SGT	25
RODRIGUEZ, ROMIRO C	1965-12-01	STOCKTON	CA	SP4	24
NERVEZA, DELMORE BYRON	1965-12-06	HILO	HI	SP5	23
DICKINSON, DANIEL ALBERT	1965-12-06	WICHITA	KS	SP4	21
GRAY, ROBERT ALLEN	1965-12-18	AVILLA	IN	SGT	35
GRIFFIN, SAMMIE	1965-12-18	PHILADELPHIA	PA	PFC	18
GUILMET, DANIEL J	1965-12-18	SEATTLE	WA	PFC	19
YATSKO, JOSEPH PAUL JR	1965-12-18	LEVITTOWN	PA	1LT	23
PETERSON, RICHARD W	1965-12-18	WEST COVINA	CA	PFC	19
FOGLE, LARY DALE	1965-12-20	LAWRENCE BURG	IN	PFC	18
GRUEZKE, JAMES A	1965-12-23	NEWBERRY	MI	WO	25
GUILLORY, JAMES CLIFTON	1965-12-27	LOS ANGELES	CA	SP4	24
JEWETT, STEPHEN DYER	1965-12-27	EAST ANDOVER	NH	SP4	23
CARLONE, JOHN JOSEPH II	1965-12-27	CHICAGO	IL	PVT	19
TAYLOR, PAUL CLIVE O	1965-12-27	SAN FRANCISCO	CA	PFC	19
KIER, CHARLES RICHARD	1965-12-27	MOUND VALLEY	KS	PFC	19
AIKEY, TIMOTHY WAYNE	1966-01-02	WARRENSVILLE	PA	SGT	19
BAKER, WALLACE EDWIN	1966-01-02	WINDHAM	OH	SSG	35
LEVY, GERALD	1966-01-02	MERIDEN	CT	SP5	20
LEWIS, GARY FRANKLIN	1966-01-02	ULEDI	PA	SP4	18
NADEAU, LARRY JOSEPH	1966-01-02	ORONO	ME	PVT	18
MORTON, JERRY WAYNE	1966-01-02	DEWEYVILLE	TX	SGT	31
MERKLEY, ELLIOTT LYNN	1966-01-02	ST CLAIR	MO	PVT	18
BIXBY, JACK DENTON	1966-01-02	GRACETON	MN	PFC	20
ALSTON, RUBEN CLEVELAND	1966-01-02	JACKSONVILLE	FL	SP4	19
MC INTIRE, WALTER EDWIN JR	1966-01-02	ANN ARBOR	MI	PFC	22
LEAKE, JOHHNY H	1966-01-02	WYOMING	NY	PFC	22
SMITH, ROBERT GEORGE	1966-01-02	CLEVELAND	OH	PFC	20

TORRES-ACEVEDO, JUVENCIO	1966-01-02	PONCE	PR	PFC	24
BARTOLF, NOEL MICHAEL	1966-01-02	ROCHESTER	NY	PFC	23
GEOGHAGEN, GEORGE EDDIE	1966-01-02	PENSACOLA	FL	SP4	19
HUGHES, JERRY NELSON	1966-01-10	MIAMI	FL	PFC	20
THOMAS, JOHN WILLIAM	1966-01-10	LEVITTOWN	PA	SP4	23
JORDAN, WILLIAM E III	1966-01-10	BANGOR	ME	SGT	24
BIRCO, JOSE GOTERA	1966-01-11	PHILIPPINES	XP	SSG	29
CAVANAGH, ARTHUR	1966-01-11	QUEENS VILLAGE	NY	SP4	20
AMATO, RICHARD C	1966-01-11	HAYWARD	CA	PFC	23
HIPP, JOSEPH EARNEST	1966-01-11	ALBANY	GA	PFC	18
MC GEHEE, NOBLE DOUGLAS	1966-01-11	MEADVILLE	MS	SSG	27
AMADOR, RAYNALD HIMENZ	1966-01-11	PUTNAN	OH	CPL	23
ROBINSON, WILLIE JAMES	1966-01-11	SEALE	AL	SP4	20
SMITH, MARVIN BONNEY JR	1966-01-11	VIRGINIA BEACH	VA	SP4	19
DAILEY, GERALD LEE	1966-01-11	SCOTTSVILLE	NY	SP4	19
HARPER, RICHARD EARL	1966-01-12	BIRMINGHAM	AL	SP4	21
KEY, ANDERSON HAROLD	1966-01-13	ORANGEBURG	SC	PFC	23
SOUSA, LAURENCE NELSON	1966-01-15	EAST BOSTON	MA	CPL	23
BOWEN, RAYMOND LEWIS JR	1966-01-24	HANNIBAL	NY	SP4	20
LOCKE, JACK ELSWORTH	1966-01-27	GARY	IN	PFC	19
BELLAMY, SIMMIE JR	1966-02-26	CONWAY	SC	PFC	19
HOSKINS, ROBERT LEE JR	1966-02-26	NORFOLK	VA	SSG	23
MITCHELL, CLARENCE	1966-02-26	NASHVILLE	TN	SGT	33
TARBELL, WILLIAM M	1966-02-26	SYRACUSE	NY	PVT	20
BERRY, ELMER EUGENE	1966-02-26	ST JOSEPH	MO	SSG	32
HIMES, JACK LANDEN	1966-02-26	PHOENIX	AZ	PFC	19
CAVINEE, RONALD C	1966-02-26	CROOKSVILLE	OH	PFC	21

FREDERICK, LAMAR DONALD	1966-02-26	TOLEDO	OH	PFC	22
CLARKE, IRVIN JR	1966-02-26	NEW YORK	NY	SP4	24
FRANK, JOHNSON FRANCIS	1966-02-26	CHARLOTTE	NC	SSG	35
BREWER, THOMAS COLEMAN JR	1966-02-26	PAGELAND	SC	SGT	30
DANIELS, CHARLIES	1966-02-26	DETROIT	MI	PSGT	37
GRAVES, EDWARD STEPHEN	1966-02-27	MINNEAPOLIS	MN	PFC	21
REILLY, JOSEPH JOHN	1966-02-27	MOUNT HOLLY	NJ	PFC	19
JENKINS, BARNETTE GARTRELL	1966-03-02	SAVANNAH	GA	PFC	18
BODELL, KENNETH A	1966-03-12	SANDY	UT	PFC	22
HERLIHY, JOHN HENRY JR	1966-03-13	NEW YORK	NY	PSGT	38
BUTLER, EARLIE JAMES JR	1966-03-14	JACKSONVILLE	FL	SSG	30
HARPER, MARVIN	1966-03-14	ST LOUIS	MO	PFC	19
TABB, PHIL	1966-03-14	COLQUITT	GA	CPT	31
SLADE, BILLY RAY	1966-03-14	HOPE MILLS	NC	SGT	22
STEGALL, ALLAN JR	1966-03-15	ATLANTA	GA	PFC	22
BEAUCHAMP, JOHN HENRY JR	1966-03-16	PRINCESS ANNE	MD	CPL	19
GIPSON, ROBERT PAUL	1966-03-16	ATHENS	GA	SP4	23
GOSSETT, WILLIAM O	1966-03-16	PHOENIX	AZ	PFC	19
BROWN, MARION C	1966-03-16	INDIANAPOLIS	IN	SGT	27
LEWIS, JERRY D	1966-03-16	OKLAHOMA CITY	OK	SP4	24
SMITH, RICHARD FLOYD	1966-03-16	ROCHESTER	NY	PFC	21
WALKER, CHARLIE C	1966-03-16	ASHBURN	GA	PFC	22
ZIONTS, CHARLES A	1966-03-16	CICERO	IL	SP4	20
THOMPSON, WILLIAM NATHANIEL	1966-03-16	MEBANE	NC	PFC	22
BELL, CHARLES ARTHUR	1966-03-16	PHILADELPHIA	PA	PFC	20
KNUDSON, KENNETH MAX	1966-03-16	SACO	MT	PFC	21
DELANO, MERWIN A JR	1966-03-17	BATH	ME	PVT	18
RODARTE, ALEXANDER D	1966-03-19	COMPTON	CA	PFC	19

FIELDS, LLOYD JR	1966-04-13	BLACKSTONE	VA	SSG	26
MARTINSON, DARRELL WAYNE	1966-05-02	MINNEAPOLIS	MN	PFC	18
MALONE, JIMMY EUGENE	1966-05-04	NORFOLK	VA	SSGT	31
MCMAHAN, JOHN EDWARD	1966-05-05	MARION	NC	PFC	21
PATRICK, RICHARD MICHAEL	1966-05-17	SAN JOSE	CA	SP4	20
WILLIAMS, JIMMY LAVERNE	1966-05-17	WETUMPKA	AL	PFC	19
GARRETT, ALLEN MORGAN	1966-05-17	HOLLAND PATENT	NY	PVT	22
WALTERS, WILLIAM E	1966-05-17	SAN DIEGO	CA	SGT	28
HARRISON, JOHNNY	1966-05-17	HEMPSTEAD	NY	PFC	21
BULLOCK, RICHARD WILLIAM	1966-05-17	RICHMOND	VA	PFC	21
BURROUGHS, WALTER L	1966-05-17	NORTH LEWISBURG	OH	PFC	19
ANDERSON, ARTIS WESLEY	1966-05-17	ATLANTA	GA	PFC	20
HAMILTON, EDWARD	1966-05-17	TAMPA	FL	SGT	24
DEDMAN, TONY	1966-05-17	LA GRANGE	IL	SP4	22
DUNCAN, KENNETH EUGENE	1966-05-17	HENDERSON	KY	PFC	21
ESPARZA, FELIX JR	1966-05-17	SAN ANTONIO	TX	PFC	19
ADAM, HOSEA DENNIS	1966-05-18	MONROE	LA	SP4	20
BULLARD, KENNY WAYNE	1966-05-19	FAIRFIELD	AL	PFC	19
KIEHL, MICHAEL RAYMOND	1966-05-19	EL CAJON	CA	PFC	21
REDMOND, CARTER	1966-05-20	PHILADELPHIA	PA	PVT	22
MOORE, GILLIAM	1966-05-20	NEW YORK	NY	PFC	19
GARDNER, JACK ELROY	1966-05-20	VACAVILLE	CA	PFC	21
GUERIN, ROBERT LOUIS	1966-05-21	PARMA	OH	SP4	19
PHELPS, WALTER WILLIAM	1966-05-21	NEW YORK	NY	SGT	27
WILSON, WILLIAM JEFFREY	1966-06-03	SANGER	CA	PFC	22
GAYMON, STEPHEN H	1966-06-03	CORCORAN	CA	PFC	19
DOZIER, DEBROW	1966-06-03	MERIDIAN	MS	PFC	20

WISNIEWSKI, CHARLES J JR	1966-06-05	UNCASVILLE	CT	PFC	19
CAMPBELL, THOMETT DARTHAN	1966-06-05	MILLINGTON	TN	PFC	21
DONION, MICHAEL	1966-06-05	LYNBROOK	NY	SGT	23
MILLS, WARD WARREN JR	1966-06-10	SHAWSVILLE	VA	PFC	21
BUCZYNSKI, GREGORY THOMAS	1966-06-10	FLEMINGTON	NJ	PFC	20
STEWART, DAVID WAYNE	1966-06-11	FOUNTAIN RUN	KY	PFC	19
SIMON, RALPH	1966-06-11	SILVER SPRING	MD	PFC	21
LOCKRIDGE, JAMES T	1966-06-12	COLUMBIA	TN	CPL	24
WILLIAMS, BILLY	1966-06-12	CHARLESTON	SC	PFC	21
LOPEZ, RENE CERDA	1966-06-12	FORT CAMPBELL	KY	SGT	25
HUDSON, RAYMOND HOYT	1966-06-15	SAN ANTONIO	TX	SGT	31
LORENZ, TERRY WAYNE	1966-06-16	LA CROSSE	WI	PFC	19
FELDER, JESSEE CLARANCE	1966-06-29	JERSEY CITY	NJ	SP4	23
HIDO, RICHARD LEE	1966-06-29	PAINESVILLE	OH	SP4	19
JONES, TOMMY ROY	1966-06-29	NASHVILLE	NC	PFC	22
BERTHEL, JOHN JOSEPH	1966-06-29	NEW YORK	NY	PFC	21
GRAVES, FRANK	1966-06-29	WASHINGTON	DC	PFC	22
FRITTS, FREDERIC WILLIAM	1966-06-29	BEAUMONT	TX	SP4	23
STEVENS, FRANCIS GEORGE	1966-06-29	ELLSWORTH	ME	PFC	21
SURETTE, PAUL JOSEPH	1966-06-29	HOLBROOK	MA	PFC	19
SMITH, LESLIE R	1966-06-29	INDIANAPOLIS	IN	PFC	20
BOWMAN, ROBERT MICHAEL	1966-06-29	WILMINGTON	DE	PFC	18
BERRY, MALCOLM CRAYTON	1966-06-29	HARTFORD	CT	PFC	20
POTTER, ALBERT RAYMOND	1966-06-29	BROWNS MILLS	NJ	SGT	27
FERRARO, DAVID ALLEN	1966-06-30	PITTSBURGH	PA	PFC	19
RIBITSCH, ERIC	1966-07-03	RIDGEWOOD	NY	PFC	23
WILKINS, TERRY KENNETH	1966-07-03	LAS VEGAS	NV	PFC	18

219

COLLINS, JULIUS JR	1966-07-03	BLACKVILLE	SC	PFC	21
NOSS, JAMES THEORDORE	1966-07-03	BRUCETON MILLS	WV	PFC	21
WILLIAMS, THEODORE JR	1966-07-04	ROBBINS	IL	PFC	19
SCARBOROUGH, ELMER WAYNE	1966-07-04	ROMULUS	MI	PFC	21
ZUKOV, STEPHEN ANDREW	1966-07-19	CARTERET	NJ	PFC	19
COLLINS, JAMES WILFORD	1966-07-27	UNION CITY	TN	PFC	22
SAMPSON, JOSEPH C JR	1966-07-27	XENIA	OH	WO	35
HUNT, JOSEPH FRANCIS	1966-07-27	LEWISBURG	PA	SSG	25
KEGLEY, JOE DAVID	1966-07-27	GREAT FALLS	MT	PFC	24
MC CRYSTAL **, JAMES LARRY	1966-07-27	LITTLE ROCK	AR	PFC	19
MC DOWELL, MELVIN WARREN	1966-07-27	DELHI	CA	PFC	18
MOORE, CARLOS DAVID	1966-07-27	HARLAN	KY	PFC	18
SCHEMEL, JERRY L	1966-07-27	DRAYTON PLAINS	MI	PFC	19
WELSH, RUTHERFORD J	1966-07-27	CANADA	XC	WO	24
REINBOTT, HAROLD W	1966-07-27	PARMA	MO	SP5	27
MARROQUIN, TOMAS JR	1966-08-11	MERCEDES	TX	PFC	21
HANEY, THOMAS WILLIAM	1966-08-14	ST PAUL	MN	PFC	25
GLOVER, FREDDIE BEE	1966-08-14	GADSDEN	AL	PFC	20
CORFMAN, DARYL RAYMOND	1966-08-14	SYCAMORE	OH	PFC	21
GALLAGHER, FRANK R	1966-08-20	LOGANSPORT	IN	PFC	19
TUCKER, WILLIE JAMES	1966-08-20	TOLEDO	OH	PFC	21
KASAI, THOMAS TARO	1966-08-20	NEW YORK	NY	PFC	20
LEWIS, MICHAEL	1966-08-22	INDIANAPOLIS	IN	PFC	22
DEMPS, HENRY VAN	1966-08-22	PLANT CITY	FL	PFC	22
LOFTON, RAYFON	1966-08-23	CHATTANOOGA	TN	PFC	21
TRAXLER, TOMMY JR	1966-09-06	CRYSTAL SPRINGS	MS	PFC	21
BARNEY, ALEXANDER LORENZO	1966-09-10	NEW YORK	NY	PFC	19
MILLER, JOSEPH LLOYD	1966-09-15	DENVER	CO	SGT	22

RANKIN, EDWARD GARRY	1966-09-16	WAYNESBORO	VA	PFC	19
RANDALL, LOUIS R	1966-09-25	COVINGTON	KY	PFC	18
WESTPOINT, THOMAS LEE	1966-09-30	CHARLESTON	SC	SGT	24
COTNEY, ELMER EUGENE	1966-09-30	LINEVILLE	AL	SP4	20
BROYLES, LANHAM ODELL	1966-09-30	OILDALE	CA	SP4	19
STUBBE, WILLIAM LEROY	1966-10-01	CENTRAL CITY	NE	PFC	21
DE MARSICO, MICHAEL JAMES	1966-10-01	WHITE PLAINS	NY	PFC	21
HEMMITT, TERRY EUGENE	1966-10-02	KANSAS CITY	MO	PFC	19
WALDRON, GEORGE ALLEN	1966-10-03	SAN JOSE	CA	PFC	20
ENGRAM, RANDAL CLYDE	1966-10-03	MIAMI	FL	1LT	23
JONES, JOHN HENRY	1966-10-04	ENTERPRISE	AL	PFC	21
PALM, JOSH JR	1966-10-05	ALEXANDRIA	LA	PFC	22
DICKERSON, JOHN GREEN III	1966-10-05	GARY	IN	PVT	19
BRANCH, DAVID WESLEY	1966-10-07	DAYTONA BEACH	FL	PFC	20
ROUNDTREE, WILLIE JUNIUS	1966-10-07	FAYETTEVILLE	NC	PFC	19
SOKOLOWSKI, FRANK MICHAEL	1966-10-07	CHELSEA	MA	PFC	18
DALOLA, JOHN FRANCIS III	1966-10-07	PENNDEL	PA	PFC	19
FREEMAN, DAVID HAROLD	1966-10-12	GADSDEN	AL	SGT	27
JONES, DOUGLAS LEE	1966-10-12	ERWIN	TN	1LT	24
GARDNER, JAMES EDWARDS	1966-10-13	KALAMAZOO	MI	1LT	25
MIKULA, EMERY GEORGE	1966-10-13	JERSEY CITY	NJ	1LT	24
MC ILVAIN, EDWARD M III	1966-10-18	WYNNEWOOD	PA	SP4	21
BURNS, LEONARD WESLEY	1966-10-18	JACKSONVILLE	FL	SP5	26
SMITH, ROBERT SR	1966-10-21	ALEXANDRIA	LA	SGT	34
BELANGER, GEORGE	1966-10-24	WATERVILLE	ME	PFC	19
RESPRESS, THOMAS	1966-10-29	TOLEDO	OH	PFC	22
BROWN, NATHANIEL	1966-10-31	CHARLOTTE	NC	SSG	27
PAPPAS, ELEFTHERIOS PANTEL	1966-10-31	NEW YORK	NY	SP4	23

CROSS, JOSEPH ALEXANDER	1966-11-15	PHILADELPHIA	PA	PFC	18
KERN, DOUGLAS DUANE	1966-11-16	BILLINGS	MT	SGT	20
JOHNSON, JAMES	1966-11-16	NORFOLK	VA	1LT	23
PALENSKE, WILLIAM ALLEN	1966-11-18	SAN JOSE	CA	PFC	23
CLARK, LORENZO	1966-12-16	MEMPHIS	TN	SFC	44
ANDREWS, COLEY	1966-12-16	MOBILE	AL	SGT	25
POWELL, RICHARD EDWIN	1966-12-19	ROYERSFORD	PA	SGT	29
RAIFORD, CHARLES LEROY JR	1967-01-01	PITTSBURGH	PA	PFC	22
REICHERT, JOSEPH R	1967-01-03	BUFFALO	NY	SSG	26
JONES, WILLIE DONALD	1967-01-10	HOMESTEAD	FL	SP4	22
STOVES, MERRITT III	1967-01-10	NORTH BIRMINGHAM	AL	PFC	19
CABBAGESTALK, EUGENE	1967-01-11	PITTSBURGH	PA	PVT	20
FLOYD, LONNIE ALLEN	1967-01-14	CHATTANOOGA	TN	SP4	19
PRINCE, JOHN R	1967-01-15	CHATTANOOGA	TN	SSG	41
LASKIN, FRANK HOWARD	1967-01-15	WASHINGTON	DC	PFC	19
ZERFASS, JEROME VINCENT	1967-01-16	BETHLEHEM	PA	PFC	20
RAMIREZ, MARIO	1967-01-16	OAKLAND	MI	SGT	23
SMITH, FRANK LEE	1967-01-16	STANWOOD	WA	PFC	25
WILKIE, ARTHUR WAYNE	1967-01-16	HENDERSON VILLE	NC	SP4	23
BRIGMAN, BILLY DEAN	1967-01-17	BARNARDS VILLE	NC	PFC	19
DYDYNSKI, STEPHEN MICHAEL	1967-01-21	HYATTSVILLE	MD	PFC	19
ZOLLER, ERIC WARD	1967-01-22	MALIBU	CA	SP4	22
ANDERSON, LEWIS CARL	1967-01-22	CHICAGO	IL	SP4	20
PENDERGIST, RONALD LYNN	1967-01-22	AUGUSTA	AR	CPL	21
COLLINS, WILLIAM ELICE JR	1967-01-23	HOUSTON	TX	SP4	19
SCHADDELEE, WILLIAM D	1967-02-01	CHICAGO	IL	SGT	23

HENDERSON, JAMES D	1967-02-01	DE FUNIAK SPRINGS	FL	PFC	22
CHIASERA, AUGUST JR	1967-02-01	NORTH TONAWANDA	NY	SP4	20
SPITTLER, IRA JAMES III	1967-02-05	SANTA MARIA	CA	SP4	21
ECKER, ROBERT RAYMOND	1967-02-05	SPRINGDALE	PA	SGT	21
CARRILLO, GEORGE J JR	1967-02-06	SAN JOSE	CA	SP4	22
CHRISTY, GILMORE WILSON	1967-02-06	TULSA	OK	SP4	21
ARMSTRONG, EVERETT	1967-02-06	NASHVILLE	TN	SGT	26
JOHNSON, FRED ARTHUR	1967-02-06	HALLANDALE	FL	PFC	20
SIMPSON, CHESTER PAUL	1967-02-06	JAMESTOWN	KY	PFC	18
DARRIGAN, RAYMOND MAURICE	1967-02-06	BRIGHTON	MA	SFC	40
HAYES, BOBBY LEE	1967-02-07	BOWLING GREEN	KY	SSG	28
SNYDER, RODGER CLAYBORN	1967-02-07	BALTIMORE	MD	SP4	20
BREWINGTON, HARVEY JR	1967-02-07	FAYETTEVILLE	NC	SSG	29
DAIGLE, BRADLEY TIMOTHY	1967-02-07	MORGAN CITY	LA	PFC	20
MEISBURGER, JOSEPH STEVEN	1967-02-08	PHILADELPHIA	PA	SP4	19
MEADOWS, MILLARD FRANKLIN	1967-02-08	BOONVILLE	MO	PFC	18
CAMPBELL, KEITH ALLEN	1967-02-08	ARLINGTON	VA	SP4	20
FORE, WILLIAM C	1967-02-11	MARION	SC	SP4	20
SLACK, CHARLES LEROY JR	1967-02-15	NEW CASTLE	PA	PFC	19
VIGO-NEGRN, LUIS	1967-02-16	SANTURCE	PR	SSG	28
JACKSON, EDWARD	1967-02-16	SCARSDALE	NY	SP4	21
KRANSHAN, TIMOTHY MICHAEL	1967-02-22	TALLMADGE	OH	PFC	19
MICKNA, JOHN RONALD	1967-02-23	OMAHA	NE	SSG	28
WATKINS, FRANKLIN ROOSEVELT	1967-02-23	MEHERRIN	VA	SSG	32
COLES, GEORGE EUGENE JR	1967-02-23	ATLANTIC CITY	NJ	PFC	18

PHILLIPS, THOMAS FRANK	1967-02-24	POMPANO BEACH	FL	CPL	21
SMITH, GARY KENNETH	1967-02-27	SANTA ANA	CA	SP4	21
RENFRO, NORMAN A	1967-03-03	OAKLAND	CA	PVT	24
BENNETT, CHARLES HERMAN	1967-03-03	FAYETTEVILLE	NC	PFC	22
SCHULTZ, PETER JOHN	1967-03-03	UTICA	MI	SP4	19
SKILES, JAMES ARTHUR	1967-03-03	NEW BRUNSWICK	NJ	PFC	22
STALTER, JOHN RAYMOND	1967-03-03	PICO RIVERA	CA	SGT	19
GAINES, MELVIN CLYDE	1967-03-03	LOS ANGELES	CA	SSG	28
ALANDT, CHARLES BYRON	1967-03-03	ROYAL OAK	MI	PFC	19
GREEN, MOSES	1967-03-03	JAMAICA	NY	SP4	21
WILSON, HERBERT JR	1967-03-03	NEW YORK	NY	PFC	19
VASQUES, SELVESTER JOE	1967-03-03	LOS ANGELES	CA	PFC	23
CALLAHAN, WELBORN A JR	1967-03-03	COLUMBUS	GA	1LT	23
STRACK, LAWRENCE	1967-03-03	RICHMOND HILL	NY	PVT	18
SAEZ-RAMIREZ, ANGEL PERFIR	1967-03-03	OROCOVIS	PR	SSG	32
CURRAN, PAUL WILLIAM	1967-03-03	EAST MILTON	MA	PFC	19
ADAMS, STEVEN JACK	1967-03-03	SPRINGFIELD	OH	PFC	18
GARRISON, EARL STANLEY	1967-03-03	BRUNSWICK	ME	PFC	18
CAIRES, CLYDE JOSEPH	1967-03-03	KALAHEO	HI	PFC	19
DRAKE, MICHAEL JOHN	1967-03-03	STANFORD	FL	PFC	18
EBALD, MICHAEL LEO	1967-03-03	PHILADELPHIA	PA	PFC	22
ANTHONY, LIONEL S	1967-03-04	LOS ANGELES	CA	PFC	21
HACKWORTH, DWIGHT LEE	1967-03-04	SAN ANTONIO	TX	PFC	18
LYERLY, RONALD WAYNE	1967-03-06	SALISBURY	NC	PFC	20
CROSS, BENNIE LEE	1967-03-07	CAIRO	IL	SGT	23
KENNEDY, CHARLES F	1967-03-07	BLYTHEVILLE	AR	SGT	32
KEITH, JAMES KELLY III	1967-03-07	CHATTANOOGA	TN	PFC	18
FRIAR, FREDDIE LYNN	1967-03-09	BLYTHEVILLE	AR	PFC	22

BARTRAM, GERALD EDWARD	1967-03-09	CHICAGO	IL	PVT	19
FURNEY, WILLIS LEE	1967-03-09	MACON	GA	SGT	20
HOLTHOFF, WILLIAM HENRY	1967-03-21	CHAMPAIGN	IL	SP4	21
MATTHEWS, ROBERT L	1967-03-22	HUNTSVILLE	AL	SP4	23
ANDERSON, CHARLES C JR	1967-03-22	BREMERTON	WA	CPT	27
EVANS, JAMES LARRY	1967-03-22	FLORENCE	AL	1LT	25
PERRY, RANDALL LAWRENCE	1967-03-23	FLINT	MI	SP4	20
GARCIA, PEDRO INCARNACION	1967-03-25	CORPUS CHRISTI	TX	SGT	19
COX, GEORGE TOLLOVAR	1967-03-25	TAMPA	FL	SGT	27
MOORE, DOUGLAS EUGENE	1967-03-25	RALEIGH	NC	SGT	24
SANDERS, DONALD RAY	1967-03-25	ELMENDORF AFB	AK	PFC	20
CARPENTERS, DOUGLAS JOE	1967-03-25	BAUXITE	AR	PFC	20
HERRON, ROCKWELL SELDEN	1967-03-25	HAWORTH	NJ	PFC	19
EVANS, JAMES WILLIAM	1967-03-25	COLUMBUS	OH	PFC	19
ANDERSON, IVY THOMAS	1967-03-26	WEST PALM BEACH	FL	SSG	33
JAMES, JOHN HENRY JR	1967-03-26	NEW YORK	NY	SP4	23
MINICK, STEPHEN MICHAEL	1967-03-26	SALISBURY	PA	SGT	19
DROWN, DAVID ALAN	1967-03-27	FAIRHAVEN	MA	SP4	28
GLASSCOCK, DAVID LEWIS	1967-03-29	ROCKWALL	TX	SP4	22
WOBLE, JOHN B	1967-04-01	WINDSOR	CT	PVT	30
DEWEY, JAMES ELLIOT	1967-04-04	GLENCOE	PA	CPL	20
PATTERSON, THOMAS	1967-04-07	SAVANNAH	GA	SGT	20
GASTON, ROSS ALLEN	1967-04-07	FAIRFIELD	AL	PFC	22
MILLER, JERRY ROBERT	1967-04-07	BALDWIN PARK	CA	CPL	19
GAMBLE, HENRY HWEY	1967-04-07	WEST PALM BEACH	FL	CPL	22
MICHAEL, DON LESLIE	1967-04-08	LEXINGTON	AL	SP4	19

OVIEDO, HIGINIO OVALLE	1967-04-08	RAYMOND VILLE	TX	PFC	22
GUYER, ALBERT MARSHALL	1967-04-08	KANSAS CITY	KS	1LT	24
THOMPSON, ROBERT JR	1967-04-08	SEPULVEDA	CA	PFC	23
LEYVA-PARRA-FRIAS, FELIX F F	1967-04-08	NORWALK	CA	PFC	19
DIXON, TERRENCE GLADE	1967-04-08	ST PETERSBURG	FL	CPL	21
HOLLAND, DOUGLAS C	1967-04-09	ANITA	IA	SP4	23
GLEASON, ARTHUR A	1967-04-09	SYRACUSE	NY	PVT	18
CULLEN, KENNETH ARTHUR	1967-04-09	PANAMA CITY	FL	2LT	22
KING, HAROLD B	1967-04-09	JONESBORO	TN	SP4	19
RAY, CHARLES	1967-04-11	DETROIT	MI	SSG	33
RABIDEAU, JOHN J	1967-04-11	EASTHAMPTON	MA	PFC	18
ELLSWORTH, NEIL ROBERT	1967-04-13	NORTHBORO	MA	PFC	19
GOHEEN, RICHARD H	1967-04-15	EVANSVILLE	IN	SP4	20
LEFFLER, RUSSELL ALAN	1967-04-16	NEW SMYRNA BEACH	FL	SP4	20
BLACKWELDER, KIT	1967-04-22	PORTLAND	OR	PFC	19
PATTERSON, TIMOTHY	1967-04-22	LUMBERTON	NC	SFT	22
CASSIDY, RAMOND SENTER	1967-04-24	PATCHOGUE	NY	SP4	19
DOMINIAK, HOWARD STANLEY	1967-04-24	CHICAGO	IL	PFC	20
CHRONISTER, JAMES VIRGIL	1967-05-01	CHICAGO	IL	PFC	18
EVANS, WADDEL	1967-05-11	HOPKINSVILLE	KY	PFC	19
LOUVRING, CARL FREDERICK	1967-05-13	LOWELL	OR	PFC	19
DUCKETT, JOSEPH L JR	1967-05-14	WASHINGTON	DC	PFC	19
BOYD, ROBERT RAY	1967-05-17	MURFREES BORO	TN	CPT	26
GERALD, WILSON TRUMAN	1967-05-17	ORRUM	NC	SGT	22
FRIGAULT, JOSEPH O	1967-05-17	CANADA	XC	SSG	40
TURNER, WILLIAM COY	1967-05-17	CHANCE	KY	SP4	21

CLAEYS, EDWARD ORAN	1967-05-17	FREMONT	CA	PFC	20
TIGHE, JOHN ROY	1967-05-17	LOMITA	CA	PFC	20
CUTRER, MARVIN EUGENE	1967-05-17	NEW ORLEANS	LA	PFC	19
HANIOTES, STEVEN MICHAEL	1967-05-17	EAST LIVERPOOL	OH	PFC	19
ALDERMAN, WINFRED	1967-05-17	BURGAW	NC	PFC	20
LEWIS, CHARLIE GRAY	1967-05-17	FAYETTEVILLE	NC	SFC	30
EDWARDS, GEORGE RAY FAYFIE	1967-05-17	PONTIAC	MI	SP5	26
FULLER, JOHNNIE CHESTER	1967-05-18	WASHINGTON	DC	SSG	26
HOWIE, NORMAN PERRY JR	1967-05-20	CONCORD	NC	PFC	20
HAGUE, GERALD CHARLES	1967-05-20	MAIDEN ROCK	WI	PFC	21
FENNESSEY, DAVID LEE	1967-05-20	BUFFALO	NY	SSG	22
JOHNSON, DAVID JOSEPH	1967-05-20	LOS ANGELES	CA	PFC	18
PROCTOR, SAMUEL JR	1967-05-22	ST SIMONS ISLAND	GA	CPL	21
CARTER, HARRY GIBSON	1967-05-30	MONTGOMERY	AL	SSG	29
BEAVERSON, HAROLD A JR	1967-05-31	CLARKSVILLE	TN	SSG	33
CARTER, LEONARD JAMES	1967-06-08	WINTHROP	IL	PFC	19
BARKER, JEFFREY LAWRENCE	1967-06-08	RIDGEFIELD	NJ	PFC	20
MEARS, CHARLES ROBERT	1967-06-16	PATTERSON	CA	SP4	21
LEATHERS, CLIFFORD W JR	1967-06-21	WRIGHT CITY	OK	SP4	19
COOK, JIMMY LEE	1967-06-21	PHOENIX	AZ	PVT	18
KELLEY, STEPHEN ALLEN	1967-06-22	ATLANTA	GA	SGT	19
NEGRO, DANIEL LEE	1967-06-22	WAKEFIELD	MI	PFC	20
HOOPER, VINS RONALD	1967-06-22	SOMERSET	NJ	SP4	20
POORE, LEONARD BURTON	1967-06-22	BEAUMONT	TX	SP4	20
PATTON, JOHN PERRY	1967-06-22	OAKLAND	CA	SGT	26
BUTLER, ALBERT JR	1967-06-22	TYLER	TX	PFC	24
JOHNSON, HARRY J	1967-06-22	TARRANT CITY	AL	SGT	22
PATTON, GEORGE	1967-06-22	NEW YORK	NY	PFC	19
WARREN, WILLIE CRAIG	1967-06-22	CROCKETT	TX	SP4	20
MC EACHIN, JOHN JR	1967-06-22	NEW YORK	NY	SP4	21

SHARBER, JOHN JR	1967-06-22	JACKSON	MS	SP4	20
ZSIGO, ALEXANDER C JR	1967-06-22	DURAND	MI	SP4	21
WALKER, CHARLIE LEWIS	1967-06-22	MUNFORD	AL	PFC	20
GIBSON, BURRELL	1967-06-22	DAYTON	OH	SP4	23
STEPHENS, DAVID ALLEN	1967-06-22	LARGO	FL	SGT	20
ALLEN, TERRY LEE ODIS	1967-06-22	KANSAS CITY	MO	PFC	19
SCHROBILGEN, WARREN H JR	1967-06-22	PACOIMA	CA	PFC	19
BOEHM, WILLIAM JOSEPH	1967-06-22	SILVER SPRING	MD	PFC	19
JOHNSON, DAVID E	1967-06-22	NATCHEZ	MS	SGT	22
MIKA, STEPHEN ADAM	1967-06-22	WILLOWICK	OH	PFC	22
MC CRAY, FRANK JR	1967-06-22	MIAMI	FL	SP4	20
SEXTON, JEFFREY ROSS	1967-06-22	MARICOPA	AZ	2LT	22
CLARK, RONALD CLEVELAND	1967-06-22	GAINESVILLE	GA	SP4	19
MC BROOM, WILLIAM STANLEY	1967-06-22	RUSSELL	NY	PFC	20
WILLIAMS, EDWIN JEROME	1967-06-22	DETROIT	MI	PFC	20
ARNOLD, JAMES	1967-06-22	GREENVILLE	SC	PFC	22
TAFAO, FA'ASAVILIGA V	1967-06-22	SAN DIEGO	CA	PFC	21
MURPHY, TIMONTHY JOHN	1967-06-22	AVENEL	NJ	PFC	19
QUARLES, FLOYD ELMER	1967-06-22	NEW YORK	NY	PFC	20
SNOW, CHARLES HARRY	1967-06-22	MEDFORD	OR	PFC	19
ROMERO, TRINE JR	1967-06-22	ROSWELL	NM	PFC	20
SAENZ, HECTOR MARIO	1967-06-22	ROSWELL	NM	PFC	20
POOR, GEORGE ALBERT JR	1967-06-22	HILLSDALE	NJ	PFC	19
HILL, ALVIN GENE	1967-06-22	BARTOW	FL	SGT	21
RIZZI, RALPH JOSEPH	1967-06-22	CANANDAIGUA	NY	SP4	20
VALDEZ, DANIEL VIRAMONTES	1967-06-22	ANTIOCH	CA	PFC	20
BUTTS, DARRELL WAYNE	1967-06-22	WICHITA	KS	PFC	19
STEIDLER, JOHNSON AUGUSTUS	1967-06-22	GIBBSTOWN	NJ	PFC	19
LITWIN, ROBERT RICHARD	1967-06-22	WILLIMANSETT	MA	PSGT	25

MAYER, WALTER CHRISTIAN	1967-06-22	SAN ANTONIO	TX	PFC	19
MUNDEN, DONALD MARTIN	1967-06-22	QUAIL VALLEY	CA	PFC	18
O'CONNOR, MICHAEL DONALD	1967-06-22	MOUNT PLEASANT	IA	SP4	20
HELLER, DAVID JUNIOR	1967-06-22	SOUTH BOONE	CO	PFC	20
JOHNSTON, RICHARD J	1967-06-22	SACRAMENTO	CA	SP4	19
HOLCOMB, DOYLE	1967-06-22	JOHNSON CITY	TN	PFC	23
STEVENS, ROBERT LOUIS JR	1967-06-22	KALAMAZOO	MI	PFC	18
WATERMAN, MICHAEL J	1967-06-22	WESTMINSTER	MA	PFC	20
ANDERSON, ERLING ALTON	1967-06-22	EAU CLAIRE	WI	PFC	22
LIMINGA, FREDERICK HUGO	1967-06-22	PONTIAC	MI	PFC	19
MUNN, WILLIAM ARTHUR	1967-06-22	DETROIT	MI	PFC	18
CAMPBELL, CARLIN MARTIN JR	1967-06-22	SAN DIEGO	CA	PFC	19
GREENE, KENNETH LAWRENCE	1967-06-22	SOMERVILLE	MA	PFC	20
LOWRY, JIMMY CLINT	1967-06-22	NOCATEE	FL	SP4	20
SMITH, LLOYD EDGAR	1967-06-22	PORTALES	NM	SP4	21
SANFORD, JAMES WALTER	1967-06-22	ORANGEBURG	SC	PFC	20
CLARK, THORNE M III	1967-06-22	LOMPOC	CA	PFC	19
BURNS, ERVIN L	1967-06-22	PROVIDENCE	KY	1LT	28
JOHNSTON, RICHARD BRUCE	1967-06-22	CANDIA	NH	SP4	21
NOE, JERRY LYNN	1967-06-22	KNOXVILLE	TN	PFC	18
CRIPE, JACK LESTER	1967-06-22	ONONDAGA	MI	SP4	18
FINNEY, BOBBY LEE	1967-06-22	BOSTON	MA	SP4	21
PREDDY, ROBERT LEE	1967-06-22	SAN BERNARDINO	CA	SP4	19
STEPHENSON, DAVID RICHARD	1967-06-22	SAND SPRINGS	OK	PFC	18
TURNER, LARRY BURNS	1967-06-22	OAKBORO	NC	SP4	21
LUTTRELL, GARY ALLEN	1967-06-22	STERLING	IL	SP4	18

JUDD, DONALD R	1967-06-22	ALEXANDER	NY	1LT	24
HOOD, RICHARD E JR	1967-06-22	WINTERHAVEN	FL	1LT	22
LIMA, KENNETH KAWIKA	1967-06-22	HONOLULU	HI	SSG	33
DE LOACH, LLOYD DWAIN	1967-06-22	DALLAS	TX	SP4	22
DE RISO, LESTER MICHAEL	1967-06-22	WARREN	RI	PFC	19
DEEDRICK, CHARLES ORVIS JR	1967-06-22	WINONA	MN	SP4	22
DESCHENES, THOMAS ALFRED	1967-06-22	FITCHBURG	MA	SP4	20
DUFFY, THOMAS BENEDICT JR	1967-06-22	GLEN ELLYN	IL	PFC	22
EGAN, TIMOTHY JAMES	1967-06-22	CHICAGO	IL	PFC	19
EMMERT, JAMES RICHARD	1967-06-22	HUNTINGTON	WV	SGT	31
ENGLE, RUSSEL WARREN	1967-06-22	MADISON	NJ	SP4	20
MC BRIDE, ELLIS A JR	1967-06-23	LITHIA	FL	1LT	23
SCHOUWBURG, GERRIT JOHN	1967-06-24	KALAMAZOO	MI	SP5	22
PARKER, MICHAEL	1967-06-27	NEW YORK	NY	PFC	20
LESTER, JAMES ROBERT	1967-06-29	STOCKTON	CA	PSGT	34
COLVIN, GENE FRANCIS	1967-07-01	FORT EDWARD	NY	SGT	20
BURCH, CLIFFORD GARLAND	1967-07-09	LANGLEY PARK	MD	PFC	19
SEXTON, WESLEY ROBERT	1967-07-09	CORNELIA	GA	PFC	21
KLEIN, SZOLTON SIGMOND	1967-07-09	ARNOLD	PA	PFC	19
WILLIAMS, WALTER DOUGLAS	1967-07-10	GLYNDON	MD	MAJ	33
BROWN, KENNETH LLOYD	1967-07-10	SHERIDAN	WY	SGT	23
CROZIER, DAVID PAUL	1967-07-10	BALTIMORE	MD	SGT	23
JOHNSON, DAVID HAROLD	1967-07-10	JONESBORO	AR	PFC	18
SAMANS, WALTER A JR	1967-07-10	RICHMOND	VA	SP4	21
SPIER, HARRY DIWAIN	1967-07-10	TYLER	TX	PFC	19
HUGGINS, FRAZIER DANIEL	1967-07-10	SEFFNER	FL	CPL	19
RETZLAFF, ARTHUR CLIFTON	1967-07-10	WESTFIELD	NJ	1LT	24
FABRIZIO, JAMES	1967-07-10	NORWALK	CT	PFC	21

MITCHELL, MICHAEL SIDNEY	1967-07-10	RICHMOND	CA	PFC	20
SHORES, MALTON GENE	1967-07-10	CLARKSVILLE	AR	PFC	19
BEACH, MYRON STANLEY JR	1967-07-10	ELMIRA	NY	SFC	29
POOLE, ORIS LAMAR	1967-07-10	SCREVEN	GA	SP4	19
SABEL, JOEL MICHAEL	1967-07-10	WEST COVINA	CA	CPL	23
SCOTT, WILLIAM ALEXANDER	1967-07-10	MAGNOLIA	NJ	SFC	38
KOFLER, SIEGFRIED	1967-07-10	VENTURA	CA	SGT	29
BOROWSKI, JOHN C	1967-07-10	CHICAGO	IL	PFC	20
JORDAN, DANIEL WALTER	1967-07-10	GRIFFITH	IN	1LT	24
SHEPHERD, FRANKLIN STEVE	1967-07-10	NORTH WILKESBORO	NC	SP4	20
TORRES, JESUS M	1967-07-10	NEW YORK	NY	SGT	19
CLARK, ROGER WILLIAM	1967-07-10	PITTSFIELD	VT	SP4	20
DARBY, JIMMY EARL	1967-07-10	OPP	AL	PFC	18
DEUERLING, WILLIAM JOSEPH	1967-07-10	N. SMYRNA BEACH	FL	SGT	23
DORING, LARRY ALLEN	1967-07-10	MANKATO	MN	SP4	21
ERWIN, ARTHUR ALBERT	1967-07-10	EUGENE	OR	SP4	19
JONES, RONALD RUSSELL	1967-07-15	NEW YORK	NY	PFC	20
DAVIS, GERALD EDWARD	1967-07-15	BETHLEHEM	PA	PFC	19
STACEY, RALPH MCGUIN JR	1967-07-20	PINOLE	CA	PFC	19
HAMBLIN, RONALD B	1967-07-20	PHOENIX	AZ	PFC	21
SORRELLS, BOBBY HORACE	1967-07-20	EAST POINT	GA	SSG	31
BARDEN, EDWARD	1967-07-25	WHITEVILLE	NC	CPL	19
SOWER, DONALD MICHAEL	1967-08-02	CAMP RED CLIFF	UT	PFC	20
MOSER, HARRY JULIUS IV	1967-08-14	BIRDSBORO	PA	SGT	18
HOLLAND, CHARLES JAMES	1967-08-18	ELIZABETH	NJ	SFC	28
BALDONI, LINDSAY DAVID	1967-08-22	DETROIT	MI	SP4	21
AUER, EDUARD ADOLPH	1967-09-19	MANSFIELD	OH	SSG	29

PERSON, DAVID EUGENE	1967-09-22	KIRBYVILLE	TX	MAJ	34
BAMVAKAIS, JOHN ROBERT JR	1967-09-28	JEFFERSON CITY	MO	SGT	20
MARTIN, TERRY LEE	1967-10-03	MINNEAPOLIS	MN	SP4	19
MEADOR, DANIEL R	1967-10-03	VINTON	VA	SP4	20
FRANKLIN, WILLIE	1967-10-14	DETROIT	MI	SSG	29
HARRIS, NATHANIEL	1967-10-18	BESSEMER	AL	SP4	20
FLECK, ROBERT LEE	1967-10-19	COSTA	WV	CPL	19
CLINE, RODNEY BARRETTE	1967-10-21	GARDEN CITY	MI	PFC	20
DUNFORD, FRANK BELLEW III	1967-10-22	COVINGTON	KY	SSG	19
SALZMAN, LAVERN LEO	1967-10-25	MONTCLAIR	CA	SGT	21
MC COY, ELEC	1967-10-25	OSWEGO	SC	SGT	20
COGGINS, LARRY FRANKLIN	1967-10-30	TROY	NC	CPL	22
CUNNINGHAM, WALTER WAYNE	1967-10-31	TRENTON	MI	SGT	23
CAVER, JOHN WAYNE	1967-10-31	LONGVIEW	TX	SGT	19
LAIRD, RICHARD FRANCIS	1967-11-06	ALEXANDER	NY	PFC	20
WRIGHT, WILLIE ALFRED	1967-11-06	CHICAGO	IL	CPL	29
STONE, RICHARD ARLAN	1967-11-06	PALO ALTO	CA	SGT	23
SHAFER, JAMES DUDLEY	1967-11-06	LIMA	OH	SGT	25
BOWERSMITH, CHARLES GEORGE	1967-11-06	MARYSVILLE	OH	PFC	19
JORGENSEN, EMORY LEE	1967-11-06	SALT LAKE CITY	UT	SP4	20
STEVENS, EDRICK KENNETH	1967-11-06	SIMI	CA	PFC	19
CORBETT, LINWOOD CALVIN	1967-11-06	HOLLIS	NY	SP4	22
MILLER, CLARENCE ALVIE JR	1967-11-06	STEGER	IL	PFC	26
MILLER, LOUIS CHARLES	1967-11-06	WATSONVILLE	CA	SP4	18
JONES, SHERMAN LAWRENCE	1967-11-06	JACKSONVILLE	FL	PFC	20
BURNEY, DAVID DRANK	1967-11-06	PALATKA	FL	PFC	19
BICKEL, ROBERT JOHN	1967-11-06	ROCHESTER	NY	PFC	19

CABRERA, JOAQUIN PALACIOS	1967-11-06	PIQUA MERIZO	GU	SSG	35
DARLING, ROBERT HARRY	1967-11-06	PITTSBURGH	PA	1LT	27
DOWDY, RUFUS JOHN	1967-11-06	SUFFOLK	VA	PFC	19
DUBB, DEWAINE V	1967-11-06	BELLINGHAM	WA	PFC	20
ELLIS, JAMES LEE JR	1967-11-06	JESUP	GA	SP4	20
KAPELUCK, JOHN MICHAEL	1967-11-08	CRESSKILL	NJ	SP4	21
BARRETO, LUIS JR	1967-11-10	NEW ORLEANS	LA	PFC	20
RILEY, CHARLES FRANKLIN	1967-11-11	ST JOSEPH	MO	PFC	25
MARTIN, LARRY	1967-11-11	CHICAGO	IL	SGT	19
GUNN, GEORGE BRUCE	1967-11-11	SCHENECTADY	NY	PFC	18
KERNS, GLENN DIRK	1967-11-11	LUMBERTON	NC	PFC	19
MARTINEZ-MERCADO, EDWIN J	1967-11-11	NEW YORK	NY	PFC	20
SHAW, GARY FRANCIS	1967-11-11	TOLEDO	OH	PFC	19
STATON, ROBERT MILTON JR	1967-11-11	JAMESVILLE	NC	SP4	19
BARNES, JOHN ANDREW III	1967-11-12	DEDHAM	MA	PFC	22
MORRIS, CHARLES H JR	1967-11-12	ALGOMA	WV	PFC	20
HARDY, ABRAHAM LINCOLN	1967-11-12	HOUSTON	TX	CPT	25
KELLEY, JERRY CONRAD	1967-11-12	ENGLEWOOD	CO	SP4	21
FOSTER, DANIEL WILLIAM	1967-11-12	ANSONIA	CT	SP4	20
ALLEN, DAN S III	1967-11-12	MEMPHIS	TN	SGT	20
FAVROTH, CHARLES	1967-11-12	NEW YORK	NY	SGT	24
BARNES, JOHN HENRY	1967-11-12	ST LOUIS	MO	PFC	20
COUCH, HAROLD EUGENE	1967-11-12	DURHAM	NC	SGT	20
CROOM, HUBERT	1967-11-12	WINONA	MS	PFC	24
THOMAS, LEONARD ALAN	1967-11-12	NEW YORK	NY	PFC	20
GUERRERO, WILEY	1967-11-12	AUSTIN	TX	PFC	19
JENKINS, JAMES EARL	1967-11-12	HIGH POINT	NC	PFC	20
ESCARENO, ARMANDO	1967-11-12	MUSKEGON HEIGHTS	MI	PFC	19

DEDEAUX, ALDON JAMES	1967-11-12	DE LISLE	MS	PFC	19
MAPLES, FRANCIS LEROY	1967-11-13	LA FERIA	TX	SP4	20
COWDRICK, HORACE W JR	1967-11-13	COLLEGE POINT	NY	PFC	19
JONES, MILFORD	1967-11-13	ST PETERSBURG	FL	PFC	21
BUNKER, DAVID ELVIN	1967-11-13	KINGSTON	NH	SP4	21
ROST, LEROY ALPHUS	1967-11-13	MOLINE	IL	PFC	19
JONES, RAY MORGAN KEITH	1967-11-13	JONESBORO	TN	SP4	20
HESS, ZAN	1967-11-13	WICHITA FALLS	TX	SP4	19
MURRAY, WAYNE PAUL	1967-11-13	POTSDAM	NY	PFC	20
WILLIAMS, LARRY KEITH	1967-11-13	TORRANCE	CA	PFC	20
FERRULLA, ROBERT SAMUEL	1967-11-13	LYNWOOD	CA	PFC	24
SCHEIBER, RICHARD ALAN	1967-11-13	HUNTINGTON	IN	SP4	25
HARDIMAN, LA FRANCIS	1967-11-13	WYANDANCH	NY	PFC	19
ROSS, ROBERT LEE	1967-11-13	WATERPROOF	LA	PFC	20
SPRINKLE, VERNON PATRICK	1967-11-13	PORTLAND	OR	PFC	19
HESTER, VANESTER LAMAR	1967-11-13	FORT PIERCE	FL	SP5	22
RAFFENSPERGER, JAMES E JR	1967-11-13	DES MOINES	IA	SP4	20
MEANS, VERNON	1967-11-13	CORDELE	GA	SGT	22
SIMMONS, WILLIE JAMES	1967-11-13	DETROIT	MI	SGT	19
MYERS, RICHARD VAUGHN	1967-11-13	GLENMOORE	PA	SP4	20
MC KOY, WILLIAM OTHELLO	1967-11-13	WILMINGTON	NC	PFC	22
SCULLY, EDWARD ANTHONY	1967-11-13	WEST POINT	NY	SP4	22
CHATMAN, NATHANIEL	1967-11-13	PITTSBURGH	PA	PFC	22
BERRY, JAMES CRAIG	1967-11-13	ROYAL OAK	MI	PFC	19
DUNN, GREGORY LYNN	1967-11-13	SANTA ROSA	CA	PFC	18
EPPS, LAMONT GEORGE	1967-11-13	BALTIMORE	MD	PFC	23
COLLINS, WILLIAM ANDERSON	1967-11-18	PEMBROKE	NC	SFC	38

BAUM, DOUGLAS BRUCE	1967-11-18	LA MESA	CA	SGT	20
WILSON, HARRY CONARD II	1967-11-18	RICHBORO	PA	SP4	20
GARCIA, RAYMOND JR	1967-11-18	SAN DIEGO	CA	PFC	21
MC GHEE, RICHARD DALE	1967-11-18	YAWKEY	WV	CPL	20
RILEY, THOMAS JAY	1967-11-18	COLUMBIA HEIGHTS	MN	SP4	19
WASHINGTON, LEONARD B JR	1967-11-18	CHICAGO	IL	PFC	20
CARMICHAEL, SAMUEL LEE	1967-11-18	CHICAGO	IL	PFC	19
TORRES, IGNACIO JR	1967-11-18	LAREDO	TX	SGT	22
MAGRUDER, DOUGLAS GRAHAM	1967-11-18	CORAL GABLES	FL	1LT	24
ROBINSON, CHARLES HARVEY	1967-11-18	ELKHART	IN	CPL	20
CRABTREE, MICHAEL ANDREW	1967-11-18	PORTLAND	OR	CPT	28
DYER, JOSEPH FRANCIS JR	1967-11-18	PITTSBURGH	PA	PFC	20
WATTERS, CHARLES JOSEPH	1967-11-19	BERKELEY HEIGHTS	NJ	MAJ	40
ROSS, WILLIAM ALLEN	1967-11-19	COLUMBUS	GA	PFC	21
HUDDLESTON, THOMAS PATE	1967-11-19	NEWNAN	GA	SP4	21
HERING, MARK RICHARD	1967-11-19	NORTH TONAWANDA	NY	SP4	20
FLYNT, JAMES WILLIAM III	1967-11-19	PITTSBORO	NC	SP4	21
KROS, ROGER ALLEN	1967-11-19	LAKE VILLAGE	IN	PVT	18
SHOOP, JACK HENRY JR	1967-11-19	RURAL RIDGE	PA	SP4	19
LA VALLEE, ROBERT C JR	1967-11-19	MIDDLETOWN	RI	PFC	20
SANDERS, ROBERT JAMES	1967-11-19	PHILADELPHIA	PA	SP4	19
SMITH, LEWIS BENJAMIN	1967-11-19	CAMDEN	NY	SP4	20
STEPHENS, HARRY EDWARD	1967-11-19	RICHMOND	VA	SP4	22
WALKER, RICHARD JR	1967-11-19	CHICAGO	IL	PFC	19
GRISSETTE, PRELOW	1967-11-19	SHALLOTTE	NC	PFC	21

ADAMS, MICHAEL EDWARD	1967-11-19	GRANITE CITY	IL	SGT	19
KOONCE, JEFFREY WAYNE	1967-11-19	UNION	NJ	SGT	20
OROSZ, ANDREW JOHN	1967-11-19	NEW YORK	NY	SP4	21
COOPER, GARY ROBERT	1967-11-19	BOSWORTH	MO	SP4	21
THOMPSON, RICHARD W	1967-11-19	ATCHISON	KS	1LT	26
LESZCZYNSKI, WITHOLD JOHN	1967-11-19	NEW YORK	NY	PFC	19
BLACKWELL, ROY JAMES JR	1967-11-19	CLINTON	SC	SP4	20
CISNEROS, MARIO ALVAREZ	1967-11-19	RIVERBANK	CA	PFC	18
SPELLER, JAMES RONALD	1967-11-19	WINDSOR	NC	PFC	18
GEORGE, GERALD LEE JR	1967-11-19	COLORADO SPRINGS	CO	SP4	18
FREDERICK, JAMES CARL	1967-11-19	MARGATE	FL	SFC	26
SMITH, DONALD EUGENE	1967-11-19	COLUMBUS	GA	1LT	27
WARD, RUDOLPH NATHINAL	1967-11-19	PORSTMOUTH	VA	PFC	22
CROXDALE, JACK LEE II	1967-11-19	LAKE CHARLES	LA	SP4	18
IANDOLI, DONALD	1967-11-19	PATERSON	NJ	SGT	21
WILLIAMS, REMER	1967-11-19	RALEIGH	NC	SSGT	31
DE HERRERA, BENJAMIN DAVID	1967-11-19	COLORADO SPRINGS	CO	PFC	19
ELLIS, MICHAEL LE ROY	1967-11-19	VALINDA	CA	SP4	21
JACOBSON, KENNETH JAMES	1967-11-20	WINSLOW	WA	SP4	20
KAUFMAN, HAROLD JAMES	1967-11-20	SPRING VALLEY	NY	CPT	26
PACIOREK, ROBERT EDWARD	1967-11-20	RAVENNA	OH	SP4	20
PAYNE, ROY CHARLES JR	1967-11-20	SAGINAW	MI	SP4	20
BROWN, HARVEY LEE III	1967-11-20	ST LOUIS	MO	SP4	21
SHOMAKER, JEROME CHARLES	1967-11-20	NEWPORT BEACH	CA	1LT	25
BENZING, BRUCE MARTIN	1967-11-20	MIAMI SPRINGS	FL	PFC	24
OGEA, WALLACE LEE	1967-11-20	BOSSIER CITY	LA	SGT	22

NOTHERN, JAMES WILLIAM JR	1967-11-20	CLARENDON	AR	SP4	20
HERVAS, AARON KAMALA	1967-11-20	MOBILE	AL	SP5	22
WOOTEN, JOHN WESLEY	1967-11-20	GARTEN	WV	SSG	24
PANNELL, JOSEPH	1967-11-20	EAST ST LOUIS	IL	PFC	20
VILLARREAL, ERNESTO	1967-11-20	DETROIT	MI	PVT	19
PATTERSON, JAMES ROBERT	1967-11-20	ORLANDO	FL	PFC	19
NOAH, JOSH CAIN	1967-11-20	HUGO	OK	SGT	23
SANCHEZ, JESSE	1967-11-20	UNION CITY	CA	SP4	24
SPAIN, ERVIN	1967-11-20	CHICAGO	IL	SP4	32
HERST, WILLIAM DONALD JR	1967-11-20	EL PASO	TX	SP4	24
WOLF, JOHN ROBY	1967-11-20	RENTON	WA	PFC	22
LANGLEY, WESTON JOSEPH	1967-11-20	HOULTON	ME	SP4	19
HASTINGS, BOBBY GENE	1967-11-20	TRUMANN	AR	PSGT	34
WILLIAMS, LEMUEL TAYLOR	1967-11-20	ST LOUIS	MO	SP4	20
POWELL, STEVEN REED	1967-11-20	DANVILLE	VA	PFC	20
TYLER, LESTER	1967-11-20	NEW YORK	NY	PFC	23
RAY, WALTER DONALD	1967-11-20	BELMONT	MA	SP4	20
BLY, ROBERT TILDON	1967-11-20	TOLEDO	OH	SP4	20
YOUNG, RONALD WAYNE	1967-11-20	TULSA	OK	SP4	26
PAGE, THELBERT G	1967-11-20	CHICAGO	IL	SP4	20
GRAY, HERBERT HOOVER	1967-11-20	GRAY	GA	PFC	21
BETCHEL, DAVID BROOKS	1967-11-20	LOS ANGELES	CA	SP4	20
GALYAN, TROY ALEXANDER	1967-11-20	CONCORD	NC	SP4	20
BUSENLEHNER, RICHARD THOMAS	1967-11-20	ROWENA	TX	1LT	21
WEBB, EARL KENNON	1967-11-20	NEW ORLEANS	LA	SP4	27
TURNER, ARTHUR JR	1967-11-20	MOUNT PLEASANT	SC	SGT	20
PINN, ARNOLD	1967-11-20	JAMAICA	NY	PFC	23
THOMPSON, NATHANIEL	1967-11-20	ST LOUIS	MO	PFC	19

SMITH, JOHN WILLIAM	1967-11-20	CELINA	OH	PFC	21
STOKES, FRANK EDWARD	1967-11-20	MONTICELLO	NY	PFC	20
TAYLOR, ERNEST RAY JR	1967-11-20	LOVELAND	OH	SP5	21
GREENWALD, DENNIS	1967-11-20	SOUTHFIELD	MI	PFC	18
LOZADA, CARLOS JAMES	1967-11-20	NEW YORK	NY	PFC	21
HALL, CLARENCE	1967-11-20	NEWPORT	KY	SP4	19
CUNNINGHAM, BRUCE WAYNE	1967-11-20	DENVER	CO	SP4	19
CAMAROTE, MANFRED FRANCIS	1967-11-20	PHILADELPHIA	PA	SGT	21
ARNOLD, LOUIS GEORGE W	1967-11-20	DETROIT	MI	PFC	19
MATTINGLY, GEORGE MICHAEL	1967-11-20	OXON HILL	MD	PFC	19
GLADDEN, MICHAEL JAY	1967-11-20	ODESSA	TX	SP4	20
MABE, ROGER DALE	1967-11-20	HAYMARKET	VA	PFC	19
RICHARDS, LEONARD JEFFREY	1967-11-20	MOUNT VERNON	IL	PFC	24
FLORES-JIMENEZ, ANGEL RAMO	1967-11-20	NEW YORK	NY	PFC	20
FARLEY, JAMES CABELL	1967-11-20	COOKEVILLE	TN	PFC	19
MURREY, TRACY HENRY	1967-11-20	MILES CITY	MT	1LT	25
FERENCE, MICHAEL WILLIAM	1967-11-20	CHICAGO	IL	PFC	19
CREWS, CHARLES RICHARD	1967-11-20	STARKE	FL	PFC	19
GARCIA, JUAN MANUEL	1967-11-20	MAMMOTH	AZ	PFC	18
HAWTHORNE, WILLIAM ALLEN	1967-11-20	EUREKA	KS	PFC	20
ORTIZ, JOHN MANUEL	1967-11-20	CHICAGO	IL	PFC	21
SPENCER, HARRY HERBERT	1967-11-20	CLEVELAND	OH	PFC	19
WADE, THOMAS JOE	1967-11-20	ANTLERS	OK	PFC	24
BAUER, GREGORY CHARLES	1967-11-20	CENTRAL BRIDGE	NY	PVT	19
HAGERTY, WILLIAM THOMAS	1967-11-20	VINEYARD HAVEN	MA	SP4	21
BEST, NEAL IRA	1967-11-20	MYRTLE BEACH	SC	PFC	19

WHITTINGTON, MERREL P	1967-11-20	TOPPENISH	WA	SP4	31
CANTU, ERNESTO SOLIZ	1967-11-20	ENCINO	TX	SP4	20
KILEY, MICHAEL JAMES	1967-11-20	LONG BEACH	CA	CPT	26
CORBETT, THOMAS LOUIS	1967-11-20	HAMPTON	VA	SP4	21
SZYMANSKI, ROBERT	1967-11-20	MILWAUKEE	WI	SGT	23
D'AGOSTINO, JOHN	1967-11-20	NEW YORK	NY	PFC	21
D'ENTREMONT, LARRY AIME	1967-11-20	KITTERY POINT	ME	PFC	19
DEGEN, ROBERT PAUL	1967-11-20	VANCOUVER	WA	PFC	19
DIANDA, CASIMIRO	1967-11-20	YUMA	AZ	PFC	20
DUNBAR, JOHN MICHAEL	1967-11-20	VILLA PARK	IL	SP4	18
KLOSSEK, GERALD	1967-11-21	NEWARK	NJ	PFC	21
MICHALOPOULOS, RAYMOND WIL	1967-11-21	PAWTUCKET	RI	SP4	21
LINDGREN, ROBERT WILLIAM	1967-11-21	MINNEAPOLIS	MN	SP4	20
RIGBY, OLIS RAY	1967-11-21	HAYS	KS	SP4	19
SMITH, JESSE E	1967-11-21	AUGUSTA	GA	PFC	23
LEE, ROY RONALD	1967-11-21	DUNN	NC	SP4	20
MANUEL, ROLAND WILL	1967-11-21	ASBURY PARK	NJ	SSG	26
HINKLE, WILLIAM CECIL	1967-11-21	GRANITE CITY	IL	PFC	20
REYNOLDS, DAVID RICHARD	1967-11-21	BUFFALO	NY	PFC	18
SHARP, VALDEZ	1967-11-22	MC LEAN	TX	PFC	20
CUBIT, BILLY RAY	1967-11-22	CHICAGO	IL	PFC	18
WILLBANKS, CHARLES EDWARDS	1967-11-22	MOUNTAIN VIEW	GA	PFC	20
PONTING, JOHN L	1967-11-22	EMPORIA	KS	SFC	31
OWENS, KENNETH GRANT	1967-11-22	ORLANDO	FL	PFC	18
IMPELITHERE, ALAN JOHN	1967-11-23	LIVERPOOL	NY	PFC	20
CATES, WILLIAM LLOYD	1967-11-23	STANFIELD	AZ	MSG	34
FLADRY, LE ROY EDWARD	1967-11-23	UNION CITY	PA	SGT	21
LANTZ, PETER J	1967-11-23	ORLANDO	FL	1LT	24
MASON, RICHARD FLOYD	1967-11-23	ERWIN	NC	PFC	19

WORRELL, JAMES R	1967-11-23	FORT LAUDERDALE	FL	PFC	20
KIMBALL, RICHARD NELSON JR	1967-11-23	GRANITE CITY	IL	PFC	24
ROERINK, GARY DOYLE	1967-11-23	PONTIAC	MI	PFC	20
MAYS, THOMAS CURTHIS	1967-11-25	HAMTRAMCK	MI	SGT	20
BARNHART, CARL RAY	1967-11-25	EAST PEORIA	IL	PFC	18
GILMORE, RONALD	1967-11-27	DOZIER	AL	SGT	19
HARTMAN, JOHN WILLIAM	1967-11-30	LONG BEACH	CA	SP4	20
WATSON, WILMER	1967-11-30	SEASIDE	CA	PFC	24
MORRIS, ROBERT L	1967-12-02	COLUMBUS	OH	SGT	19
CULLEN, MARK JAMES	1967-12-08	NIAGARA FALLS	NY	PFC	19
MILLER, IVAN DEAN JR	1967-12-10	FORT WAYNE	IN	PFC	19
BURGESS, DONALD RAY	1967-12-13	TULSA	OK	PFC	20
MC CORD, MICHAEL RAYE	1967-12-13	CARMI	IL	SP4	18
HAMILTON, PAUL GEORGE JR	1967-12-13	DES MOINES	IA	PFC	21
PARSONS, RONALD ALLEN	1967-12-24	YORK	ME	PFC	23
SANDERS, FRANCIS EUGENE	1967-12-25	AUGUSTA	MI	PFC	19
ARRINGTON, JOHN ROBERT	1967-12-27	COLUMBUS	IN	PFC	19
FULLER, MICHAEL DAVID	1967-12-27	DES MOINES	IA	PVT	19
HALL, BRUCE	1967-12-27	MIDLAND	TX	SP4	19
HEGLER, MOSE JR	1967-12-27	MAGAZINE POINT	AL	PFC	19
HOLLIMAN, TED DELANE JR	1967-12-27	GREENSBORO	NC	CPL	19
KNOX, IRVILLE J	1967-12-27	STURGIS	MI	PFC	21
MINOR, MICHAEL JAMES	1967-12-27	COLUMBUA	OH	CPL	18
OWENS, BEN	1967-12-27	INDIANAPOLIS	IN	SGT	20
SCHWELLENBACH, GARY RALPH	1967-12-27	CHICO	CA	CPL	19
KLINDT, DAN THOMAS	1967-12-27	ASTORIA	OR	PFC	19
GREENWOOD, FRANCIS DAVID	1967-12-27	OXFORD	IN	PFC	19

EDDY, RICHARD NELSON	1967-12-27	BUFFALO	NY	SP4	20
ADAMS, CLARENCE MATTUE	1967-12-30	DETROIT	MI	SSG	25
CURTIN, JOHN HENRY	1968-01-02	ELMHURST	IL	1LT	24
BORNMAN, DONALD WAYNE	1968-01-05		IL	SGT	20
HEEREN, DARREL WAYNE	1968-01-07	MAYWOOD	CA	SGT	20
SCHMIDT, STEVEN WARREN	1968-01-10	ANAHEIM	CA	SGT	20
RIGGINS, BILLY G	1968-01-10	GREENSBORO	NC	SSG	39
HILL, LARRY EDWIN	1968-01-15	WEST POINT	GA	CPL	21
BIFFLE, JOE LESLIE JR	1968-01-21	GAINESVILLE	TX	SP4	19
BLOOM, LAWRENCE CLIFFORD	1968-01-26	EXETER	NH	SGT	20
JOHNSON, JIMMY LEROY JR	1968-01-26	RUTHERFORD	NC	SGT	22
FOLEY, JAMES WILLIAMS	1968-01-26	OMAHA	NE	SP4	22
FINCH, TERRY DEAN	1968-01-26	PORTLAND	OR	CPL	19
STANLEY, DENNIS RALPH	1968-01-28	CLINTWOOD	VA	SGT	19
THOMSON, STUART HAROLD	1968-01-29	MILWAUKEE	WI	SFT	30
MC KEE, JACK ROGER	1968-01-30	NEEDLES	CA	SGT	19
LOCHRIDGE, ROBERT ERIC	1968-01-30	OLYMPIA	WA	SGT	21
TIGNER, JOHN HENRY	1968-01-30	COLUMBUA	GA	SSG	20
MARTINOVSKY, MILOSLAV JOSE	1968-01-30	GERMANY	XG	SSG	35
LA ROUCHE, JAMES MICHAEL	1968-01-30	GARDEN CITY	MI	SGT	22
WALL, JIMMIE PAUL	1968-01-30	MONTICELLO	AR	CPL	24
WHITBECK, ROBERT EARL	1968-01-30	ALEXANDRIA	VA	LTC	38
BODISON, JAMES CALVIN	1968-01-30	ROUND O	SC	PFC	19
GREENE, LAWRENCE DOUGLASS	1968-01-30	FORT KNOX	KY	1LT	25
SWINNEA,1 THOMAS HENRY	1968-01-30	BEEVILLE	TX	SGT	20
WESOLOWSKI, ALVIN JOHN JR	1968-01-30	CUPERTINO	CA	PFC	20

241

FROEHLICH, NORBERT LOUIS	1968-01-30	BELFIELD	ND	CPL	20
CERVANTEZ, EDWARD EDDY	1968-01-30	CHICAGO	IL	CPL	21
ROSS, GENE AUTRY	1968-01-30	DALLAS	TX	PFC	21
SZUTZ, BRAD JOHN	1968-01-30	LOMA LINDA	CA	PFC	20
PETERS, ROBERT CHARLES	1968-01-30	ROUND LAKE	IL	CPL	20
FOOTE, PETER	1968-01-30	NORTH ADAMS	MA	SGR	20
DE PRIEST, DAVID WAYNE	1968-01-30	LYNCHBURG	VA	SP4	19
ELLIOTT, ARTHUR FLOYD	1968-01-30	SALEM	OR	PVT	19
MADRID, ERNEST	1968-01-31	MC NARY	AZ	SGR	20
SERREM, MARK MAC DONALD	1968-01-31	CARMEL	CA	1LT	23
WEBER, JOHN KNUTE	1968-02-03	ST PAUL	MN	SSG	21
WILLINGHAM, JOHN DAVID	1968-02-04	SALISBURY	MD	SP4	31
MONDRAGON, BENJAMIN ALLEN	1968-02-04	DENVER	CO	SP4	19
JARVIS, WILLIAM THOMAS	1968-02-05	SAVANNAH	GA	SP4	21
SHERMAN, VICTOR P JR	1968-02-10	NEW YORK	NY	PFC	20
PINHEIRO, JEFFREY ANTONE	1968-02-11	SOUTH DARTMOUTH	MA	SGT	20
COKER, JAMES LEE	1968-02-12	PHOENIX	AZ	PFC	20
SUTHERLAND, BOBBY COLLINS	1968-02-12	MEDDELTON	GA	SP4	20
WAGNER, RICHARD EDWARD	1968-02-12	MOSCOW	OH	SGR	22
LOPEZ-GARCIA, GEOVEL	1968-02-12	NEW YORK	NY	CPL	20
VOJIR, JAMES PAUL	1968-02-12	JACKSON HEIGHTS	NY	PFC	19
HESTER, ELVESTER JR	1968-02-13	GREENSBORO	NC	PFC	20
PORT, GARY CRAIG	1968-02-13	SAN RAFAEL	CA	PFC	19
CAMPION, EUGENE MICHAEL	1968-02-13	MINNEAPOLIS	MN	SGR	26
REIGLE, AARON HENRY	1968-02-13	HERSHEY	PA	SGT	25
DAUGHTON, JOSEPH D JR	1968-02-14	SAN LEANDRO	CA	PFC	20
PYLE, JOHN WILLIAM	1968-02-14	CHICAGO	IL	SSG	20

SCHAP, FRANK JOSEPH	1968-02-20	BALTIMORE	MD	1LT	26
OLSZEWSKI, JOHN MICHAEL	1968-02-27	PHILADELHPIA	PA	PFC	19
O'CONNOR, FREDERICK J. JR	1968-02-27	SOMERVILLE	MA	PFC	19
MINO, ROBERT E	1968-02-27	NEW YORK	NY	PFC	22
KENNEDY, RAYMOND O	1968-02-27	INDIANAPOLIS	IN	PFC	22
STEWART, SAMUEL KAY	1968-02-29	SAN DIEGO	CA	PFC	19
NAHODIL, DONALD A JR	1968-03-03	SHAMOKIN	PA	PFC	19
ORTIZ, DOMINGO	1968-03-03	NEW YORK	NY	PF	21
GARNER, JACKIE WAYNE	1968-03-03	GADSDEN	AL	PVT	19
OGLE, DAVID ROBERT	1968-03-03	LYNDON	KS	SP4	20
ROSS, CHARLES GREGORY	1968-03-03	TAYLORVILLE	IL	CPL	18
JONES, LAWRENCE EDWARD	1968-03-03	DENVER	CO	PFC	22
LATTMAN, DONALD WAYNE	1968-03-03	ST PAUL	MN	PFC	20
JUSTINIANO, VICTOR A JR	1968-03-03	NEW YORK	NY	PFC	20
DUCKER, RONALD EUGENE	1968-03-03	SPARTANBURG	SC	SSG	23
JACKSON, ROBERT EUGENE	1968-03-04	PUEBLO	CO	SP4	20
BOYKIN, PRENTIS BARNEY JR	1968-03-04	VANCOUVER	WA	PFC	20
WALKER, ROBERT HARVEY	1968-03-04	SPUR	TX	SP5	23
HALL, GARY DODDS	1968-03-04	VERNAL	UT	SP5	21
ABERNATHY, ROBERT WILLIAM	1968-03-04	ROCKVILLE	MD	SP4	20
KIDD, DONNY RAMON	1968-03-04	SIOUX FALLS	SD	PFC	38
ACHOR, TERRENCE WILLIAM	1968-03-04	WHITTIER	CA	PFC	20
FOSTER, WILLIE FRANK	1968-03-04	ANDERSON	SC	PFC	20
MASON, WILLIAM PAUL	1968-03-04	HORSHAM	PA	PFC	20
ROMAN, JEREMIAS	1968-03-04	NEW YORK	NY	PFC	19
RIOS, ROBERTO PENA	1968-03-04	SAN ANGELO	TX	PVT	18
KIOVUPALO, ROBERT W JR	1968-03-04	DETROIT	MI	PFC	19
DEL CAMP, ADRIAN LEROY	1968-03-04	MILWAUKEE	WI	MAJ	34
VOGEL, GARRITY	1968-03-06	CHASKA	MN	PFC	26

BEALL, CHARLES RICHARD	1968-03-06	DE BARY	FL	SP4	20
BROWN, WARREN GENE	1968-03-06	DETROIT	MI	PFC	20
JATICH, GARRY LEE	1968-03-06	AKRON	OH	SP4	19
SCHUH, DAVID MICHAEL	1968-03-06	ELCHO	WI	SGT	20
ROGAN, JAMES PAUL	1968-03-08	SALT LAKE CITY	UT	MAJ	28
SULLIVAN, JOHN JOSEPH	1968-03-08	WATERTOWN	MA	PFC	19
MULLER, HAROLD BRADLEY	1968-03-13	MC KINLEYVILLE	CA	SGT	21
MOORE, MICHAEL KEITH	1968-03-13	PHILADELPHIA	PA	SSG	20
WEBB, TERRY EMERSON	1968-03-13	GROVE CITY	OH	CPL	20
BIERNACKI, JAMES RICHAD	1968-03-14	CHULA VISTA	CA	SGT	20
POPE, THOMAS ROBERT	1968-03-14	LA MIRADA	CA	PFC	20
CHESTER, HENRY J JR	1968-03-14	DETROIT	MI	PFC	19
GUNTHER, JOHN JACOB	1968-03-14	MELBOURNE	FL	SGT	20
FERGUSON, MICHAUEL DON	1968-03-14	RIVERSIDE	CA	SP4	21
YOUNG, ERNEST HAROLD III	1968-03-14	DOWNEY	CA	PFC	20
HARRISON, JIMMIE RAY	1968-03-14	DE KALB	IL	MS	32
LUCERO, PATRICK ARNOLD	1968-03-14	PUEBLO	CO	SP4	19
ELLIS, HARRY JOSEPH III	1968-03-14	ATCO	NJ	SGT	21
MIDDLETON, STEVEN ALFRED	1968-03-15	ST STEPHEN	SC	SGT	19
MERRILL, WELDON BRNARDO	1968-03-16	PENROSE	NC	SFC	26
JOHNSON, DAVID ARTHUR	1968-03-16	YUMA	AZ	SGT	19
WHEELER, MICHEL T	1968-03-16	EMMETT	ID	CPL	19
ZIMMERMAN, TERRY	1968-03-16	NEW YORK	NY	SGT	19
BERNHART, CARL HANS	1968-03-16	RICHMOND	OH	CPL	20
JOHNSON, HENRY L	1968-03-16	ROCKFORD	IL	CPL	28
SMITH, HOWARD BRUCE	1968-03-16	NEW CANAAN	CT	PFC	18
DICKSON, MARK LANE	1968-03-16	ST CLAIR SHORES	MI	SP4	19
GROOMS, RICHARD J	1968-03-17	ATLANTA	GA	SP4	24
BURR, DANIEL LEE	1968-03-17	MILWAUKEE	WI	SGT	24

BLACKSHEAR, JAMES GUY	1968-03-17	ATLANTA	GA	SP4	19
TREMBLAY, PATRICK JOSEPH	1968-03-17	CONESUS	NY	PFC	18
FERA, JOHN ANTHONY	1968-03-18	DANVERS	MA	1LT	23
COFRAN, WILLIAM EARL	1968-03-18	HOMEWOOD	IL	SGT	20
MABE, TOMMY DARRELL	1968-03-18	WINSTON-SALEM	NC	SGT	18
MERCHANT, CARL LEE	1968-03-18	CORINTH	NY	SGT	24
WUSTERBARTH, CLINTON CARL	1968-03-18	MANITOWOC	WI	CPL	20
BARR, JAMES DAVID	1968-03-18	CARTHAGE	NC	CPL	19
SPEIGHT, FRANKLIN ELLIOTT	1968-03-18	CURRITUCK	NC	2LT	23
JONES, LARRY WILLIAM	1968-03-20	GREENSBORO	NC	CPT	25
LUNA, ROBERT	1968-03-22	ALAMEDA	CA	SGT	21
MANEY, RALPH WARREN	1968-03-22	PEABODY	MA	SGT	19
MURRAY, THOMAS J	1968-03-22	NEW YORK	NY	SP4	22
GEARHART, DONALD LEE	1968-03-24	PITTSBURGH	PA	SSG	28
WRIGHT, SYLVESTER JR	1968-03-26	JEANERETTE	LA	PFC	19
WANAMAKER, JOHNNY WAYNE	1968-03-26	NASHVILLE	TN	CPL	19
WENRICK, PHILIP BRUCE	1968-03-29	COLUMBUS	GA	PFC	20
AUDILET, FRANKLIN DELANO	1968-04-01	YORKTOWN	TX	WO	31
PHILYAW, LAWRENCE EDWARD	1968-04-02	BOWDENS	NC	SSG	25
BONNEY, JOHN CLAIR	1968-04-03	VANDERCOOK LAKE	MI	CPL	19
HUGHES, DENNIS FOX	1968-04-10	HERRIN	IL	PFC	20
ROBERTS, CLAUDE	1968-04-11	DELRAY BEACH	FL	PFC	20
JOLES, RICHARD WADE	1968-04-12	NEW ORLEANS	LA	SP5	21
PARLIAMENT, KIM RANDLE	1968-04-15	LIBERTY	IN	CPL	19
WHITE, ARNOLD SYLVANUS	1968-04-15	PHILADELPHIA	PA	CPL	18
GASKINS, WILBUR CORNELL	1968-04-18	WILSON	NC	PFC	20
ULMAN, EDWARD DELBERT	1968-04-20	FLINT	MI	CPL	19

GLIDDEN, ROBERT WAYNE	1968-04-20	BEMIDJI	MN	PFC	19
NULL, RICKY LEE	1968-04-20	LEMOYNE	PA	PFC	19
GUTRICK, DONALD MAURICE	1968-04-24	NANJEMOY	MD	CPL	20
BERRY, DAVID JOE	1968-04-28	BELLFLOWER	CA	SP4	21
STRICKLIN, THOMAS GRADY	1968-04-28	MINNEAPOLIS	MN	PFC	18
D'AGOSTINO, JOHN R JR	1968-04-30	GREEN BAY	WI	SGT	21
HARLAND, WAYNE LYNN	1968-05-01	TEXARKANA	TX	SGT	20
LANGHAM, HOLLAND IRWIN	1968-05-03	TYLER	TX	CPL	18
MOBLEY, SUTTON JR	1968-05-04	WILMINGTON	NC	SP4	19
MORAN, JOHN WILLIAM	1968-05-04	PITTSBURGH	PA	CPL	20
DURHAM, JOHN MELVIN	1968-05-04	GRAND LEDGE	MI	SSG	20
MOORE, JIMMY RAY	1968-05-04	SAN FRANCISCO	CA	CPL	21
BACKES, BRUCE RICHARD	1968-05-05	TITUSBILLE	NJ	SP4	21
FERGUSON, JAMES DONAHUE	1968-05-05	WEST PLAINS	MO	SGT	20
HARBISON, SHERRON EVERETT	1968-05-05	FLINT	MI	SGT	21
ROOD, CRAIG ALLEN	1968-05-05	MINNEAPOLIS	MN	SP4	20
WEBB, FRANK WRIGHT	1968-05-05	KENBRIDGE	VA	1LT	21
HINTON, DENNIS EDWARD	1968-05-05	ENGLEWOOD	CO	1LT	24
STEPHENSON, DONALD RAY	1968-05-05	SHELBYVILLE	TN	SP4	20
ALLEN, ROBERT SAMUEL	1968-05-05	NORTH BERGEN	NJ	CPL	20
WELLS, ROBERT SAMUEL	1968-05-05	LITTLE ROCK	AR	SP4	20
LOWE, DONALD EVERETT	1968-05-05	TACOMA	WA	CPL	21
HILLMAN, RONALD ARWED	1968-05-05	TEXAS CITY	TX	CPL	20
ROBINSON, FRANCIS JOSEPH	1968-05-05	NEW ORLEANS	LA	SGT	19
TABOR, BRUCE WAYNE	1968-05-05	AURORA	CO	PFC	18
POFF, ELBERT DARRELL	1968-05-05	MULLENS	WV	SP4	19
LESKA, ROBERT JOHN	1968-05-05	TRUMBULL	CT	SGT	20
HENNING, ARTHUR ROBERT	1968-05-05	LAKE TOMAHAWK	WI	CPL	18

GREEN, RICHARD AL	1968-05-05	CHICAGO	IL	PFC	18
DENNISON, CORTLAND ELLIS	1968-05-05	CAE CITY	KY	CPL	20
DULAC, MALCOLM CYRIL	1968-05-05	DEXTER	ME	1SG	36
CRANDALL, RODNEY ALLEN	1968-05-06	DETROIT	MI	SP4	21
BULLARD, KARL LEE	1968-05-06	MIAMI	FL	1LT	20
STEWART, LONNY LAWRENCE	1968-05-06	NORWALK	CA	SGT	21
MUNDY, ROBERT HAL	1968-05-06	ANNISTON	AL	SP4	22
BRISCOE, LARRY	1968-05-06	DENVER	CO	SGT	21
CROCKETT, FREDDIE ISIASH	1968-05-06	HOPEWELL	VA	PFC	20
CLINGERMAN, JOSEPH ALLAN	1968-05-06	YOUNGSTOWN	OH	PFC	19
KELLY, LARRY LEE	1968-05-06	HAYWARD	CA	PFC	20
HUMPHREY, VICTOR JAMES	1968-05-06	BAYTOWN	TX	PFC	20
MC GINTY, LAWRENCE MICHAEL	1968-05-06	PHILADELPHIA	PA	PFC	19
FOX, THOMAS AMISS	1968-05-06	RICHMOND	VA	CPL	18
ALDRICH, LAWRNECE LEE	1968-05-06	FORT WORTH	TX	SP4	20
WAIDE, DONALD GILES	1968-05-07	CLAYTON	NM	SGT	22
GEROME, MICHAEL ANTHONY	1968-05-07	RESEDA	CA	SGT	21
CANAPP, GARY EDWARD	1968-05-08	BALTIMORE	MD	CPL	19
BRENKER, ECKHARD GERHARD	1968-05-08	YORK	PA	CPL	21
DARDEN, PAUL L JR	1968-05-08	SNOW HILL	NC	SGT	20
SPROULE, WILLIAM C JR	1968-05-10	FOLCROFT	PA	1LT	23
ZIMMERMAN, ROGER	1968-05-10	DEERFIELD	IL	SSG	24
GRAY, WARREN	1968-05-10	INGLEWOOD	CA	SGT	21
OWENS, ROBERT LEE	1968-05-10	BEAUFORT	SC	SGT	22
BROWN, JAMES SCOTT	1968-05-10	PRESCOTT	AZ	CPL	19
RYLEE, JAMES SIDNEY	1968-05-11	GLENMOORE	PA	SP5	27
HONEYCUTT, DONALD EUGENE	1968-05-11	CADILLAC	MI	SGT	25

GOOCH, CALVIN LIONEL	1968-05-11	BURKEVILLE	TX	CPL	20
BRONCZYK, LAWRENCE JOSEPH	1968-05-12	GILBERT	MN	SGT	19
MANSFIELD, PATRICK LEROY	1968-05-12	TUCSON	AZ	CPL	18
BARNES, ALLEN ROY	1968-05-13	AGUILA	AZ	SP4	21
ORTEGA, ANIBAL JR	1968-05-15	NEW YORK	NY	SGT	20
FOY, THOMAS WALTER	1968-05-15	BALTIMORE	MD	CPT	23
QUINN, STEPHEN WAYNE	1968-05-17	VIRGINIA BEACH	VA	CPL	19
FIELDS, JULIAN THOMAS	1968-05-17	PIKEVILLE	KY	SGT	21
HERRERA, FRANK G	1968-05-17	MESA	AZ	SGT	19
REEVES, MICHAEL DAVIS	1968-05-20	ABSECON	NJ	CPL	20
KOWALESKI, GREGORY STANLEY	1968-05-20	RIVERSIDE	NJ	GT	21
MITCHELL, LARRY LEON	1968-05-20	VALDOSTA	GA	SP4	19
WOOD, DONALD CHARLES	1968-05-20	PHILADELPHIA	PA	PFC	18
PASCAL, IVAN KIMOKEO	1968-05-23	HONOLULU	HI	PFC	20
LEVINGS, JAMES M	1968-05-23	NEW TOWN	ND	SGT	19
FOX, GARY GUANE	1968-05-24	SHERIDAN	WY	CPL	18
HOSKINS, DANNY	1968-05-25	TRENTON	OH	CPL	25
GOUGH, LINWOOD	1968-05-25	PHILADELPHIA	PA	CPL	24
BRICE, WILLIAM FRANCIS JR	1968-05-27	DOVER	NJ	SGT	23
STEELE, PATRICK MATTHEW	1968-05-27	ROSEVILLE	MI	CPL	19
BOYD, SAM HENRY	1968-05-28	FORT MILL	SC	CPL	20
KAAKIMAKA, ALGERNON P JR	1968-06-01	HONOLULU	HI	SGT	20
POE, JESSIE GERALD	1968-06-02	KINGSTON	IL	SGT	19
RAMON, DENNIS MICHAEL	1968-06-02	SANDUSKY	OH	SP4	19
VANDEVENDER, JOSEPH	1968-06-02	NEWPORT	RI	CPL	21
STROHM, TIMOTHY LAWRENCE	1968-06-02	ENTRPRISE	OR	PFC	20
MURRAY, MARVIN WINSTON	1968-06-03	NEW YORK	NY	CPL	21
NASTOR, TONY VALDEZ	1968-06-05	SAN JOSE	CA	CPL	21

HOOKS, DAYTON JOSEPH	1968-06-07	MULLINS	SC	SGT	19
ROSE, LAWRENCE OLIVER	1968-06-10	NEW YORK	NY	PFC	20
SOLANO, PORFIRIO SAM	1968-06-13	AVONDALE	CO	SSG	21
WOOLEY, HENRY EUGENE	1968-06-13	BANKS	AR	SGT	21
FERGUSON, JERRY ROGER	1968-06-13	HARRIMAN	TN	SGT	24
WHITE, LEONARD RAY	1968-06-13	WATSONVILLE	CA	CPL	21
BERRY, CHARLIE E	1968-06-17	ATLANTA	GA	SGT	21
TOWNSEND, ROOSEVELT	1968-06-17	MATHEWS	AL	CPL	24
WEDGEWORTH, WILLIAM THOMAS	1968-06-17	CLEVELAND	OH	CPL	24
FUJIMOTO, DONALD SHUICHI	1968-06-17	STOCKTON	CA	SGT	22
KENNEDY, MICHAEL JOSEPH	1968-06-17	FORT LAUDERDALE	FL	PFC	19
BEDSOLE, CHARLES ARTHUR	1968-06-17	SEVERNA PARK	MD	1LT	20
STROUD, ALLEN SHEFFIELD	1968-06-17	GARNER	NC	CPL	20
SISLER, WILLIAM DOUGLAS	1968-06-19	MORGANTOWN	WV	SGT	21
BELL, DAVID THOMAS	1968-06-20	WILLOUGHBY	OH	CPL	19
SMITH, DAVID II	1968-06-23	ELIZABETH TOWN	NC	SP4	20
WALKER, MICHAEL EARL	1968-06-27	FREDERICKS BURG	OH	CPL	19
SMITH, LARRY HAYS	1968-06-29	JACKSON	MS	CPL	23
TREMBLAY, ALAIN JOSEPH	1968-07-07	HEMPSTEAD	NY	SFC	32
STROUSE, GARY LEE	1968-07-10	VESTAL	NY	SGT	21
TILLOTSON, ROBERT VIRTUS	1968-07-10	HELENA	MT	PFC	19
TREVARTON, LARRY GEORGE	1968-07-10	LONGMONT	CO	PFC	20
LUKES, THOMAS BURTON	1968-07-13	PONTIAC	MI	SGT	20
PILLOW, RONALD EDWARD	1968-07-13	HUGHES	AR	CPL	20
TAYLOR, RICHARD BERRY	1968-07-14	MIDWAY PARK	NC	PFC	19
LARSEN, MICHAEL CONRAD	1968-07-19	CEDAR RIVER	MI	CPL	18
STELL, JAMES ARTHUR	1968-07-20	POINT MARION	PA	CPL	20

ORTIZ-BURGOS, JOSE ALBERTO	1968-07-23	WEST NEW YORK	NJ	CPL	19
WITZEL, ROBERT CHARLES	1968-07-23	SPRING VALLEY	NY	CPL	21
FRANCKOWIAK, JOSEPH RALPH	1968-07-27	HUNTINGTON PARK	CA	CPL	24
GRAVES, JERRY LEE	1968-07-28	MEXICO	MO	CPL	21
SACK, GERALD DUANE	1968-07-30	MANKATO	MN	CPL	19
MURRAY, DARNELL PATRICK	1968-08-04	ANNISTON	AL	SSG	23
TYLER, LARRY JEROME	1968-08-08	GALVESTON	TX	SGT	20
PORTIS, ANTHONY JEROME	1968-08-15	LAUREL	MS	CPL	19
NEAL, WILBERT HOYT JR	1968-08-17	NASHVILLE	TN	SGT	19
RUSSELL, PETER LOWELL	1968-08-22	PORT ARTHUR	TX	SGT	24
BALES, CHARLES ROBERT	1968-08-22	BAXLEY	GA	SP4	19
CARLSON, JAMES BLAIN	1968-08-22	LAKEVIEW	OR	SSG	20
GETTER, WAYDELL	1968-08-22	LUFKIN	TX	SSG	22
MEARS, PETER JOSEPH JR	1968-08-22	BRAINTREE	MA	CPL	19
GARCIA, RAMON	1968-08-23	ALBUQUERQUE	NM	SSG	21
WHITLEY, FREDDIE LEE	1968-08-23	ST LOUIS	MO	CPL	19
GUTIERREZ, ALBERT R JR	1968-08-24	SAN ANTONIO	TX	PFC	21
ABERNATHY, DANIEL OWEN	1968-08-24	BURLINGTON	NJ	1LT	21
FUNSTON, JOSEPH ERNEST	1968-08-25	GALENA	IL	CPL	19
MULVEY, FRANCIS TRAINOR	1968-08-25	FENNIMORE	WI	CPL	23
KRYSKE, LEO NEA	1968-08-25	MISHAWAKA	IN	SFC	36
WALKER, THOMAS JAMES	1968-08-25	GASTONIA	NC	CPL	20
RICHARDSON JIMMIE JENKINS	1968-08-27	FLORENCE	SC	CPL	18
HASKETT, EDWARD O DAY	1968-08-30	ST PETERSBURG	FL	PVT	19
JAWOROWICZ, LARENCE FRANK	1968-09-05	ST PERERSBURG	FL	PVT	20
PARKER, HERMAN JR	1968-09-05	GRAY SUMMIT	MO	PFC	18
BROWN, DAVID CARLTON	1968-09-07	FORT MONROE	VA	CPT	24
GRISMER, EDGAR JOSEPH	1968-09-07	LOUISVILLE	KY	SSG	19
WINTERS, STEVEN ANDREW	1968-09-07	TULSA	OK	CPL	20

KARR, DAVID RAY	1968-09-07	QUITMAN	MO	SFC	25
GILRAY, ROBERT BRUCE JR	1968-09-07	CHATHAM	NJ	2LT	23
EVANS, CECIL VAUGHN	1968-09-07	SALISBURY	MD	SSG	20
FRAZER, KENNETH CHARLES	1968-09-09	CHESTER	IL	SGT	22
ELLIOTT, ROBRT THOMAS III	1968-09-09	ANCHORAGE	AK	1LT	23
HUFFMAN, DAVID KEITH	1968-09-11	SPEEDWAY	IN	SGT	22
HUSTEAD, TERENCE MICHAEL	1968-09-13	MORAGA	CA	SGT	25
WELCH, RICHARD WILLIAM	1968-09-13	WILMINGTON	MA	PFC	18
BENZ, ROBERT JOSEPH	1968-09-13	SYRACUSE	NY	SP4	22
MORAN, LONZO JOSEPH JR	1968-09-13	LAWTON	OK	PFC	20
LEWIS, GARY LEE	1968-09-13	FORT MADISON	IA	PVT	22
UNDERWOOD, HARRY WILLIAM	1968-09-14	ST LOUIS	MO	PVT	19
OWENS, CHARLES EDWARD	1968-09-17	GASTONIA	NC	CPL	19
PAULK, ELIAS JOHNSON	1968-09-19	OCALA	FL	SSG	20
HULSLANDER, ROSS THOMAS	1968-09-19	GAINESVILLE	FL	CPL	20
SCHULTZ, JAMES CHESTER	1968-09-19	CHICAGO	IL	CPL	19
BROCK, THOMAS DEAN	1968-09-23	GREENVILLE	SC	SGT	20
CARTER, GREGORY	1968-09-23	COLUMBUS	OH	SGT	21
HARING, KARL RICHARD	1968-09-24	AURORA	IL	SGT	19
WPLFF, RICHARD GLEN	1968-09-24	NEWARK	NJ	SP4	20
HACEK, JAMES DAVID	1968-09-26	CRYSTAL LAKE	IL	CPL	20
TOBEY, MICHAEL JAMES	1968-09-26	GREENFIELD	MA	SGT	19
LESANDO, NICHOLAS PETER JR	1968-09-26	GREENWOOD	NY	CPL	21
FILIPPELLI, ALFRED ANDREW	1968-09-26	WOODSIDE	NY	CPL	20
REEDER, PHILIP DALLAM	1968-09-27	BEAUMONT	TX	PFC	19
WEBB, VIRGIL JUNIOR	1968-09-27	MARYSVILLE	OH	CPL	26
LAWTON, EDWARD LESTER	1968-09-27	THERMOPOLIS	WY	CPL	19
MASON, CHARLES JOSEPH L	1968-09-27	WASHINGTON	DC	PVT	20

251

HAMM, DONALD CURTIS	1968-10-09	MOBILE	AL	SGT	20
STEWART, GREGORY WILLIAM	1968-10-09	TUCSON	AZ	CPL	23
WIEST, JOHN ROBIN	1968-10-12	BILLINGS	MT	CPT	28
VANDERHOFF, GEORGE A JR	1968-10-16	OAK RIDGE	NJ	CPL	19
PORTER, TIMOTHY MICHAEL	1968-10-24	PITTSBURGH	PA	1LT	20
RUSSELL, RONNIE LEN	1968-10-28	STONE PARK	IL	PFC	18
COUNIHAN, MICHAEL BRENDAN	1968-11-01	HYDE PARK	MA	SGT	22
NICHOLS, PHILIP LARRY	1968-11-02	CLAY	WV	2LT	24
MANN, CHARLES CLIFTON JR	1968-11-05	MALVERN	AR	SGT	20
GREENE, LLOYD ROLLAND	1968-11-05	ST LOUIS	MO	PVT	19
SANTIAGO, TIMOTEO MUNOZ	1968-11-05	SAN BENITO	TX	CPL	21
SUGGS, JOHN FENTON JR	1968-11-05	FARMINGTON	MO	PFC	23
BURDETT, LANNY JOE	1968-11-06	BALTIMORE	MD	SGT	21
FYALL, VERNON ROBERT	1968-11-06	PORT ROYAL	SC	CPL	19
THOMAS, ALLEN WALKER	1968-11-08	SAN MARCOS	TX	CPL	20
RABEL, LASZIO	1968-11-13	MINNEAPOLIS	MN	SSG	29
MORRIS, THOMAS WE	1968-11-13	HAYWARD	CA	CPL	20
KIMBLE, EDDIE CLAUDE	1968-11-16	MCDONOUGH	GA	SGT	20
ROWLAND, GEORGE CLAYTON JR	1968-11-17	OWENSBORO	KY	1SG	31
HAVEKM RUCGARD TGINAS	1968-11-17	ATWATER	CA	SGT	19
MAY, ROY EDWARD	1968-11-17	SACRAMENTO	CA	SGT	19
ROCK, GERALD FRANCIS	1968-11-17	GRAND RAPIDS	MI	CPL	19
REEVES, RAYMOND STANLEY JR	1968-11-19	ST PAUL	MN	SGT	21
DESROCHERS, ROBERT ALAN	1968-11-19	DARTMOUTH	MA	SP4	20
WASILOW, JOHN STEPHEN	1968-11-24	MYRTLE BEACH	SC	CPL	19
RINEHART, JOSEPH LESTER	1968-12-02	WASHINGTON	DC	CPL	20
HARASON, JOHN EDGAR	1968-12-02	PHILLIPSBURG	NJ	CPL	19
PEGGS, ALBERT LEE	1968-12-04	CHICAGO	IL	CPL	23

FOX, ROBERT CHARLES	1968-12-05	ORANGE CITY	FL	CPT	29
MOLTON, KENNETH WAYNE	1968-12-07	BIRMINGHAM	AL	CPL	20
LANGLER, STEPHEN DOUGLAS	1968-12-11	MUSKEGON	MI	SP5	19
WALKER, WILLIE C	1968-12-12	TRENTON	NC	CPL	20
WARNER, GARY ALLEN	1968-12-14	JERRY CITY	OH	PFC	20
WISSELL, LAWRENCE JAMES	1968-12-21	HEBRON	IL	CPT	23
FORKUM, GARRY MICHAEL	1968-12-22	INGLEWOOD	TN	SGT	19
HAYES, THOMAS	1968-12-27	SHIPROCK	NM	SGT	21
BYRD, BILLIE	1968-12-29	FAYETTEVILLE	NC	SGT	20
BROWN, WILLIAM LEROY	1968-12-29	PHILADELPHIA	PA	PFC	19
MORRISSEY, JAMES JOSEPH	1968-12-29	PHILADELPHIA	PA	CPL	20
CILLINS, ELTON BRADLEY	1968-12-30	FORT WAYNE	IN	CPL	20
WHITE, STEPHEN O MEARA	1968-12-30	CHICAGO	IL	SGT	21
TUTTLE, KENNETH ALLEN	1968-12-31	MARTINS FERRY	OH	CPL	19
GOLD, ERIC STUART	1969-01-05	CHARLOTTE	NC	SGT	19
PACK, ROBERT VAN	1969-01-07	DUNCAN	OK	CPT	24
NANCE, SHIRL BRAD	1969-01-07	SALT LAKE CITY	UT	SSG	20
DAVIS, CHARLIE	1969-01-07	WINSTON SALEM	NC	CPL	19
OWENS, WILBERT	1969-01-12	CLEVELAND	OH	PVT	20
KELLY, JAMES MICHAEL	1969-01-12	OWINGS MILLS	MD	SGT	19
ROUNTREE, GLEN EVERETT	1969-01-13	WILLIAMSBURG	KY	SSG	27
BAILEY, SCOTT JAY	1969-01-15	SALT LAKE CITY	UT	SGT	19
CHENOWETH, AUSTIN RAY	1969-01-15	DOVE CREEK	CO	CPL	21
AYERS, JOHNNIE MARVIN	1969-01-17	ELKVIEW	WV	SP5	19
HICKS, FRANK EDWARD	1969-01-19	POMONA	CA	SGT	18
BROWN, LARRY	1969-01-20	BALDWIN	FL	SP4	23
TUCKER, GREGORY CHARLES	1969-01-24	SANTA CLARA	CA	CPL	20
JORDAN, PAUL ROBERT	1969-01-24	SACRAMENTO	CA	SGT	21
DEERINWATER, BRUCE EDWARD	1969-01-25	MC ALESTER	OK	SSG	21
BRADFORD, SHERMAN DUANE	1969-01-26	ARLETA	CA	SGT	19

O'NEAL, JERRY LEE	1969-01-26	FLINT	MI	CPL	20
EVANS, WILLARD JAMES	1969-01-26	TOLEDO	OH	SGT	20
CULWELL, JIMMY LEE	1969-01-29	LUBBOCK	TX	SGT	19
RUSH, JOSEPH BRADLEY	1969-01-31	DUNN LORING	VA	SGT	19
LAMB, EDWARD ALAN	1969-01-31	DUNDALK	MD	SP4	20
RAMIREZ, HILDEFONSO M	1969-01-31	WATSONVILLE	CA	CPL	26
REBITS, JOHN RAYMOND	1969-02-03	BERKLEY	MI	SGT	21
PARKER, DAVID WAYNE	1969-02-06	STONE MOUNTAIN	GA	SGT	21
SMITH, JAMES ROBERT	1969-02-07	LONG ISLAND	NY	CPL	20
CUMBO, LINWOOD RAY	1969-02-07	JACKSON	NC	PFC	20
DAVENPORT, ROBERT MALCUM	1969-02-07	MANTECA	CA	SGT	23
GATES, RICHARD PALMER	1969-02-13	JOHNSTOWN	NY	SP4	25
RIVERA-GARCIA, WILLIAM	1969-02-15	NEW YORK	NY	SGT	22
VENABLE, ELTON RAY	1969-02-19	HOLDENVILLE	OK	SGT	20
LAUREANO-LOPEZ, ISMAEL	1969-02-21	NEW YORK	NY	SP4	23
PIERCE, JOSEPH HOWARD JR	1969-02-22	JACKSONVILLE	FL	SGT	20
WHITE, JAMES LEE	1969-02-23	NEW YORK	NY	PVT	21
MC QUINN, BYRON DEAN	1969-02-24	COUNCIL BLUFFS	IA	CPL	19
HOLLAND, RUSSELL JAMES	1969-02-25	CLAYTON	NM	CPL	20
OLIPHANT, JOSEPH B JR	1969-02-25	VENTNOR CITY	NJ	PFC	20
BATCHELOR, MARTIN T JR	1969-02-25	BETHEL	NC	SGT	20
LANCTOT, RICHARD LOUIS	1969-02-25	PROVIDENCE	RI	SGT	19
THOMAS, DAVID EUGENE	1969-02-25	MABLETON	GA	CPL	20
ANDREWS, ARTHUR LEE	1969-02-25	SOPCHOPPY	FL	SSG	22
BARTLETT, ARTHUR WAYNE SR	1969-02-25	DALLAS	TX	SFC	34
MARQUEZ, GERALDO	1969-02-28	LAVEEN	AZ	SGT	20
BARNES, MARVIN DONALD	1969-02-28	ALTURAS	CA	SSG	25
WALTERS, JOHN EDMOND	1969-03-02	PARSONS	KS	CPL	19
CRAIG, WILLIAM THOMAS JR	1969-03-08	BATTLE CREEK	MI	SSG	22

WILSON, RUDOLPH	1969-03-09	AMSTERDAM	GA	PVT	23
PANGELINAN, GREGORIO L	1969-03-09	MONGMONG	GU	CPL	25
DOSECK, RICHARD ALLEN	1969-03-10	ST MARYS	OH	PFC	18
PEARSALL, RICHARD MARK	1969-03-16	PONTIAC	MI	SGT	20
SMITH, LARRY DEAN	1969-03-20	RINGGOLD	GA	SSG	30
KAWAMURA, TERRY TERUO	1969-03-20	WAHIAWA	HI	CPL	19
KOCK, EUGENE JOHN GEORGE	1969-03-22	BREDA	IA	SGT	20
PELLETIER, RICHARD WILLIAM	1969-03-24	GREENVILLE	NH	SSG	19
WELLS, ROBERT OLIVER	1969-03-36	KILEEN	TX	SGT	19
LINDLEY, BOBBY PAT	1969-03-36	HOUSTON	TX	PFC	21
GREEN, WILLIE FRANK	1969-03-36	RIVERVIEW	FL	CPL	21
WILLIAMSON, WILLIAM CURTIS	1969-03-30	CENTRAL ISLIP	NY	CPL	21
GRIFFIS, MICHAEL DANIEL	1969-04-07	PHILADELPHIA	PA	SP4	20
KELLEY, LARRY MILTON	1969-04-07	BLYTHEVILLE	AR	SGT	20
MITCHELL, THOMAS VICTOR	1969-04-07	PITTSBURGH	PA	SGT	21
BIRD, KENNETH ROBERT	1969-04-07	MONROVIA	CA	SGT	19
GRAY, JOHN TERRY	1969-04-07	ELLISVILLE	MS	SP4	20
PYLE, LARRY GENE	1969-04-07	FORT WORTH	TX	CPL	20
COCHRAN, ROBERT MC LAIN JR	1969-04-07	SARASOTA	FL	SP4	19
BEERS, JACK BLAINE	1969-04-07	CLARKSVILLE	TN	SFC	34
GODOY, PETER JR	1969-04-07	LOS ANGELES	CA	PFC	20
DEAL, FLOYD ANDREW	1969-04-07	GLOBE	AZ	SGT	18
DYE, TIMOTHY ELDEN	1969-04-07	MARION	OH	SP4	20
JONES, MARYUS NAPOLEON	1969-04-12	LACKEY	VA	SFC	33
PANARESE, ROLAND JOHN	1969-04-19	JACKSONVILLE	NC	SP4	22
COOKE, LARRY HOUSTON	1969-04-19	CASTRO VALLEY	CA	SSG	21
LONGORIA, JOE GILBERT	1969-04-19	SAN ANTONIO	TX	SGT	19
HANNON, RICHARD LAMAR	1969-04-19	ROCK HILL	SC	CPL	22
BRADLEY, ROBERT RICHARD	1969-04-19	MOSES LAKE	WA	PVT	20

BOTTOMS, HAROLD GENE	1969-04-19	SPRINGFIELD	IL	SGT	20
THOMAS, CHARLES	1969-04-19	TAMPA	FL	SP4	20
KOEFOD, RODGER MAGNUS	1969-04-27	MOSCOW	ID	CPL	20
CARTER, WALTER CORBIN	1969-04-27	REISTERSTOWN	MD	SP4	23
WELSH, DANIEL	1969-04-28	CARTHAGE	MS	SGT	19
MALONE, HERBERT LEE	1969-04-28	CARTHAGE	MS	SGT	19
LISBON, JOHNNY	1969-05-01	ELLIOTT	SC	SSG	28
JONES, PAUL	1969-05-03	FORT PIERCE	FL	SP4	20
WRIGHT, GARY WAYNE	1969-05-03	HAYES	VA	SP4	18
ELLIS, JAMES MARION	1969-05-05	HONEA PATH	SC	SGT	20
KLANIECKI, EDWARD MATTHEW	1969-05-09	FANWOOD	NJ	SP4	20
SANDERS, DONALD ROBERT JR	1069-05-10	DAYTON	OH	SSG	23
MYERS, R C	1969-05-11	JACKSON	MS	SGT	23
BELL, ARTHUR FREDERICK	1969-05-12	GREENVILLE	MS	CPL	23
LOVE, JOHN ARTHUR	1969-05-13	LIBRAL	KS	SGT	20
DICKERSON, WILLIAM CLINT	1969-05-13	WILLCOX	AZ	SSG	23
WADDLE, SAMMIE WAYNE	1969-05-14	BREMEN	AL	SGT	25
WINTERS, WILLIAM JOHN	1969-05-14	BOONVILLE	NY	SSG	23
YAZZIE, DAN	1969-05-15	CONTINENTAL DIVIDE	NM	SP4	20
VALENCIA, AMADO ACOSTA	1969-05-15	AUSTIN	TX	SP4	24
ROBSON, TIMOTHY FRANCIS	1969-05-20	GREEN BAY	WI	CPL	21
BARTH, THOMAS FREDERICK	1969-05-20	LAKEWOOD	CA	CPL	18
SWANSTROM, DOUGLAS GAYLORD	1969-05-21	ELLINGTON	NV	SSG	21
MARTINEZ, ENRIQUE	1969-05-22	EL PASO	TX	CPL	20
COOKE, CALVIN EDWARD	1969-05-22	PETERSBURG	VA	CPL	19
SIGNOLTZ, ROBERT H JR	1969-05-26	NORTH SPRINGFIELD	VA	CPT	23
JANKE, KEITH BRIAN	1969-05-28	ASHLAND	WI	SSG	26
TAYLOR, CLARENCW	1969-05-28	GREENVILLE	AL	CPL	25

GRUBB, STEVE FREEMAN	1969-05-28	FABER	VA	CPL	22
HAMILTON, VIRGIL VERN	1969-05-30	BROOKSVILLE	FL	SGT	20
COLLINS, JEROE LISTON	1969-05-30	MAGNOLIA SPRINGS	AL	CPL	21
BECKER, JAMES FRANCIS	1969-05-30	PHOENIX	AZ	CPL	20
ALEXANDER, WILLIAM LEE	1969-05-31	FLINT	MI	CPL	19
OWEN, STEVEN CRAIG	1969-05-31	LONG BEACH	CA	SP5	22
WASHINGTON, ALBERT B JR	1969-06-01	ASBURY PARK	NJ	CPL	23
HOPKINS, JAMES HARRISON	1969-06-04	MARIETTA	GA	SP4	20
GARCIA, JOE ROBERT	1969-06-04	AUSTIN	TX	CPL	22
WELCH, NORMAN GENE	1969-06-05	SPLENDORA	TX	PSG	28
ERVIN, JERRY LYNN	1969-06-08	CLARKSVILLE	TX	PFC	21
WHITE, MICHAEL ALAN	1969-06-09	EL DORADO	KS	SSG	19
PARRISH, ROGER ALAN	1969-06-10	MANHATTAN	KS	1LT	21
FARMER, CHARLIE WILL JR	1969-06-11	LA GRANGE	GA	SSG	21
HARDY, PHILLIP DEAN	1969-06-11	MOUNT OLIVE	NC	CPL	18
MATLOCK, WILLIAM TRAVIS	1969-06-12	NACOGDOCHES	TX	SGT	20
PETTIS, LORENZO RICHARD	1969-06-12	WEST PALM BEACH	FL	CPL	19
CLATFELTER, ROBERT DENNIS	1969-06-12	SPRINGFIELD	IL	PFC	20
KAZMIERCZAK, ROBERT JOSEPH	1969-06-14	LACKAWANNA	NY	CPL	20
SAWYER, JAMES EVERETT JR	1969-06-14	LACONIA	NH	CPL	21
WALLACE, EUGENE KENNETH	1969-06-18	FAYETTEVILLE	NC	SSG	31
BATTERSON, JOHN PEDDIE JR	1969-06-19	LARCHMONT	NY	SP4	22
ROGERS, JERRY EUGENE	1969-06-21	DEMOREST	GA	SGT	20
PERMERTER, MICHAEL JAMES	1969-06-22	MIDLAND PARK	NJ	CPT	24
JOHNSON, JAMES ALLEN	1969-07-01	JERSEY CITY	NJ	CPL	23
KEIL, DUANE RICHARD	1969-07-03	ADRIAN	MI	SGT	20
BLANCHFIELD, MICHAEL R	1969-07-03	ARLINGTON HEIGHTS	IL	SP4	19

KIMBROUGH, GOLSBY JR	1969-07-06	PHILADELPHIA	PA	SGT	20
CARDONA, RONALD WILIAM	1969-07-06	GARDNER	MA	SSG	19
JONES, ERVIN	1969-07-06	TALLAHASSEE	FL	SGT	22
SPEARS, JERRY WAYNE	1969-07-06	MEMPHIS	TN	SPL	20
COLEY, BRUCE EDWARD	1969-07-07	FREEHOLD	NJ	SGT	21
GREVILLE, LEONARD GEORGE	1969-07-07	CRESCENT CITY	CA	PFC	19
GENTRY, BOBBY LEE	1969-07-08	WINCHESTER	KY	PFC	19
ANDERSON, STEVE	1969-07-10	NEWARK	NJ	CPL	22
HOLEMAN, RONALD STEVEN	1969-07-13	SANTA MONICA	CA	PFC	18
MENDEZ, THEODORE SR	1969-07-14	ANTWERP	OH	SSG	34
BRASTER, CHARLES DAVID	1969-07-14	SEMINOLE	OK	SGT	20
LEE, JAMES HOWARD	1969-07-15	LOCKPORT	NY	SP4	19
BRAITHWAITE, ARNIM N	1969-07-15	NEW YORK	NY	CPL	22
REYES, HENRY R	1969-07-15	PORTERVILLE	CA	SGT	22
ERICSON, WILLIAM F II	1969-07-15	ROXBURY	CT	1LT	25
STEMBRIDGE, WAYLAND DAN	1969-07-19	ANACONDA	MT	SGT	22
THOMAS, MICHAEL OLIVER	1969-07-26	ALEXANDRIA	VA	SGT	21
DURAN, ALFONSO MARQUEZ	1969-07-26	COLORADO SPRINGS	CO	SGT	19
JACKSON, JAMES CLEVELAND	1969-07-27	CHESTER	SC	CPL	20
HAMBY, JACKIE DWAYNE	1969-07-28	BONO	AR	SGT	22
BEVERFORD, TIMOTHY WAYNE	1969-07-28	LOS ANGELES	CA	SP4	19
GIVENS, ROY NATHANIEL	1969-07-29	NEWPORT NEWS	VA	SGT	20
MURRAY, LARRY	1969-07-29	FAYETTEVILLE	NC	SGT	22
RENDON, JOSEPH	1969-07-31	PUEBLO	CO	SGT	21
WILLIAMS, HAROLD DAVID	1969-08-01	LOS ANGELES	CA	SSG	21
CASTILLO, THOMAS	1969-08-01	SANTA MARIA	CA	SGT	25
WALTHERS, FRANK DANIEL	1969-08-01	MORTON GROVE	IL	CPL	20
MC DERMOTT, TERRANCE M	1969-08-03	HARTFORD	CT	1LT	23

MILLINGER, GLEN ALLAN	1969-08-03	OAK HARBOR	OH	SGT	20
BARRON, DANNY LANCE	1969-08-05	CARBON HILL	AL	CPL	24
LARSON, RANDOLPH LOUIS	1969-08-11	MILWAUKEE	WI	SP4	20
OXENDINE, RODNEY GLENN	1969-08-12	YORKTOWN	VA	CPL	21
FORDHAM, JERRY LEE	1969-08-13	EASTMAN	GA	SP4	19
BARRINGTON, PAUL V JR	1969-08-13	RIVIERA BEACH	FL	SP4	24
FIELDS, HERMAN THURSTON	1969-08-14	WINTERVILLE	GA	SP4	20
MITCHELL, ROBERT STEVENS	1969-08-14	ROGERS	AR	PFC	18
ROBERTS, PAUL MICHAEL	1969-08-15	MELBOURNE BEACH	FL	PFC	19
FRAKES, JERRY ALLEN	1969-08-16	FAIRFIELD	IA	SGT	21
BASSIGNANI, WILLIAM JOHN	1969-08-18	NEWFANE	VT	1LT	26
GOMEZ-DIAZ, RIGOBERTO	1969-08-18	LOS ANGELES	CA	SGT	20
GAFTUNI, ROBERT ERNEST	1969-08-25	SACRAMENTO	CA	SGT	20
STRAZZANTI, ALAN PETER	1969-08-25	NORTHFIELD	OH	SGT	19
GENTRY, TERRANCE NEIL	1969-08-25	MAN	WV	SGT	20
AYERS, CARL BRACY JR	1969-08-29	CHICAGO	IL	CPL	20
MC ALLISTER, CAMERON TRENT	1969-09-07	OMAHA	NE	SSG	28
SMITH, THOMASLEROY	1969-09-11	OMAHA	NE	CPL	21
RYAN, JERRY VAN	1969-09-11	WALNUT CREEK	CA	CPL	20
CAGLE, RANDY GRAHAM	1969-09-11	MENLO	GA	CPL	18
SQUIER, WILLIAM RUSSELL JR	1969-09-13	BROWNELL	KS	SSG	20
PYPNIOWSKI, LARRY	1969-09-16	STATIO	NJ	CPL	20
LOWE, WALTER BEDFORD JR	1969-09-16	GARDEN CITY	TX	SSG	22
SERVANTEZ, JOSEPH ANTHONY	1969-09-17	INKSTER	MI	SGT	21
RODRIGUEZ, ENCARNASTION	1969-09-17	LA MIRADA	CA	SGT	21
LABRECQUE, ROBERT WILLIAM	1969-09-18	RIVIERA BEACH	FL	CPL	18

TRACY, JOHN WAYNE	1969-09-18	SEMINOLE	OK	SSG	35
DYER, MARTIN BARRY JR	1969-09-19	NEW YORK	NY	SGT	20
HAGER, ROBERT LEE JR	1969-09-22	KANNAPOLIS	NC	CPL	20
TOMPKINS, JAMES ERVIN	1969-09-25	WASHINGTON	DC	SSG	28
HENNEGHAN, ROBERT LEE	1969-09-27	COWARD	SC	SGT	22
NEWSOME, JOHNNY	1969-09-27	LOS ANGELES	CA	CPL	20
GARRETT, HENRY WAYNE	1969-10-01	MONTVALE	VA	SSG	21
ULIBARRI, EDWARD ANTHONY	1969-10-01	SALINAS	CA	CPL	19
CANNING, RICHARD BRUCE	1969-10-04	MEMPHIS	TN	SSG	24
SHROBA, THOMAS MICHAEL	1969-10-04	CHICAGO	IL	SSG	21
GLOVER, LARRY RAY	1969-10-07	NEW WHITELEAND	IN	SSG	21
GRAHAM, JAMES HENRY	1969-10-09	GARDEN GROVE	CA	SGT	21
O'NEAL, TONY LEE	1969-10-09	GAY	GA	CPL	20
CANNON, RONALD LAMER	1969-10-11	ALBANY	GA	SP4	18
WILLIAMS, FRANK NORMAN	1969-10-13	DALZELL	SC	CPL	20
TAYLOR, JOHN HENRY	1969-10-18	JACKSON	TN	CPL	20
APPLETON, DANNY ELBERT	1969-10-21	SANGER	CA	SP4	19
REYNOLDS, HARVEY CLAUDE	1969-10-22	LOUISVILLE	KY	SSG	37
BISHOP, WILLIAM BUEL II	1969-10-22	KNOXVILLE	TN	SGT	22
TOKARSKI, STANLEY RICHARD	1969-10-23	NEW YORK	NY	SGT	20
YAMASHITA, MELVIN MASAICHI	1969-10-24	HONOLULU	HI	SGT	23
PARR, KEITH MASON	1969-10-26	MOUNT CARMEL	IL	SGT	19
KOPKE, ROGER JOSEPH	1969-10-30	GREEN BAY	WI	SSG	21
LAU, JOEL THOMAS	1969-11-01	MINNEAPOLIS	MN	SSG	20
MANGUM, SAM HENRY	1969-11-01	HITCHCOCK	TX	SGT	19
HAGOOD, JOHN ROBERT	1969-11-01	ARCADIA	NE	1LT	24
ROSS, JAMES ARTHUR	1969-11-01	CANTON	OH	SFC	26
STEFFE, MICHAEL WILLIAM	1969-11-03	BALTIMORE	MD	SP4	20

BEAVER, JAMES CLARKE	1969-11-04	DOLTON	IL	CPL	22
LARACUENTE, ERNESTO LUIS	1969-11-04	NEW YORK	NY	PFC	21
HOLMES, THOMAS EUGENE	1969-11-06	WALHALLA	SC	CPL	18
COOK, DAVID RICHARD	1969-11-07	BALTIMORE	MD	CPL	19
SHIRMANG, RICHARD	1969-11-07	CHICAGO RIDGE	IL	1SG	35
SHIPLEY, THOMAS FREDERICK	1969-11-08	SALE CREEK	TN	SGT	21
REYES, EDWARD THOMAS	1969-11-08	SAN LEANDRO	CA	CPL	20
SEEKFORD, DANIEL LEONARD	1969-11-11	BALTIMORE	MD	SSG	20
MEADOWS, JOHN WILLIAM	1969-11-11	ALBUQUERQUE	NM	SSG	22
LINDSEY, DENNIS PAUL	1969-11-11	MILFORD	MI	SSG	23
SERNA, ERNEST	1969-11-11	SAN PABLO	CO	SGT	22
BURKHART, WALTER GUY	1969-11-11	FORT LAUDERDALE	FL	CPL	21
LOGAN, GORDON WESLEY JR	1969-11-12	ANACORTES	WA	CPL	20
SCHOOLER, STEVEN THOMAS	1969-11-13	EAST WENATCHEE	WA	SP4	19
PLAMBECK, PAUL WANDLING JR	1969-11-13	AUSTIN	TX	CPL	22
JORENS, EVERETT RALPH JR	1969-11-15	ST LOUIS	MO	SGT	21
MC NEIL, WILLIE DAVIS	1969-11-17	OLIVE BRANCH	MS	CPL	19
SHERMAN, REX MARCEL	1969-11-19	ROMNEY	WV	CPL	18
LUNSFORD, JAMES WILLIAM JR	1969-11-29	CHILLICOTHE	OH	SGT	19
EPPERSON, ROY ALLEN	1969-11-29	PHOENIX	AZ	CPL	19
BOSSOM, JOHN AUSTIN	1969-11-30	PORTLAND	OR	CPL	20
PARKER, ROBERT KENNETH	1969-11-30	NEWBURYPORT	MA	SGT	21
JONES, THOMAS HOWARD	1969-11-30	TENNILLE	GA	SGT	21
TRUJILLO, FRANCISCO M	1969-12-02	LIVINGSTON	CA	CPL	21
PETRS, DANIEL ALLEN	1969-12-05	CLEVELAND	OH	SGT	21
DEAN, ANTHONY WILLIAM	1969-12-09	EVANSVILLE	IN	SGT	20
GHEE, JAMES FITZROY	1969-12-10	BALTIMORE	MD	CPL	20

WHITLATCH, WILLIAM CARL JR	1969-12-12	MOUNDSVILLE	WV	SGT	25
KULIK, CASIMIR	1969-12-12	EAST DETROIT	MI	SGT	21
MC MILLEN, RONALD DEAN	1969-12-16	HAMILTON	IL	SP4	19
SNELL, RALEIGH JOHN JR	1969-12-16	FLUSHING	NY	SGT	20
BUCCILLE, RICHARD GARY	1969-12-20	PITTSBURGH	PA	SP4	22
MAGEE, MITCHELL JR	1969-12-26	GARU	IN	CPL	21
SCIBELLI, THOMAS ANTHONY	1969-12-27	NEW HYDE PARK	NY	SSG	26
BAN, HERMAN HALEMANU	1970-01-04	HALAULA	HI	SGT	22
HU, PATRICK HOP SUNG	1970-01-05	HONOLULU	HI	SGT	20
SCHMIDT, RICHARD CARL	1970-01-05	JOHNSON CITY	NY	SSG	26
SOLIS, FELIX	1970-01-08	NEW YORK	NY	SGT	20
HIBBLER, RICHARD WAYNE	1970-01-09	ROSENBERG	TX	SP5	32
GUERRO, JOSE F JR	1970-01-09	ANAHEIM	CA	SGT	20
LEWIS, TEDD MCCLUNE	1970-01-09	DALLAS	TX	MAJ	34
STEFKO, WILLIAM CHARLES	1970-01-09	BAYONNE	NJ	1LT	22
JACKSON GERALD ARTHUR	1970-01-09	JACKSONVILLE	FL	2LT	21
CONNERS, LEE ALEXANDER	1970-01-14	KENNEDY	NY	SGT	24
COLGLAZIER, DONALD ROBERT	1970-01-18	HAVELOCK	NC	1LT	23
EDWARDS, STEVEN FRANK	1970-01-18	DE SOTO	IA	SGT	21
MC DAID, JOHN MURL	1970-01-19	ITHACA	MI	SGT	20
PHILLIPS, WILLIAM LEROY	1970-01-20	TOCCOA	GA	CPT	24
GASKO, ROBERT JHN JR	1970-01-20	MAYS LANDING	NJ	PFC	20
QUICK, GEORGE DEWEY JR	1970-01-22	BENNETTSVILLE	SC	PFC	20
MULLENS, ROBRT JOSEPH JR	1970-01-23	NEW YORK	NY	1LT	24
MOORE, DENNIS WESLEY	1970-01-26	BODINES	PA	SGT	27
WASHINGTON, LAWRENCE O	1970-01-26	HENDERSON	KY	SSG	28
BRYSON, TERRY ADAM	1970-02-02	GREENSBORO	NC	PFC	20
BURNLEY, JOHN MOORE	1970-02-04	PINE BLUFF	AR	SGT	20

SMITH, WILLIAM	1970-02-05	SATELLITE BEACH	FL	CPL	18
MARTIN, RALPH	1970-02-05	BURLESON	TX	CPL	22
MILLNER, CARLTON BRANDARD	1970-02-07	KEELING	VA	CPL	18
BERRY, CHARLES RAY	1970-02-09	WICHITA FALLS	TX	SSG	22
KULIKOWSKI, EDWARD JOSEPH	1970-02-10	SIMPSON	PA	CPL	19
MEZA, JESUS JAMES	1970-02-13	SAN BERNARDINO	CA	AP4	21
KELLY, JOHN WILLIAM SIDNEY	1970-02-15	DETROIT	MI	CPL	24
COONS, GREGORY MAC	1970-02-15	SIOUX CITY	IA	SGT	20
O'CONNELL, ROBERT GENE	1970-02-15	CAMP SPRINGS	MD	CPL	20
MURPHY, WILLIAM JOSEPH	1970-02-16	NEW CASTLE	DE	SGT	19
HARDING, DAVID LEE	1970-02-18	ROHNERT	CA	SGT	20
WOOD, DARRELL GEORGE JR	1970-02-19	CORVALLIS	OR	1LT	22
LONG, JOE	1970-02-27	BALTIMORE	MD	SFC	34
DEL GRECO, VICTOR JR	1970-03-02	MANCHESTER	CT	SGT	21
GOLSON, ANTHONY	1970-03-03	SALLEY	SC	CPL	20
PARKER, JAMES ALLEN	1970-03-04	PRINCE FREDERICK	MD	SGT	21
CHAVARRIA, JOHN MAREZ	1970-03-04	LAMAR	CO	CPL	18
STANLEY, JAMES MITCHELL	1970-03-04	GADSDEN	AL	CPL	20
PETRECHKO, EDMUND A JR	1970-03-04	RICHMOND	MO	CPL	19
CAREY, RONALD DUANE	1970-03-05	ROMNEY	IN	GT	21
SHIPMAN, ROBERT DUANE	1970-03-06	DANVILLE	IL	SSG	26
ADAMS, PAUL VERNON	1970-03-07	DETROIT	MI	SGT	20
ROEST, DOUGLAS RAY	1970-03-13	KENOSHA	WI	SGT	19
URQUHART, THOMAS	1970-03-13	NEW YORK	NY	CPL	19
RUTTIMANN, ALLAN	1970-03-13	CANOGA PARK	CA	SGT	19
ALLEN, DANNY RAY	1970-03-16	GULFPORT	MS	SGT	18
RODRIGUEZ, ROBERT	1970-03-16	WICHITA FALLS	TX	SGT	24
SUMTER, FORREST DARRYL	1970-03-16	OKLAHOMA CITY	OK	CPL	19

DE LA CRUZ, FERNANDO	1970-03-16	HARLINGEN	TX	SSG	23
MOHR, RICHARD ALLEN	1970-03-17	BARTO	PA	SGT	20
KIPP, RAYMOND SIDNEY	1970-03-17	OKLAHOMA CITY	OK	SP4	21
DICE, ROBERT FLOYD	1970-03-17	AKRON	OH	CPL	20
PARKER, LARRY	1970-03-21	WINNEMUCCA	NV	SSG	30
JORDAN, LARRY LEON	1970-03-24	CHICAGO	IL	PFC	18
PICKETT, MALCOLM JEROME	1970-03-25	CHICAGO	IL	PFC	18
FRANCIS, PAUL JAMES	1970-03-28	COLUMBUS	GA	1LT	30
INSLEE, RAYMOND STEPHEN	1970-03-29	LEVITTOWN	NY	SGT	19
FLOYD, ROBERT GENE	1970-04-01	FORT MYERS	FL	SGT	22
WHEELHOUSE, CLIFTON P JR	1970-04-01	VIRGINIA BEACH	VA	SGT	19
WELCH, DAVID	1970-04-01	OAKLAND	FL	CPL	20
YOUNG, JOHN EDWARD	1970-04-01	SANTA CLARA	CA	CPL	20
WILSON, THOMAS EDWARD	1970-04-01	MOUNT MORRIS	MI	SSG	20
DOWD, CARTER WAYNE	1970-04-01	LILBURN	GA	SSG	21
DAVIS, MARCUS RAYMOND	1970-04-04	EVARTS	KY	SSG	23
RUYBAL, DANNY GILBERT	1970-04-11	AVONDALE	CO	CPL	19
SILBAS, ROSENDO FLORES	1970-04-11	SAN JOSE	CA	PVT	21
CLICKNER, MICHAEL	1970-04-11	WABBASHA	MN	SGT	20
SANTOS, RAFAEL SALAS	1970-04-12	AGANA	GU	SSG	23
DOWNING, JOHN FREDERICK	1970-04-16	REDWOOD CITY	CA	SSG	19
COLON-SANTOS, RAFAEL	1970-04-17	HAMILTON	NJ	SGT	21
BRIGHT, RALPH NORTH	1970-04-21	DOCTORS INLET	FL	CPL	22
POWERS, JOHN ROGER	1970-04-25	CHEHALIS	WA	SGT	23
RISTINEN, ARMAND ERVIN	1970-04-25	BURLINGTON	IA	SSG	22
BYRNS, GERALD WINSTON JR	1970-04-27	DUNCAN	OK	SSG	24
JACKSON, EDWARD JR	1970-05-01	DURHAM	NC	SFC	33
SHERMAN, JOHN CALVIN	1970-05-02	SEASIDE	CA	SSG	19

LESTER, GRADY RUDOLPH JR	1970-05-02	WICOMICO CHURCH	VA	SSG	21
KNAUS, JOHN RICHARD	1970-05-07	NEWARK	NJ	SGT	20
PLUMB, CHARLES DONALD JR	1970-05-07	JACKSON	MI	SSG	21
CAPASSO, JOHN ALAN	1970-05-07	ROCKVILLE	MD	SGT	20
RAY, MICHAEL WAYNE	1970-05-12	SWARTZ CREEK	MI	CPL	19
BONEY, ALLEN LEWIS	1970-05-12	WARSAW	NC	SSG	22
FOSTER, STEEN BRUCE	1970-05-12	WAUKEGAN	IL	SSG	22
MEADE, DAVID ERNEST	1970-05-15	PORTLAND	OR	1LT	21
MC NULTY, CHARLES RICHARD	1970-05-16	MC LEAN	VA	SSG	22
GRAHAM, HARVEY GENE	1970-05-18	INDIANAPOLIS	IN	SP4	25
BARNETT, CARL TAYLOR	1970-05-18	BLUFFTON	IN	SSG	24
FULLER, FLOYD EDWARD JR	1970-05-19	LEXINGTON	MS	CPL	20
WHEELER, JAMES CHRISTOPHER	1970-05-20	ONEONTA	NY	SP4	20
MOULTON, LESTER NEAL	1970-05-25	VICTOR	ID	1LT	28
KERNAN, MICHAEL ROBERT	1970-05-25	PEARL RIVER	NY	SGT	20
BRUYERE, PETER NORBERT	1970-05-25	CANADA	NC	SP4	19
BIRDWELL, GEORGE ALFRED	1970-05-25	DE LAND	FL	SP4	19
CLAYTON, TOMMY MAKIN	1970-05-25	LOS ANGELES	CA	PVT	22
RODRIGUES, RICHARD	1970-05-25	FALL RIVER	MA	CPL	18
FLORES, RAMON JR	1970-05-25	CLEVELAND	OH	CPL	20
BATCHELOR, CHARLES EDWARD	1970-05-25	JACKSON	TN	CPL	19
OLIVO, RAFAEL	1970-05-25	NEW YORK	NY	SP4	19
SMITH, CURTIS	1970-05-25	CHICAGO	IL	SP4	19
LAWRENCE, BILLY EVERETT	1970-05-25	JACKSONVILLE	FL	CPL	20
DOLAN, JAMES EDWIN	1970-05-25	SCITUATE	MA	SP4	23
MYERS, DONALD WAYNE	1970-05-25	HOUSTON	TX	SGT	20
FERRELL, BILLY	1970-05-29	YPSILANTI	MI	SP4	19
CLARK, JOHN JAMES	1970-06-02	SPOKANE	WA	LTC	37

GIUSTA, JOSEPH MICHAEL	1970-06-02	WESTLAND	MI	CPL	18
TILLOU, JOHN FREDERICK JR	1970-06-04	YUMA	AZ	CPL	20
HALL, DONALD DALE	1970-06-07	URBANA	OH	CPL	19
TAFOYA, VICTOR ARNALDO	1970-06-07	TOOELE	UT	CPL	18
OLLILA, DONALD WARREN	1970-06-08	STURGIS	SD	SGT	21
ROBINSON, JOHN	1970-06-08	JAMAICA	NY	CPL	22
TOMSIC, MICHAEL PATRICK	1970-06-09	PUEBLO	CO	SP5	19
MC MAHAN, DANIEL JACKSON	1970-06-09	CLEVELAND	OH	SGT	20
OVERBECK, PHILIP MOREY	1970-06-10	STURGEON BAY	WI	1LT	22
LE LEAUX, MICHAEL JAMES	1970-06-14	WESTWEGO	LA	SP4	18
STOLTZ, STEVEN RAY	1970-06-18	HAMPTON	IA	SGT	20
COWAN, HAROLD EUGENE	1970-06-23	CAHOKIA	IL	CPL	19
WATSON, THOMAS EDWARD	1970-06-24	LOS ANGELES	CA	PFC	20
MC GINN, JOHN ARTHUR	1970-06-28	SILVER SPRING	MD	SGT	20
HUDNALL, WILLIAM LEON	1970-06-29	RICHMOND	VA	PFC	20
RAMOS, STEPHEN KEALOHA	1970-06-30	HONOLULU	HI	PFC	19
KISCADEN, MICHAEL EDWARD	1970-07-01	LANCASTER	PA	SSG	19
SECOR, WILLIAM DALE	1970-07-02	BIRMINGHAM	AL	SP4	23
DAVIS, SHERMAN PONDEXTER	1970-07-02	SUGAR CITY	CO	SGT	20
SOWERS, RANDAL GENE	1970-07-02	TOLEDO	OH	PVT	18
BURDETTE, HILBURN M JR	1970-07-12	SIMPSONVILLE	SC	SGT	19
CANDRL, BRUCE CHARLES	1970-07-14	ST LOUIS	MO	SGT	23
KRUEGER, GREGORY KEITH	1970-07-17	GARRISON	ND	SGT	21
SLAUGHTER, KENNETH WESLEY	1970-07-22	MURFREESBORO	NC	1LT	21
SUNIGA, JOHN ANTHONY JR	1970-07-24	DENVER	CO	PFC	18
OSTER, ROBERT DALE JR	1970-07-26	GARDEN CITY	MI	SP4	20
CALMESE, ALBERT	1970-07-27	ST LOUIS	MO	CPL	20
ATKINS, DOUGLAS PAUL	1970-07-27	ANN ARBOR	MI	PFC	19
PEREZ, JOSE MANUEL	1970-07-28	BROWNSVILLE	TX	SP	21

CLEVERLEY, WILLIAM BERT	1970-07-28	DETROIT	MI	PFC	19
LAVELLE, JOHN JOSEPH	1970-07-29	MIDWEST CITY	OK	SP4	20
HILTERBRAN, DANNY LEE	1970-07-29	MIDWEST CITY	OK	SP4	20
MC CRAY, PLEASANT JR	1970-07-29	ST LOUIS	MO	CPL	22
HAYES, HAROLD UTAH	1970-07-30	NEELYVILLE	MO	SFC	31
HILDERBRANT, PHILLIP JAY	1970-07-31	EDMORE	MI	SGT	21
BUSCH, ERIC PETER	1970-08-07	CHICAGO	IL	SP6	25
CRAWFORD, JOHN NELSON JR	1970-08-07	KANSAS CITY	MO	SP6	29
MAC NAUGHT, ROBERT WILLIAM	1970-08-07	WARWICK	RI	1LT	26
CLIMER, DAVID LEROY	1970-08-08	COLUMBUS	OH	SP4	20
BAXLEY, DENNIS WAYNE	1970-08-09	ORANGE	CA	SGT	22
KUBELUS, ANTHONY GEORGE JR	1970-08-10	SCRANTON	PA	SP4	19
JACKSON, BEN JR	1970-08-15	LOS ANGELES	CA	PFC	23
HUGHES, FURMAN DAVID	1970-08-20	HAMMOND	IN	PVT	20
JASSO, JOHN	1970-08-25	RUDOLPH	OH	SP4	19
BATES, MELVIN CARROLL JR	1970-08-29	BALTIMORE	MD	SGT	20
BLENKINSOP, WILLIAM DARWIN	1970-08-29	COEUR D'ALENE	ID	CPL	19
COATES, EMORY THERON	1970-09-05	INDIANOLA	IA	SP4	21
MORENO, JESUS JR	1970-09-06	CORPUS CHRISTI	TX	SP4	20
BROOKS, LARRY EUGENE	1970-09-06	DETROIT	MI	CPL	20
PADILLA, EDDIE JACK	1970-09-07	STEVENSON	CA	CPL	19
AARON, EUGENE ALLEN	1970-09-07	TAMPA	FL	PFC	19
SVEEN, BRENT WILLIAM	1970-09-07	FARGO	ND	PFC	18
ENGLISH, GLENN HARRY JR	1970-09-07	CORNWELLS HEIGHTS	PA	SSG	30
ASEP, MICHAEL	1970-09-08	NEW YORK	NY	SP4	21
FRIEND, GARY RALPH	1970-09-09	HARPER	OR	SGT	19
LEWIS, ELTON	1970-09-09	INDEPENDENCE	LA	PFC	18
CAMPBELL, WILSON	1970-09-10	LAURINBURG	NC	CPL	19
ADAMS, MERRITT	1970-09-10	FAYETTEVILLE	NC	SGT	20

HARPER, HAROLD OWEN	1970-09-12	GRAND RAPIDS	MI	SGT	20
MATHEWS, CHARLES DONALD	1970-09-12	GRAND HAVEN	MI	SP4	20
MARSHALL, DENNIS CRAIG	1970-09-13	WOOSTER	OH	CPL	19
WALDRON, JAMES TAYLOR	1970-09-13	MINNEAPOLIS	MN	SGT	20
GENTRY, DENNIS WAYNE	1970-09-13	ATHENS	GA	SGT	20
CLAYTON, CURVIN	1970-09-13	DURHAM	NC	SP4	20
WATSON, TYRONE CALVIN	1970-09-13	PHILADELPHIA	PA	SSG	28
SEDA, PABLO ISREAL	1970-09-15	NEW YORK	NY	PVT	21
KEENEY, JOSEPH FRANK	1970-09-16	BALTIMORE	MD	PVT	21
WELLS, ROGER ORRIE	1970-09-17	PLEASANTVILLE	PA	CPL	20
LAWRENCE, TORY DRAKE	1970-09-19	MURPHYS	CA	CPL	22
HENSLEY, MARK ALAN	1970-09-19	GREAT FALLS	MT	CPL	20
SHIPE, THOMAS ALLEBACH	1970-09-19	VENETTA	PA	CPL	22
OVERWEG, ROGER DALE	1970-09-19	ZEELAND	MI	SGT	20
JINDRICH, STEVEN FREDERICK	1970-09-22	DENVER	CO	SP4	20
SEGAR, CALVIN RUSSELL	1970-09-22	BISBEE	AZ	PFC	18
RATLIFF, BILLY HARRISON	1970-09-24	POMEROYTON	KY	SGT	20
UPRIGHT, BRIAN DALE	1970-10-04	STARRUCCA	PA	SP4	18
GADDIE, DAVID JR	1970-10-04	HOPE MILLS	NC	SSG	28
LARSON, DAVID WAYNE	1970-10-04	FUNK	NE	PFC	22
BAKER, ROBERT BENTON JR	1970-10-12	PASADENA	TX	SGT	22
MILLER, RALPH PETERSON III	1970-10-19	DETROIT	MI	1LT	26
MARSH, HAROLD CLIFTON	1970-10-19	LAURINBURG	NC	SSG	21
DICKEY, JAMES WHEELER	1970-10-21	ALEXANDRIA	VA	SGT	20
PATINO, ROBERTO LERMA	1970-10-22	CORPUS CHRISTI	TX	SGT	30
DOMINE, MANUEL DE LEON	1970-10-25	FORT SILL	OK	SGT	24
GERMAIN, JAMES THOMAS	1970-10-29	ST JAMES	NY	1LT	26
LAYPORTE, OSCAR ROBERT	1970-10-30	CANTON	OH	CPL	21
REED, PAUL EDWARD	1970-10-31	FRANKLIN	PA	SSG	30
MARCHESI, JIMMY EUGENE	1970-10-31	LITTLETON	CO	PFC	23
TAYLOR, WENDELL	1970-11-02	ENFIELD	NC	SGT	20

LANZARIN, LEONARD ALLAN	1970-11-04	SAN FRANCISCO	CA	SP4	20
ROBERTS, WALTER JAMES	1970-11-05	FLINT	MI	SP4	21
HERNANDEZ-RODRIGUEA, RUBENEDID	1970-11-06	ISBELA	PR	SSG	24
HEAGGANS, THURSTON CONRAD	1970-11-15	TROUTMAN	NC	CPL	20
ZERGGEN, FRANCIS ALBERT	1970-11-20	PHILADELPHIA	PA	CPL	19
FLEMING, WILLIAM ELGIN JR	1970-11-20	MISSOULA	MT	SP4	20
JOHNSON, JAMES JR	1970-11-20	PENSACOLA	FL	SGT	23
O'BOYLE, TERRENCE PATRICK	1970-11-20	NORFOLK	VA	SGT	22
DALE, DENNIS HUMPHREY	1970-11-20	BALTIMORE	MD	PFC	20
SCHOENBERG, RICHARD C	1970-11-21	PALMYRA	NJ	CPT	23
BRADLEY, THOMAS REUBEN	1970-11-21	TARBORO	NC	SP4	21
KAVICH, ROBERT DALE	1970-11-22	JEFFERSON TOWN	KY	CPL	18
PAULICH, PATRICK JAMES	1970-11-30	RACINE	WI	PVT	20
COILEY, CHARLES ROBERT	1970-11-30	OLD TOWN	ME	PFC	18
CURTIS, JOSEPH PAUL	1970-12-17	HOLLYWOOD	MD	SSG	25
RAMM, FERENC JOHN	1970-12-17	DANVILLE	IL	SGT	32
CRAIG, CLAYTON GEROME	1970-12-18	LESTER	AL	SGT	23
CRANSON, ROBERT DORIAN	1970-12-18	BANGOR	ME	SP4	20
SEMPSROTT, BRUCE GORDON	1970-12-18	INDIANAPOLIS	IN	PFC	20
MYERS, TONY HOWARD	1970-12-22	KANSAS CITY	MO	SP4	21
SMITH, GARY WAYNE	1970-12-23	TOLEDO	OR	SGT	21
SIMS, HENRY JAMES	1970-12-31	FORT PIERCE	FL	SGT	28
HUDSON, THOMAS HAROLD	1971-01-01	ST CHARLES	MO	SP4	21
TRESTER, DAVID ALEXANDER	1971-01-03	WEAVERVILLE	CA	SP4	22
WILSON, JONATHAN TRAXLER	1971-01-03	RICHMOND	VA	SP4	19
MIKE, STEVEN	1971-01-06	GALLUP	NM	PFC	20

HILL, GERALD WILLIAM	1971-01-07	MILFORD	OH	SP4	10
BROWN, RICK SAMUEL	1971-01-07	MESA	AZ	SGT	21
NELSON, RUSSEL COURTNEY	1971-01-07	MINNEAPOLIS	MN	CPL	20
BOOTS, STEPHEN ELDON	1971-01-07	DES MOINES	IA	SSG	27
TABOR, RICHARD EUGENE	1971-01-07	CHEYENNE	WY	SP4	21
JONES, BENNIE FRANK	1971-01-09	BRIGHTON	MA	PFC	20
ROBINSON, CLINTON CURTIS	1971-01-09	BALTIMORE	MD	SP4	20
RUSHLOW, RICHARD LEONARD	1970-01-11	LINCOLN PARK	MI	SGT	21
NELSON, EARL	1971-01-16	MEMPHIS	TN	SSG	26
MENDALL, CARLTON JOSEPH	1971-01-16	HYDE PARK	MA	1LT	24
SHOVER, BRUCE CHARLES	1971-01-16	MARIETTA	OH	PFC	20
JIM, MARTIN JR	1971-01-16	MAYETTA	KS	PFC	19
CUTTING, JERRY WOODROW	1971-01-23	DAVENPORT	IA	SGT	21
ROCHA, JOSE MARKE	1971-02-07	MILWAUKEE	WI	CPL	22
PEACE, CHARLES LAMONT	1971-02-07	SHARON HILL	PA	CPL	21
MICHAEL, JAMES ALBERT	1971-02-13	GAINESVILLE	GA	SGT	21
METZLER, PERRY	1971-02-14	DETROIT	MI	PFC	30
MITCHELL, LARYY GENE	1971-02-22	COLORADO SPRINGS	CO	CPL	18
KEYS, MICHAEL HENRY	1971-02-24	MANSON	WA	SP4	21
QUINONES-RODRIQUEZ, LUIS A	1971-02-25	NEW YORK	NY	PVT	22
WOODS, WILLIAM STEPHEN	1971-02-25	MAULDIN	SC	CPL	20
HART, RANDOLPH GUY JR	1971-02-28	MONROE	LA	SGT	21
KUPKOWSKI, JOHN WALTER	1971-02-28	BLASDELL	NY	SGT	26
LAMB, HOWARD SIDNEY	1971-02-28	GADSDEN	AL	SGT	20
STOCKETT, RICHARD LEE	1971-03-02	MESA	AZ	SGT	20
SALDANA, RICHARD DAVID	1971-03-02	OXNARD	CA	SP4	20
BROOKS, JESSIE MICHAEL	1971-03-02	IRVINGTON	AL	SSG	20
MULKEY, HERBERT EUGENE JR	1971-03-02	MOUNT AIRY	MD	PFC	18

MORGAN, GEORGE ROBERT	1971-03-07	MOBILE	AL	SGT	23
BLAIR, TERRY LEE	1971-03-07	KANSAS CITY	MO	SP4	20
FRICKE, PATRICK LOYAL	1971-03-07	LE CLAIRE	IA	SGT	19
SMITH, DAVID HUGH	1971-03-11	LOS ANGELES	CA	CPL	19
STONE, GREGORY MARTIN	1971-03-24	TORRANCE	CA	CPL	21
VENCEL, ALBERT ALLEN	1971-03-26	WARREN	OH	CPL	20
ERICKSON, KENT DOUGLAS	1971-03-29	ST LOUIS PARK	MN	PVT	19
WILLIAMS, HARRIS LEE	1971-03-31	MULLINS	SC	CPL	20
PARNELL, BILLY RAY	1971-03-31	WINNIE	TX	CPL	18
MC LHERN, MICHAEL SHEA	1971-03-31	GARY	IN	PFC	18
YOUNGERMAN, JOSEPH MICHAEL	1971-04-02	DAYTON	OH	PVT	22
BEST, ARTHUR	1971-04-03	KENANSVILLE	NC	SSG	39
BUTT, GARY	1971-04-03	CANADA	XC	SSG	19
KISER, ROBERT JESSE	1971-04-03	STAMFORD	CT	SSG	21
ROG, EDWARD JOSEPH JR	1971-04-03	CHICAGO	IL	SP4	19
WARBINGTON, HOWARD OTTO	1971-04-03	PASCAGOULA	MS	SSG	21
BOROWSKI, WAYNE ROY	1971-04-03	FAYETTEVILLE	NC	CPL	18
SUEDMYER, LARRY DEAN III	1971-04-04	TULELAKE	CA	SGT	20
CABE, PAUL PHILIP	1971-04-05	GUILD	TN	SGT	18
TAYLOR, DONNIE CARL	1971-04-06	GRAND RAPIDS	MI	SGT	23
THOMAS, CHARLES F IV	1971-04-08	PALM BAY	FL	CPT	24
MC DONALD, MARTIN TERRANCE	1971-04-10	PHILADELPHIA	PA	SGT	20
HENDERSON, GREG NEAL	1971-04-10	BUTTE	MT	CPL	24
KING, JACK LLOYD	1971-04-10	DEER PARK	TX	SSG	21
CHANNEL, BILLY GENE	1971-04-10	KANSAS CITY	MO	SGT	19
THOMAS, JAMES RONALD	1971-04-17	NEW ORLEANS	LA	SGT	21
YUGEL, LOUIS ARTHUR	1971-04-21	THORNTON	CO	SP4	19
FERGUSON, LOWELL VERNON JR	1971-04-24	AVON PARK	FL	SGT	20
BLANTON, BILL EDWARD	1971-04-24	DAYTON	OH	SGT	21

ALVAREZ, BERNARDO RODRIGUEZ	1971-04-24	JACKSON	MI	CPL	20
MC CANN, FRANCIS JOSEPH JR	1971-04-26	GLENOLDEN	PA	CPL	20
PEEL, LAWRENCE RAY	1971-04-28	KANSAS CITY	KS	SP4	19
BORJA, JUAN SANTOS	1971-04-28	AGANA	GU	SSG	30
WILCOX, CHARLES THOAS	1971-05-08	CHAGRIN FALLS	OH	SP4	22
LLOYD, MARTIN ROGER	1971-05-08	GREEN CITY	MO	SP4	20
KIRCHNER, GARYALLEN	1971-05-08	BELLEVILLE	MI	PFC	20
CADIEUX, THOMAS PAUL	1971-05-09	LA GRANGE PARK	IL	SGT	21
CAMPBELL, DAVID DANA	1971-05-10	MACEDONIA	OH	SGT	19
MARTIN, STEVEN LARRY	1971-05-11	FRESNO	CA	SP4	22
NAVARRETE, JOB JR	1971-05-16	FAYETTEVILLE	NC	SGT	21
HUMPHREY, HARVEY EDWARD	1971-05-26	BARNET	VT	CPL	21
SWEENEY JOSEPH EDWARD	1971-05-29	PHILADELPHIA	PA	CPL	21
BARNES, MITCHELL ODELL	1971-05-30	COLUMBIA	TN	SGT	21
MILLER, LARRY LEE	1971-06-05	EDGERTON	MO	SGT	20
BRYANT, MAURICE HERBERT	1971-06-08	COAHOMA	MS	CPL	20
SEXTON, HUGH AMES JR	1971-06-09	DENTON	NC	SGT	20
BREWSTER, CARL WARDEN	1971-06-10	FOREST	OH	SGT	20
CONNIFF, THOMAS JOSEPH	1971-06-11	LOS ANGELES	CA	SGT	21
HAYES, JOSEPH D	1971-06-13	WEED	CA	SP4	21
HART, ERNEST DWIGHT JR	1971-06-17	FRESNO	CA	PFC	26
PATTERSON, RICHARD STUART	1971-07-06	TOLEDO	OH	PVT	21
GOFF, ALAN SHERMAN	1971-07-06	BAKERSFIELD	CA	PFC	19
WATKINS, MICHAEL	1971-07-12	NEW YORK	NY	PVT	20

Glossary

The following is a list of military terms and slang found throughout this book. I have attempted to briefly explain each on its initial use. These words and terms, while not always politically correct, are used for authenticity and realism; they tell it like it was. Any group of people isolated by physical, legal, or social boundaries creates its own vocabulary; the following was ours.

81-mm mortar—standard infantry mortar of U.S. in Vietnam, capable of firing high explosives, phosphorus, and illumination flares. Using rapid fire, the tube could project as many as twenty-seven rounds per minute.

122-mm rocket—a Russian-supplied rocket supplied to the Vietcong.

175-mm gun—self-propelled gun; range: 38,000 meters (approximately twenty-three miles).

201—military personnel file.

airborne—qualified paratrooper/parachutist.

AIT—Advanced Individual Training, the period following basic training.

AK-47—Soviet-bloc assault rifle, 7.62 x 39 MM caliber, also known as Kalashnikov AK-47.

ammo—ammunition.

Article 15—summary disciplinary judgment on a soldier by a commander, usually resulting in a fine or confinement.

ARVN—Army of the Republic of Vietnam.

AWOL—absent without official leave.

battalion—approximately 500 personnel.

beaucoup—French term for "very many."

Black Hat—airborne training cadre distinguished by their black, baseball-style caps.

booby trap—an explosive charge or other device engineered by the enemy to kill or cause injury when triggered.

boonies, boondocks, brush, bush—slang for jungle area away from cities or civilization.

brigade—between 2,000 and 4,000 personnel.

butter bar—a second lieutenant, in reference to his gold bar insignia.

caribou—an unarmed army transport plane.

central highlands—a 20,000-square-mile plateau at the southern edge of the Truong Son Mountains where nearly one million Montagnard tribesmen produce coffee, tea, and vegetables.

Charlie—nickname for the VC and NVA.

chopper—helicopter, so called for the sound it makes.

civvies—civilian clothing.

claymore mine—two-pound, remote-control mine.

CO—commanding officer.

Cobra—helicopter gunship; AH-1-J-Vietnam, heavily armed attack helicopter, usually carrying 7.62 Gatling guns, 2.75-inch rocket launchers, and 40-mm grenade launchers.

Communist—follower of the philosophical writings of Karl Marx and Friedrich Engels and dedicated to overthrowing non-Communist societies.

company—a military unit comprised of approximately 120 personnel.

CP—command post.

CS grenades—riot-control gas grenades.

Davy Crockett—light, mobile, rapid-response army low-yield nuclear weapon; also the name of now-disbanded units trained to fire the weapon.

dust-off—medical evacuation by helicopter or helicopter ambulance.

extraction—withdrawal of troops by helicopter from an operational area.

firebase—forward artillery position for supporting ground units.

firefight—exchange of small-arms fire from opposing units.

FNG—"fuckin' new guy," slang for a new arrival in Vietnam.

fragmentation hand grenade—M-35/new M-67; effective killing radius of five meters; casualty radius of fifteen meters; can project fragments up to 230 meters.

gook—derogatory term for North Vietnamese Army and/or Vietcong.

Green tracers—color trail left by AK-47s (Communist-issued ammo).

grunts—infantryman, referring to the sound he makes when lifting his heavy rucksack.

hand grenade—*see* fragmentation hand grenade.

helicopter gunship—*see* Cobra.

Head Hunter One—the radio call sign for the platoon lieutenant of Second Platoon of Charlie Company of the Second Battalion 503rd Infantry of the 173rd Airborne Brigade.

Head Hunter One Kilo—the radio call sign for the sergeant in charge of the squad in which Dennis Hendrix served as temporary RTO.

Ho Chi Minh Trail—a vast network of roads and trails running from North Vietnam, down through Laos, Cambodia, and South

Vietnam, and terminating just northwest of Saigon. It made up the transportation route that enabled the NVA to replace its losses of manpower, arms, and equipment.

hooch—slang for barracks or living quarters made of mud and straw.

howitzer—155-mm artillery gun that fires shells at targets that cannot be reached by flat trajectories; range of up to 11,000 meters (almost eight miles).

hump—hike with heavily loaded rucksack.

KIA—killed in action.

Kit Carson Scouts—North Vietnamese Army defectors who "helped" the U.S.

klick—kilometer; 0.62137 miles.

LAW—light anti-tank weapon; a one-shot, disposable rocket launcher; a miniature bazooka with a 66-mm-shaped charge.

LRRP—Long Range Reconnaissance Patrol.

LRRP Ration—packet of the dehydrated food that U.S. troops carried on patrol.

LZ—landing zone; a clearing in the jungle large enough to accommodate forward combat units.

M-14—standard-issue 7.62-caliber semiautomatic/automatic rifle.

M-16—standard-issue 5.56-caliber semiautomatic/automatic rifle.

M-60—light 7.62-caliber machine gun, a primary infantry automatic weapon.

M-79—a grenade launcher; also known as a "thumper" for the sound it made when launched.

M-35 Super Frag—fragmentation grenade.

mama-san—an elderly female in the tribal structure who headed the family unit.

medevac—medical evacuation by helicopter; *see also* dust-off.

MIA—missing in action.

MOS—Military Occupational Specialty.

nuclear weapon—a bomb, shell, rocket, or guided missile employing nuclear fission or fusion as its destructive force.

NVA—North Vietnamese Army.

papa-san—an elderly Vietnamese father.

paratrooper—a solider trained to use a parachute for descent from an aircraft into a battle area or area behind enemy lines.

platoon—approximately thirty to forty personnel.

point man—the lead soldier of the patrol.

posttraumatic stress disorder—emotional disorder occurring after a wound, combat, or tragic happening.

Purple Heart—an award issued to military personnel wounded in action against a hostile force.

PX—post exchange, a military department store.

R&R—rest and recreation.

red leg—artillery, referring to the artillery uniform worn during the Civil War.

RTO—radiotelephone operator.

punji pit—camouflaged hole filled with sharpened bamboo stakes.

rucksack—metal-framed backpack.

sit rep—situation report.

slack man—the second man in a patrol.

smoke roll—main and reserve parachutes that fail to open, and that looks like a stream of smoke.

spider hole—a camouflaged fighting position used by NVA/VC.

stand-down—a period of rest following completion of a field mission.

squad—approximately nine to eleven personnel; *see also* company.

thumper—*see* M-79.

VC—*see* Vietcong.

Vietcong—South Vietnamese Communist guerrillas.

zap—kill.

zapper—a Vietnamese who sacrificed his/her own life to kill their enemy.

I would like to give a special thanks to Lt. Colonel Ron De Laby, Army National Guard, retired.

His constant encouragement and friendship gave me the strength to place on paper all of the memories I had buried long ago. He insisted that the American people know what the true war in Vietnam was like for hundreds of thousands of young men and women who fought that war.

His contributions to the final preparation of this book were invaluable.

Thank you so much, Ron.

"ALL THE WAY, SIR!"

Printed in the United States
39488LVS00002BA/1-99

9 781420 879971